A Practical Guide to

Enterprise Architecture

The Coad Series
Peter Coad, *Series Editor*

———■———

- David J. Anderson
  Agile Management for Software Engineering:
  Applying the Theory of Constraints for Business Results

- David Astels
  Test Driven Development: A Practical Guide

- David Astels, Granville Miller, Miroslav Novak
  A Practical Guide to eXtreme Programming

- Andy Carmichael, Dan Haywood
  Better Software Faster

- Donald Kranz, Ronald J. Norman
  A Practical Guide to Agile Unified Process

- James McGovern, Scott W. Ambler, Michael E. Stevens,
  James Linn, Vikas Sharan, Elias Jo
  A Practical Guide to Enterprise Architecture

- Jill Nicola, Mark Mayfield, Michael Abney
  Streamlined Object Modeling: Patterns, Rules, and Implementation

- Stephen R. Palmer, John M. Felsing
  A Practical Guide to Feature-Driven Development

About the Series

The Coad Series is a growing collection of practical guides "from the trenches." The series focuses on key "must be addressed" IT pain points, felt by leaders around the globe. The series is especially suited for CIOs, IT department managers, technology leaders, and change agents. The Coad Series addresses the four dimensions of successful IT: technology, process, people, and vision. For the series, Peter Coad personally selects authors and topics and then mentors the authors at a strategic level along the way.

About the Series Editor

Peter Coad (pronounced "code") is senior vice president and chief strategist of Borland (http://www.borland.com) Software Corporation. Coad collaborates with fellow Borland execs in formulating long-term business and product strategies. Peter also represents Borland worldwide as a thought leader, industry luminary, and evangelist among CXOs, technical department managers, and developers.

Peter is globally recognized as an accomplished business strategist, model builder, and thought leader. As business strategist, Peter formulates long-term competitive strategies for Borland. Previously, as Chairman, CEO, and President of TogetherSoft, he led in growing that company 11.6 times revenue in the span of two years, overall profitably. As model builder, Peter has built hundreds of models for nearly every business imaginable, fully focused on building-in strategic business advantage. As thought leader, Peter writes books (six to date) on building better software faster; he speaks at industry events worldwide; and he is the Editor-in-Chief of The Coad Series, published by Prentice Hall; in addition, Peter was an invited speaker on business strategy at the 2003 "Future in Review" conference.

Coad attended the Stanford Executive Program for Growing Companies and received a Master of Science in Computer Science (USC) and a Bachelor of Science with Honors in Electrical Engineering (OSU).

WWW.WWISA.ORG

The Worldwide Institute of Software Architects (WWISA) is a non-profit professional organization dedicated to establishing a formal profession of software architecture and providing information and services to software architects and their clients—analogous to the formation of the American Institute of Architects roughly 140 years ago. The essential tenet of WWISA is that there is a perfect analogy between building and software architecture, and that the classical role of the architect needs to be introduced into the software construction industry.

The architect, whether designing structures of brick or computer code, forms the bridge between the world of the client and that of the technical builders. This critical bridge has been missing from the software industry, resulting in a decades-long software crisis. Entire software structures are dysfunctional or have been scrapped entirely—before seeing a single "inhabitant." We have simply been building huge, complex structures without architects, and without blueprints.

WWISA was established in 1998 and now has over 1,500 members in over 50 countries. Membership is open to practicing and aspiring software architects, professors, students, CIOs, and CEOs. Members participate to promote training and degree programs, develop architectural standards and guiding principles, and work toward creating a standard body of shared knowledge. We are our client advocates; clients are our driving force. We hope to become the clients' bridge to successful software construction by helping them leverage the full range of technology.

A Practical Guide to Enterprise Architecture

James McGovern
Scott W. Ambler
Michael E. Stevens
James Linn
Vikas Sharan
Elias K. Jo

PRENTICE HALL
PTR

PRENTICE HALL
Professional Technical Reference
Upper Saddle River, NJ 07458
www.phptr.com

Library of Congress Cataloging-in-Publication Data

Practical guide to enterprise architecture / James McGovern . . . [et al.]—1st ed.
  p. cm.
Includes bibliographical references and index.
  ISBN 0-13-141275-2
1. Computer architecture. 2. Computer systems—Design. I. McGovern, James,

QA76.9.A73P753 2003
004.2'5—dc22

2003021138

Editorial/production supervision: *Carlisle Publishers Services*
Cover design director: *Jerry Votta*
Art director: *Gail Cocker-Bogusz*
Interior design: *Meg Van Arsdale*
Manufacturing manager: *Alexis R. Heydt-Long*
Manufacturing buyer: *Maura Zaldivar*
Executive editor: *Paul Petralia*
Editorial assistant: *Michelle Vincenti*
Development editor: *Jim Markham*
Marketing manager: *Chris Guzikowski*
Full-service production manager: *Anne R. Garcia*

PRENTICE
HALL
PTR

© 2004 by Pearson Education, Inc.
Publishing as Prentice Hall Professional Technical Reference
Upper Saddle River, New Jersey 07458

Prentice Hall PTR offers excellent discounts on this book when ordered in quantity for bulk purchases or special sales. For more information, please contact: U.S. Corporate and Government Sales, 1-800-382-3419, corpsales@pearsontechgroup.com. For sales outside of the U.S., please contact: International Sales, 1-317-581-3793, international@pearsontechgroup.com.

Second Printing

ISBN 0-13-141275-2

Pearson Education LTD.
Pearson Education Australia PTY, Limited
Pearson Education Singapore, Pte. Ltd.
Pearson Education North Asia Ltd.
Pearson Education Canada, Ltd.
Pearson Educación de Mexico, S.A. de C.V.
Pearson Education—Japan
Pearson Education Malaysia, Pte. Ltd.

About Prentice Hall Professional Technical Reference

Contents

Contents
—

Acknowledgments

This book would not be possible without the keen eye of our acquisitions editor, Paul Petralia, and Peter Coad. Many thanks go to our development editor, Jim Markham, who has spent many hours refining our manuscript and the delicate procedure of linguistic hygiene.

This textbook's author team has benefited from early reviews by very talented visionaries within our profession. Input came from all parts of the world from people with diverse backgrounds: from professionals who work in large enterprises to professors at major institutions of higher learning; from people who believe in heavyweight processes to those who have embraced agile methods; from those whose native tongue is English, to those who speak such joyous languages as Arabic, Chinese, French, Portuguese, and Spanish, as well as others; and from those who are lowly developers to those who are senior executives.

We deeply appreciated the feedback received from the following people (company affiliations are included where permitted):

- Paul Clements (Senior Member of Technical Staff), Software Engineering Institute, Carnegie Mellon University
- Russ Rufer, Silicon Valley Patterns
- Charlie Mead, (Director) Healthcare Information Architecture, Oracle
- Alan Inglis (Director of Enterprise Consulting), The Infrassistance Company
- Leon Kappelman (Director Information Systems Research Center), University of North Texas
- Celia Redmore, BMC Software, Atlanta, Georgia
- Marcello Kai (IT Analyst), IBM
- Joe Schurman (Independent Consultant)
- David Dossot (Team Leader), Atos Origin, Luxembourg
- Spiro Lecatsas (CTO), Pitstop IT
- Taran Rampersad (Software Engineer), KnowProSE.com, Trinidad & Tobago
- Jean Sirica (Architect), Hartford Financial Services
- Deklan J. Dieterly (Software Developer)
- Todd J. Johnsgard (Human Factors Engineer)

- Gerrit Muller (Senior Research Fellow), Embedded Systems Institute, Netherlands
- Robert H. Shanahan (Chief Software Architect), Northern Solutions Software
- Hubert Smits (Senior Consultant), Vision Consulting, Scotland
- Eugen Coca (Professor of Computer Architecture), University Stefan cel Mare, Romania
- Marié-Louise Dercksen (Business Architect), Comparex, South Africa
- Rik Manhaeve, Belgium
- Jason Garbis (Senior Product Manager), IONA
- Phillip Ohme
- Alfred Smith (Application Architect), State Information Technology Agency, South Africa
- Lucas Persona (Computer Scientist), Widesoft Sistemas, Brasil
- Sirigere Sanjeev, Siemens AG
- Charles Hawk, FedEx
- John Lamb (Enterprise Architect), Hartford Financial Services
- Sean McBreen (Lead .NET Architect), Cap Gemini Ernst & Young, United Kingdom
- Cordell Carter II (Management Consultant), IBM
- Raul Abril (Program Management Director), Teradata (a division of NCR)
- Nitish Verma (Enterprise Architect), Essense Networks Ltd, New Zealand
- G. Michael Zimmer (Senior Coordinator), Methods and Procedures, British Columbia, Canada
- Harm Smit (Advanced Projects Manager), SYLLEM, Toulouse, France
- Marilyn Littman (Professor), Nova Southeastern University, Florida
- Alexander Schmid (Enterprise Architect), Munich, Germany
- Rathan Dhariwal (Software Architect), Computer Horizons
- Bob Corrick (Developer Skill Manager), Virgin Money, Norwich, England
- Sergio Villagra (Professor), Universidad de Buenos Aires, Argentina
- Xijia (Frank) Chen (Tech Lead), Verizon Wireless, California
- Peter Booth (Software Architect), Major Financial Institution, New York City
- Dirk Muthig (Department Head), Fraunhofer Institute for Experimental Software Engineering (IESE), Kaiserslautern, Germany
- Anders Aspnäs (Solution Architect), Fujitsu Invia OY, Turku, Finland
- Dr. Shane D. Shook (Manager, Information Risk Management), KPMG LLP

- Gordon Tulloch (Application Development Manager), Province of Manitoba, Winnipeg, Canada
- Lisa Crispin (Manager, QA), KBToys.com, Denver, Colorado
- Huet Landry (Software Process Improvement Manager), Unisys, Virginia
- Thomas M. Cagley Jr. (Principal), TMConsulting Services, Ohio
- Claudio Ochoa (Senior Software Engineer), NEC, San Luis, Argentina
- Charles Poon-Teck Ling, Ph.D. (Service Provider, Architect, and Principal Consultant), Sun Microsystems Pte Ltd, Singapore
- Nitish Verma (Enterprise Architect), Essense Networks
- Bruce Beller (Project Manager), Beller Consulting, Inc., Pennsylvania
- Horia Slusanschi (Enterprise Architect), Unisys, Wellington, New Zealand
- Marlyn Kemper Littman (Professor), Nova Southeastern University, Florida
- Paolino Madotto (Manager), KPMG, Rome, Italy
- Mark R. Nelson (Professor), Rensselaer Polytechnic Institute, Troy, New York
- Sharad Patel (Consultant), KPMG, London

The author team has benefited immensely in its profession by reading papers from industry luminaries and have incorporated collected thoughts on enterprise architecture and agile methods into this book. Those luminaries include the following:

- Dana Bredemeyer
- Ruth Malan
- Douglas Barry
- Paul Harmon
- Peter Herzum
- Kent Beck
- Alistair Cockburn
- Ward Cunningham
- Martin Fowler
- Jim Highsmith
- Ron Jeffries
- Jon Kern
- Clive Finkelstein
- Steve Mellor
- Ken Schwaber
- Jeff Sutherland

James McGovern

It is much easier to write a book when others believe you can. My deepest thanks to Sherry: my true love and constant source of inspiration. To my parents, James and Mattie Lee, for bringing me up and always supporting me. Universal greetings to my family: Daisy, Annika, Pamela, Demesha, Aunt Jesse, Soogia, Kenrick, Kiley, Nicholas, Ian, Alex, Kelon, and Keifer. To my perfect son, Little James: I am going to get you.

Thanks to all my coworkers at Hartford Financial Services who never stopped being interested in Enterprise Architecture and the progress of this book. Furthermore, I thank the readers of my previous works for their suggestions, praise, letters of admiration, and gratitude.

Scott W. Ambler

I would like to acknowledge all architects within the industry who have been successful in getting their organizations to adopt agile methods for enterprise architecture, as well as the industry thought leaders who have continued to make this a worthwhile profession.

Michael E. Stevens

On a personal note, I thank my wife, Rhonda, and daughter, Katie, for their encouragement and understanding during the writing of this book. I also thank my mother, Doris, and father, Ed, for their support. On a professional note, I thank my coworkers James McGovern, Jeff Ryan, Tom Sorensen, Damon Rosenthal, Geetha Yogaratnam, and professors Houman Younessi and Charles Pelletier for their roles in shaping my philosophy of software development. Lastly, I thank Frank Hauser for recognizing my programming aptitude and inspiring me to study and pursue a career in computer science.

James Linn

I thank my wife, Terria, for her kind forbearance as I worked my way through this project. I also thank James McGovern and Michael Stevens for setting examples of what enterprise architects should be.

Vikas Sharan

I acknowledge numerous industry thought leaders, far too many to list here, who have made enterprise architecture a truly multidisciplinary profession. I also acknowledge my wife and son for their support and patience. I would neither have written this book nor done much in life had I not been married to Ritu. Had my son Shubhankar not looked at me in awe when I told him that I might be writing a book, I would not have pushed myself to write at all.

Elias K. Jo

My thanks go out to my colleagues and friends who I have worked with and grown with through my technology career. In particular, I call out to Abdi Oday, you are *the* architect. To Tony Yi, you help me connect the dots between business and technology. To Brian Walter, who believes I know what I'm talking about, and to Jerry Wen, who called my first program a "virus."

I also thank my friends and family who have listened to my technology ideas even though I suspect they don't know what I'm talking about. Thanks Mom, Dad, Q, and Linda. Also, thanks to my dear Susan, who let me write much of my work at her place (which is much nicer than mine).

I'd also like to thank the other members of this author team. Your help and feedback have supported me immensely through the whole writing process.

Foreword

Once upon a time, a learned scientist, working in his laboratory, placed a beaker of liquid on a Bunsen burner. Picking up another beaker, he poured its contents into the first. As the temperature of the resulting mixture rose, its color started to change, and it suddenly effervesced, giving off the most wondrous aroma.

"Eureka!" the scientist shouted and ran from the lab to carry the good news to his superiors.

"We must go into production at once!" said the CEO. "We can sell two billion gallons this year alone!"

So a construction team was commissioned to build a two-hundred-foot-high Bunsen burner and a two-hundred-and-twenty-foot-high platform on which to place a half-million-gallon beaker, together with a five-hundred-foot crane to lift a second beaker into the air so that it could be poured into the first to mix the ingredients.

Well, no, that would be beyond absurd. An experiment in a lab is quite different from full-scale production. It is curious, then, that enterprise systems are sometimes built using the same architecture as one would use for an experiment. That, too, is beyond absurd. Enterprise systems are different from "dining room LAN" systems, but the difference lies in architecture, not design. Too often, however, architecture is confused with design. Architecture expresses the characteristics, structures, behavior, and relationships that are common across a family of things. Design expresses in detail how a specific member of a family will be built.

Architecture and design are always present. Much of the time, however, they are buried in the mind of the programmer. Now if all programmers were expert architect/designers, if all had long and fruitful experience with enterprise systems, if all enjoyed mind-meld with other programmers working on this and other related projects, and if no one after them ever had to maintain or build other enterprise systems, the invisibility of architecture and design would be irrelevant, and the world of IT would be quite different. But they aren't, they haven't, they don't, and they do.

Thus both architecture and design must be overt and separate. Architecture is produced by knowledgeable professionals who communicate, inspire, and lead. Design alone is not enough. Design of an enterprise system must be appropriate to the extrafunctional requirements of such systems—scalability, integratability, flexibility, buildability, and so on—which are specified by architecture.

One important reason enterprise systems often fail is that architecture and design are conflated. Other human endeavors are just as complex as enterprise systems, and yet they don't demonstrate anything close to the failure rate of large IT projects. Why is this? My answer is that the significant deficiencies within the IT industry currently occur in three major areas:

- Architecture at the enterprise level (enterprise architecture)
- Tools to support enterprise architecture
- Organization to support enterprise architecture

The Burning Need for Architecture

Designing an enterprise system is difficult. It requires a great deal of knowledge and skill. In other industries, much of the knowledge required by professionals is taught before they enter work. Such industries can be said to be "institutionally knowledgeable." This knowledge is often separated into specific areas of concern. In the building industry, architects learn that factory design is quite different from apartment design, which again is different from church design and office block design. Again, engineers understand that designing disk drives is quite different from designing airplanes (although both involve aerodynamics). Vehicle designers understand that 18-wheeler design is different from designing a family automobile. Each area has its own architecture, and design of specific products conforms to that architecture.

Within an industry, each area of concern is characterized by what can be called its "architectural approach." (Richard Hubert calls this "architectural style." See *Convergent Architecture*, Wiley, 2002). Projects whose products have the same architectural approach have a great deal in common, while those involving products with differing architectural approaches will have much less in common. This is so even though the techniques and tools used in projects may be similar. Design of a specific product is informed, constrained, and defined by the architectural approach within which that design happens. Techniques that are common across areas (and sometimes across industries) are important, but more important are the different applications of those techniques to each architectural approach.

The knowledge needed to produce something varies according to the architectural approach required by the customer, and customers will often specify the architectural approach: Thus, you'll hear "I want a family automobile" and seldom if ever "I want a vehicle."

Our industry is burdened by technique, and it is light on architectural approach. Yet it is obvious that a stand-alone GUI application is quite different from an enterprise system, and both are quite different from a factory automation control system. Each represents a different architectural approach, and for projects within each architectural approach, a great deal of knowledge is commonly applicable. Still, many IT projects begin with the professionals having a tool kit full of techniques, without the knowledge required for the given architectural approach. Some of this knowledge has to be learned painfully within the context of the project. Inevitably, many projects fail to deliver the required knowledge, as project architects are required to learn by themselves.

We need to capture that knowledge and make it available within our industry. This book is an important contributor to fulfilling this need.

The least computerized part of any organization is probably the IT application development organization. But wait a minute! Don't they have expensive PCs at every desk, networked together, and equipped with expensive software development tools? Well, yes. Yet many are still in the cottage industry stage of industrialization. It's as if a group of engineers were asked to build a new model of automobile, using their tools of trade—welding torches, lathes, shears, and so on. A design is given to them, detailed to the last nut and bolt, but there's no production line tailored to produce the architectural approach of "family auto." So they build their own production line (or infrastructure), devoting 80 percent of their efforts to it and only 20 percent to producing the required number of autos. When they finish, way over budget and time, their production line is thrown away because it was built for that one particular model.

In the same way, application developers may have good tools and deep skills, but without an architectural approach to inform, constrain, and define their efforts, each project must define its own enterprise architecture, as well as produce its own infrastructure, "glue" code, process customization, and so on (the production line). Today's tools support specific skills and techniques, usable across different architectural approaches. However, we do not have tools that support a specific architectural approach—what might be called "architecture support tools." Perhaps this is why our development processes are so fragmented: A usable process is specific to an architectural approach. Hence any general-purpose process must require extensive tailoring and customization. When was the last time you saw a general-purpose Customer Relationship Management (CRM) process marketed as the answer for your CRM people's process needs? To be effective, processes must be specific—down to the bottom-level procedures, and they must be oriented to producing the thing you want to produce. Lack of such orientation is why over-heavy processes, many of which seem to be (and indeed are) purposeless, are being widely rejected today.

We need tools that support the architectural approach required by enterprise systems. This book describes many of the requirements for such tools.

Now consider an IT department that has a number of experienced enterprise architects, capable and motivated developers, and excellent tools and processes, including enterprise architecture support tools. Is this enough? Alas, no. Enterprise architecture also needs a human organization within which the architecture can thrive, grow, and be effective. Effectiveness is measured in how much application development projects find their work reduced.

Many IT departments are organized on a project (or product) basis. Aside from some basic common infrastructure, such as the hardware, operating system, and Database Management System (DBMS), each project decides everything else for itself. Many initiatives I've seen have been staffed and equipped in this way, only to founder on what is perhaps the most difficult part: human organization. A successful approach to this problem is to organize into two major areas. One area provides the development and run-time infrastructure for building and deploying enterprise applications, while the other produces enterprise applications. This latter organization is rigorous in pushing as many common aspects of technology, development, and enterprise architecture approach as possible to the former organization. This form of organization is radically different from most in the industry today.

Whatever organization is finally settled on, the important point is that we organize to support a particular endeavor. If the organization does not directly support and enable that endeavor, then failures are, sadly, to be expected. Applying enterprise architecture such that application development projects are successful requires thought to be given to human organization.

This book addresses organization as it relates to enterprise architecture.

Why This Book Is Important

Today, the encouraging coalescence of opinion among leaders in enterprise architecture is that many enterprise systems have the same architectural approach—although not all express it in this way. A similar convergence addresses the kinds of techniques, patterns, and designs that are independent of specific application domains and that enable effective production of responsive, scalable, flexible, and unifiable enterprise applications. This book is important because in many ways it epitomizes that convergence. It addresses the whole range of knowledge required for successful enterprise systems and pulls together many strands, from the essential data foundation (the part of a system that persists when the machine is turned off) through run-time software design, architectural separation of concerns, and scalability patterns, to the much-neglected area of user interface. Of equal importance, it addresses not only what should be built but also how, from tools and modeling, to development process and methodology, to the product line approach, to agile development, and it includes the important question of human organization.

Moreover, what shines through the book is the sheer hardheaded practicality and competence of the authors—based on years of experience. This work contains much of the knowledge—or pointers to knowledge—that a budding enterprise architect needs, expressed in a readable, relevant, and nondidactic presentation. It is also an ideal textbook—a foundation work— for a graduate course in enterprise architecture. In fact, I suspect it could well become an important part of the institutional knowledge about enterprise systems within our fascinating and vibrant industry.

Oliver Sims
Mortimer West End
May 2003

Preface

In today's business climate, the rules of competition have changed. Organizations are forced to eliminate the process of reinventing the wheel each time a new business problem arises that forces the enhancement of an existing system or implementation of a new one. Enterprise architecture is the practice that allows organizations to build foundations they need to survive and adapt to present and future business challenges. Sound enterprise architecture supports the ability to stay agile, provides for increased return on investment, and creates a framework for making future technology decisions.

Enterprise architecture identifies the main components of an organization and how components in the organization's nervous system function together to achieve defined business objectives. These components include personnel, business processes, technology, financial information and other resources. If decisions about components and their interrelationships are uncoordinated, minimally effort and resources will be duplicated; performance and management problems will arise and will result in the loss of agility. Enterprise architecture done correctly will ensure the choice of appropriate components and will specify how each component will operate together in a fluid manner that increases organizational efficiencies.

Enterprise architecture is one of the most challenging roles in information technology today. Many aspects of the role are technical while much more of it is about interaction. Many people who have this position have significant responsibility but do not have authority or control. Enterprise architecture as an area of study allows one to focus on interesting, complex problems, to advance on the corporate ladder, and to maintain technical competencies while making a colossal difference to the enterprise.

Enterprise architecture requires skill sets not normally taught in university curriculum or acquired on the job. Even good architectures are rarely accepted without formidable challenges. The successful architect has to overcome any aversion to politics and become the evangelist of architecture in the eyes of its various stakeholders. Architects cannot simply buy into any vision that is articulated. Any involvement in the implementation of enterprise architecture requires one to understand it. The most successful architecture will have an architect that can describe the motivation behind architectural choices. Likewise, a successful architecture has an architect who leads the architecture team, the development team, the technical direction of the enterprise, and sometimes the organization itself. The primary focus of this book is to be a guide and trusted advisor to those who want to be successful in this role.

Why Enterprise Architecture?

A wise enterprise architect once worked for a very well-respected organization (name intentionally withheld). He was passionately engaged in a conversation with a senior executive about what direction the organization should take with its information systems. His recommendations fell on deaf ears until he asked the executive three very simple questions:

- How can we have a viable customer relationship management strategy when we do not even know where all of our customer's data reside?
- How does our technology spending equate to enabling our strategic business goals?
- Does our organization have an operational process model?

As you can surmise, the answers to these questions were not known. Many executives in information technology are not knowledgeable about what it takes to guide the architecture in the direction that results in the biggest bang for the buck. Sadly, many executives have lost control of the ship they steer, which has resulted in bloated infrastructures and conclusions being made on whims rather than on sound principle-based judgment and experience.

In many organizations, the annual budget cycle starts with clueless, disruptive questions such as "How many servers do we have?" or "Let's get the new Intel 3333 GHz machines as desktops." None of these statements is appropriate for a discussion about enterprise architecture. A good architecture addresses the following:

- The organization's business and information needs
- Leverage of the synergistic relationship between return on investment (ROI) and total cost of ownership (TCO)
- The ability to support migration from the current state (as-is)
- The ability to support easy migration to the organization's desired future state
- Ways to support the business objectives of reducing costs, improving operational service, and increasing revenue

Many organizations will claim to have an architect who creates architecture. Others will attempt to buy a nicely packaged architecture from one of the Big Five consulting firms without having a clue as to what they are getting. If your architecture does not address the following principles, you may be doing more harm than good:

- Data are separated from logic (business functions).
- The principles of modularity are observed by ensuring that each component within the enterprise architecture performs only one or two discrete tasks.
- Functions are separated into differentiated tasks that are generic and self-contained.
- The architecture is self-documenting. If it isn't, something is wrong.

Meta Architecture
Concentration is on high-level decisions that influence the structure of the system. Selection and Tradeoffs occur here.
Architecture
Definition of the structure, relationships, views, assumptions and rationale are created for the system. Decomposittion and separation of concerns occur here.
Guidelines
Creation of models, guides, templates and usage of design patterns for the system. At this stage, frameworks are used and standards are employed. Providing guidance to engineers so the integrity of the architecture is maintained occurs here.

Architecture / Construction

- All data and artifacts that are generated by an organization are managed and maintained by the same organization.
- The architecture is technically feasible and can be implemented at a reasonable cost within a reasonable time frame.
- The architecture is traceable from business requirement to technology implementation.
- Logical architecture is separated from physical architecture.

The term *architect* was derived from the building trade. The building of a corporation's nervous system is directly comparable to building a house. One may say, "I have no clue about how to build a $50 million dollar skyscraper, let alone a $50,000 house." Yet the response to both tasks is simple: They are accomplished by creating blueprints.

Blueprints show how a house will be constructed. They provide multiple views, each expressing its own level of detail. One view of the house may include all the electrical circuits that are of extreme value to an electrician. Likewise, the plumber will need a blueprint to show where all the pipes and water should go. Enterprise architecture diagrams the blueprints for all of the people within an organization so they know how to build an agile enterprise. The enterprise architecture blueprint is meant to provide sufficient detail to allow the idea to become a reality when put in the hands of skilled professionals, much as a house blueprint does.

We do not mean to imply that building a skyscraper is as easy as building a house. A decade ago, Garlan stated, "As the size and complexity of software systems increases, the design problem goes beyond the algorithms and data structures of the computation: designing and specifying the overall system structure emerges as a new kind of problem. . . . This is the software architecture level of design." [Garlan 1992].

Building an Enterprise Architecture

| Business |
| Information |
| Operational Organizational |
| Architectural |
| Infrastructure |

Enterprise architecture within this context seeks to solve for intellectual manageability. Architecture of large projects and their complexity arise from broad scope, massive size, novelties of the minute, currently deployed technologies, and other factors. The goal of enterprise architecture in this situation is to provide a manner to hide unnecessary detail, simplify difficult-to-understand concepts, and break down the problem into better-understood components (decomposition).

Complexity also arises within organizations due to processes used in building the system, the number of people who are involved with construction, the introduction of the possibility of outsourcing and geographically dispersed teams, and the organizational funding model. Ideally, enterprise architecture can assist, but not eliminate, the management of the process by providing clearer separation of concerns, enhancing communications, and making dependencies more manageable.

Building enterprise architecture is difficult but not impossible, as long as one sticks to architectural principles. The architectural blueprint defines what should be built, not how or why. Project plans document the how, and their creation is best left to individuals who have studied project management. The why is best left to one's business customer, as all architecture should be business-driven.

A word of advice: A good architecture provides agility but also provides constraints. A highly successful architecture will remove points of decision from those who are traditionally accustomed to having a free-for-all, making decisions impulsively or reacting to the opinions of those who are uninformed. Good architects will see things that make their heads hurt, but their aspirin is in knowing that their hard work and persistence will result in the reduction of future problems. Helping others see the value of enterprise architecture is crucial, as it brings benefit to the enterprise even if decisions have local consequences.

About This Book

The idea for this book came about during a lunchtime conversation between two of its authors. They were reminiscing about why the computer field was the only field in which one could become a manager, director, or even vice president without any computing experience. During this lunchtime conversation, we compared the computer field to such other professional fields as accounting, the practice and enforcement of law, and medicine.

Imagine that the town you live in is looking to hire a new police chief. Can you have confidence in the chief if he has never been a police officer? Furthermore, what if the prospective chief does not know how to use a gun and has no knowledge of proper investigation procedures? Extend this concept by envisioning a former McDonald's manager applying to be a partner at an accounting or law firm simply because he is a leader. The partners in the legal and accounting fields are leaders, but they also retain current knowledge of their professions and can argue a case or balance one's books. With relevant experience, the prospective police chief is a leader, too, and most likely remembers how to write a parking ticket and perform other cop-on-the-street duties.

Getting to the root of this problem cannot be done quickly. Unlike other fields, in the computer field you can have the title of architect but not necessarily know your job. The information technology field is constantly evolving and ever-changing. For the motivated, it requires long hours reading numerous books by the thought leaders of the industry. Even for the most diligent, the goal of achieving knowledge and enlightenment may never be fulfilled.

Many businesses are faced with such challenging problems as technology changing rapidly, employees with limited skill sets, smaller budgets, and less tolerance for failure. The only way one can be successful in this new order is to learn a new strategy. Today's businesspeople no longer have the opportunity to learn from their failures.

This book presents several provocative alternatives and serves as a leader, teacher, and guide to help you manage the chaos. It will challenge both the conventional and the contrarian's wisdom. This book is written by some of the brightest information technology thought leaders with the purpose of helping you create an agile enterprise using techniques learned on the battlefield of life.

Come to success.

The goal of this book is to share insight gathered by industry thought leaders in an easy-to-read and practical style. This book contains many leading-edge examples that illustrate how enterprise architecture can be applied to existing business and technology issues to help one focus on how to think concretely about enterprise architecture while providing solutions to today's problems. The following topics are covered within this book:

Content of This Book

- Systems architecture
- Software architecture
- Service-oriented architecture
- Product-line practice
- Methodology
- Enterprise unified process
- Agile architecture
- Agile modeling

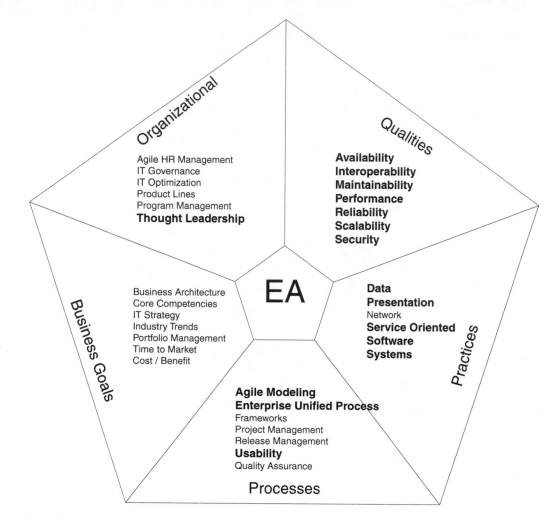

Figure P-3
McGovern/Stevens pentagon for architecture agility.

- Presentation tier architecture
- User experience and usability
- Data architecture
- Thought leadership

Authors and readers alike have their own religion when it comes to the best way a given topic should be explained. The examples contained within this book will not be blow-by-blow descriptions of the subjects. There are books better suited for this goal. We shall strictly focus on content that provides an additional value-added experience.

The author team also believes this book is not one to curl up with and read from cover to cover. The topics contained within this book mandate further study and even implementation before they can be fully appreciated.

Audience

This book is suitable for all information technology professionals who have the passion and discipline to study technology to the level required for successful implementation. Ideally, the reader of this book should be a project manager, senior developer, software architect, or enterprise architect employed by a Fortune 1000 organization or by a consulting firm that serves these enterprises. This book is also suitable for such information technology executives as chief information officers (CIO), chief technology officers (CTO), and others within the IT technology management chain.

Since *architect* is not a title one is granted based merely on the number of years on the job, this author team has intentionally avoided making any references to years of experience in the profession. We assume that the reader has basic familiarity with emerging technologies and their use in solving existing problems. We provide references in Appendix E hat the readers may refer to if they are interested in drilling deeper into any particular topic.

Disclaimer

The advice, diagrams, and recommendations contained within this book may be used however you desire, with the sole exception that you may not claim you were the author. The publisher, authors, and their respective employers do not provide any form of warranty or guarantee this book's usefulness for any particular purpose.

This book is 100 percent error free. Not! If you believed us even for a second, I have a suspension bridge in my backyard that I would like to sell you. The author team and editors have worked very hard to bring you an easy-to-understand, accurate guide on enterprise architecture. If you find any mistakes in this book, please contact us at eaauthors@architectbook.com.

This book uses a fictitious auto manufacturer to help illustrate examples. All companies, organizations, products, domain names, email addresses, people, places, and events depicted herein are fictitious. No association with any real company, organization, product, domain name, email address, person, place, or event is intended or should be inferred.

In Summary

Developing an enterprise architecture is a difficult task. It requires refinement of overlapping and conflicting requirements; invention of good abstractions from those requirements; formation of an efficient, cost-effective implementation; and ingenious solutions to isolated coding and abstraction evils. Additionally, enterprise architects must manage all this work up to a successful finish, all at the lowest possible cost in time and money. The only way this can be truly accomplished is by remaining agile.

In an agile approach, architects assume responsibilities beyond modeling and conceptual design. They must minimally serve as technical advisors to project managers. This is analogous to industrial engineers and their relationships to architects in the construction fields.

Many of the thoughts presented will assume an agile approach to explaining the solutions to the problems presented. An understanding of agile methods for software development will help readers become more successful in implementing practical enterprise architecture.

chapter 1

Systems Architecture

The first requisite for success is the ability to apply your physical and mental energies to one problem incessantly without growing weary.

Thomas Edison (1847–1931)

Systems architecture can best be thought of as both a process and a discipline to produce efficient and effective information systems.

It is a process because a set of steps is followed to produce or change the architecture of a system.

It is a discipline because a body of knowledge informs people as to the most effective way to design.

A system is an interconnected set of machines, applications, and network resources. Systems architecture unifies that set by imposing structure on the system. More importantly, this structure aligns the functionality of the system with the goals of the business.

Systems architecture encompasses the infrastructural layer of Figure 1–1.

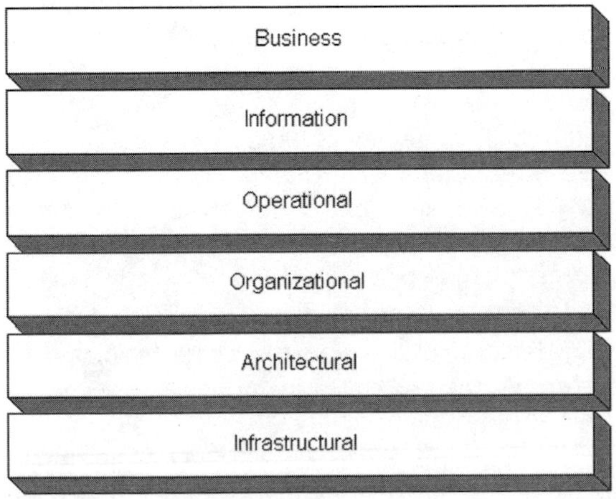

| Business |
| Information |
| Operational |
| Organizational |
| Architectural |
| Infrastructural |

Figure 1–1
Enterprise architecture model.

The basic purpose of systems architecture is to support the higher layers of the enterprise architecture. In many companies, the software and hardware represent a significant portion of the enterprise's total assets. It is important that enterprise architects do not equate their duties with the objects, the applications, or the machines that comprise their domain. The fundamental purpose is to support and further the business objectives of the enterprise. Hardware and software objects are fundamentally transient and exist only to further the purposes of the business.

Systems architecture is also used as part of the process of keeping the enterprise architecture aligned with the business goals and processes of the organization. It is important to understand the technical details of the infrastructure and the applications running within it but also to have the knowledge to participate in the process of architectural change with the enterprise architectural team. That involves the following:

- Defining the structure, relationships, views, assumptions, and rationales for the existing systems architecture and the changes in relationships, views, assumptions, and rationales that are involved in any changes required for moving from what is to what is desired.
- Creation of models, guides, templates, and design standards for in use in developing the systems architecture.

Canaxia Brings an Architect on Board

Let us set the stage for further discussion by focusing on Canaxia. As part of Kello James's engineering of Canaxia's enterprise architecture, James has brought on board an architect, the first one in Canaxia's history.

We are sitting in on a seminal meeting with some of Canaxia's C-level executives and Myles Standish, the new architect. He is being introduced to a semi-skeptical audience. It will be Myles's task in this meeting to establish the value to Canaxia of systems architecture and, by extension, a systems architect. As part of his charter, Myles was given oversight responsibility for recommended changes in the physical infrastructure and for the application structure of the enterprise. That means he will be part of the architecture team as Canaxia evolves.

Myles begins his remarks by giving a quick rundown of what his research has uncovered about the state of Canaxia's systems architecture. The discussion proceeded as follows:

- Myles noted that a large part of Canaxia's fixed assets, like those of most large corporations, is in the applications and machines that comprise Canaxia's systems architecture. The corporations in Canaxia's business environment that best manage their systems architectures will thereby gain a competitive advantage.
- He noted that the majority of the budget of the information technology (IT) department is swallowed by costs related to Canaxia's infrastructure. At the present time, most of these costs are fixed. If Canaxia wishes to gain any agility in managing its information technology resources, it will have to put into its systems architecture the necessary time, effort, and attention to sharply reduce those costs.

- Major business information technology functionality at Canaxia, Myles pointed out, is divided among silo-applications that were, in some cases, created three decades ago. Here, Myles was interrupted by an executive vice president who asked, "You are not going to tell us that we have to rewrite or replace these applications are you? We have tried that." Myles firmly replied that he had no plans to replace any of the legacy applications. Rather than replace, he was going to break down the silos and get the applications talking to each other.

- The terrorist attack that completely destroyed the World Trade Center in New York City has put disaster recovery on the front burner for Canaxia. Systems architecture issues are crucial to a disaster recovery plan (DRP). (The systems architecture aspects of data recovery planning are discussed later in this chapter.) As part of his presentation, Myles briefed the business side on the systems architecture section of a disaster recovery plan that had been developed by the architecture group.

- Myles then discussed the issues surrounding storage. He asked the executives if they realized that, at the rate that Canaxia's data storage costs were rising, by 2006 the cost of storage would equal the current IT budget. The stunned silence from the executives in the room told Myles that this was new information for the executive team. Myles then said he would also ask them for their support in controlling those costs and thereby gaining a further competitive advantage for Canaxia.

> Data storage and the issues surrounding it are discussed later on in this chapter.

- The recent flurry of bankruptcies among large, high-profile companies has led to the imposition of stringent reporting rules on the top tier of publicly owned companies in the United States. These rules demand almost real-time financial reporting capabilities from IT departments. Canaxia is one of the corporations subject to the new reporting stringencies. Myles bluntly told the gathered managers that the current financial system was too inflexible to provide anything more than the current set of reports and that the fastest those reports can be turned out is monthly. Myles next stated that accelerated financial reporting would be a high priority on his agenda. This brought nods from the executives.

- Myles also brought up the issue that visibility into the state of Canaxia's infrastructure is an important component of a complete view of the business. Myles intended to build a reporting infrastructure that allowed line managers and upper-level management to have business intelligence at their disposal so they could ascertain if the system's infrastructure was negatively impacting important business metrics, such as order fulfillment. In the back of his mind, Myles was certain that Canaxia's antiquated systems architecture was the root cause of some of the dissatisfaction customers were feeling about the auto manufacturer. He knew that bringing metrics of the company's infrastructure performance into the existing business intelligence (BI) system was an important component in restoring customer satisfaction levels.

The cumulative impact of thousands of low-level decisions has encumbered Canaxia with an infrastructure that doesn't serve business process needs and yet devours the majority of the IT budget. In many cases, purchase decisions were made just because the technology was "neat" and "the latest thing." "Under my tenure that will stop," Myles stated firmly. "We are talking about far too much money to allow that. Moving forward, how well the project matches with the underlying business process, and its return on investment (ROI) will determine where the system infrastructure budget goes."

Then the subject of money—the budget issue—came up. "You are not expecting a big increase in budget to accomplish all this, are you? No money is available for budget increases of any size," Myles was informed. He responded by pointing out that the system infrastructure of an enterprise should be looked at as an investment: a *major* investment, an investment whose value should increase with time, not as an object whose value depreciates. The underperforming areas need to be revamped or replaced. The areas that represent income, growth, or cost-reduction opportunities need to be the focus.

After the meeting, both Kello and Myles felt greatly encouraged. Both had been involved in enterprise architecture efforts that had faltered and failed. They both knew that the prime reason for the failure was an inability to engage the C-level managers in the architecture process and keep them involved. This meeting made it clear that, as far as Canaxia's top management was concerned, the issues of increased financial reporting, disaster recovery, and cost containment were on the short list of concerns. Myles and Kello knew that they would have the support they needed to build their architecture. They also knew that that architecture would have to translate into fulfillment of Canaxia's business concerns.

Architectural Approach to Infrastructure

It is important to take a holistic view of all the parts in a system and all their *interactions*.

We suggest that the most effective path to understanding a system is to build a catalogue of the *interfaces* the system exposes or the *contracts* the system fulfills. Focusing on the contract or the interface makes it much easier to move away from a preoccupation with machines and programs and move to a focus on the enterprise functionality that the systems must provide. Taken higher up the architecture stack, the contract should map directly to the business process that the system objects are supposed to enable.

When done properly, creating and implementing a new systems architecture or changing an existing one involves managing the process by which the organization achieves the new architecture as well as managing the assembly of the components that make up that architecture. It involves managing the disruption to the stakeholders, as well as managing the pieces and parts. The goal is to improve the process of creating and/or selecting new applications and the process of integrating them into existing systems. The payoff is to reduce IT operating costs by improving the efficiency of the existing infrastructure.

Additional Systems Architecture Concerns

The following are some considerations to take into account when building a systems architecture to support the enterprise:

- The business processes that the applications, machines, and network are supposed to support. This is the primary concern of the systems architecture for an enterprise. Hence, an architect needs to map all the company's business processes to the applications and infrastructure that is supposed to support it. This mapping should be taken down the lowest level of business requirements. In all likelihood, a 100 percent fit between the business requirements and the implementation will not be possible.

- Any part of the overall architecture that is being compromised. Areas that often suffer are the data and security architectures and data quality. The data architecture suffers because users don't have the knowledge and expertise to understand the effects of their changes to procedure. Security architecture suffers because security is often viewed by employees as an unnecessary nuisance. Data integrity suffers because people are pressured to produce more in less time and the proper cross-checks on the data are not performed.

- The stakeholders in the systems architecture. The people involved, including the following:
    - The individuals who have created the existing architecture
    - The people tasked with managing and enhancing that architecture
    - The people in the business who will be affected positively and negatively by any changes in the current systems architecture
    - The business's trading partners and other enterprises that have a stake in the effective functioning and continued existence of this corporation
    - Any customers dealt with directly over the Internet

The needs and concerns of the stakeholders will have a large impact on what can be attempted in a systems architecture change and how successful any new architecture will be.

- The context that the new system architecture encompasses. In this text, *context* refers to the global enterprise realities in which systems architects find themselves. If you're a company that is limited to a single country, language, and currency, you're the context will probably be relatively simple. Canaxia is a global corporation, and its stakeholders speak many different languages and live in a variety of time zones; thus its corporate culture is a complex mix of many regional cultures. This diversity is, on balance, a positive factor that increases Canaxia's competitiveness.

- The data with which the systems architecture deals.

> See Chapter 11, Data Architecture, for full details about data architecture considerations.

Working with Existing Systems Architectures

All companies have not had a single person or group that has had consistent oversight of the businesses systems architecture. This is the situation that Myles found himself in. Canaxia's systems architecture wasn't planned. The company had gone through years of growth without spending any serious time or effort on the architecture of its applications, network, or machines. Companies that have not had a systems architecture consistently applied during the growth of the company will probably have what is known as a *stovepipe architecture*.

Suboptimal architectures are characterized by a hodgepodge of equipment and software scattered throughout the company's physical plant. This equipment and software were obtained for short-term, tactical solutions to the corporate problem of the moment. Interconnectivity was an afterthought at best. Stovepipe architecture is usually the result of large, well-planned projects that were designed to fill a specific functionality for the enterprise. These systems will quite often be mission critical, in that the effective functioning of the company is dependent upon them. Normally these systems involve both an application and the hardware that runs it. The replacement of these systems is usually considered prohibitively expensive. A number of issues accompany stovepipe architecture:

- The systems don't fit well with the business process that they are tasked with assisting. This can be due to any of the following:
  - The software design process used to build the application imperfectly capturing the business requirements during the design phase
  - The inevitable change of business requirements as the business's competitive landscape changes

> See Chapter 5, Methodology Overview, Chapter 6, Enterprise Unified Process, and Chapter 8, Agile Modeling, for more depth on software development processes.

- The monolithic design of most stovepipe applications making it difficult to rationalize discrepancies between business processes and application functionality.
- The data not integrating with the enterprise data model, usually due to vocabulary, data format, or data dictionary issues.

See Chapter 11, Data Architecture, for a more complete discussion of the data architecture problems that can arise among stovepipe applications.

- Stovepipe applications definitely not being designed to integrate into a larger system, be it a result of enterprise application integration (EAI) or supply-chain management.

- It is difficult to obtain the information necessary for business intelligence or business process management.

- The marriage of application and hardware/operating system that is part of some stovepipe applications creating a maintenance and upgrade inflexibility that results in stovepipe applications having a high total cost of ownership (TCO).

Many times it is useful to treat the creation of enterprise systems architecture as a domain-definition problem. In the beginning, you should divide the problem set so as to exclude the less-critical areas. This will allow you to concentrate your efforts on critical areas. This can yield additional benefits because smaller problems can sometimes solve themselves or become moot while you are landing the really big fish. In the modern information services world, the only thing that is constant is change. In such a world, time can be your ally and patience the tool to reap its benefits.

Systems Architecture Types

Few architects will be given a clean slate and told to create a new systems architecture from scratch. Like most architects, Myles inherited an existing architecture, as well as the people who are charged with supporting and enhancing it and the full set of dependencies among the existing systems and the parts of the company that depended on them. It must be emphasized that the existing personnel infrastructure is an extremely valuable resource.

Following is an enumeration of the systems architecture types, their strengths, their weaknesses, and how to best work with them.

Legacy Applications

Legacy applications with the following characteristics can be extremely problematic:

- A monolithic design. Applications that consist of a series of processes connected in an illogical manner will not play well with others.

- Fixed and inflexible user interfaces. A character-based "green screen" interface is a common example of a legacy user interface (UI). Interfaces such as these are difficult to replace with browser-based interfaces or to integrate into workflow applications.

- Internal, hard-coded data definitions. These data definitions are often specific to the application and don't conform to an enterprise data model approach. Furthermore, changing them can involve refactoring all downstream applications.

- Business rules that are internal and hard-coded. In such a situation, updates to business rules caused by changes in business processes require inventorying applications to locate all the relevant business rules and refactoring affected components.
- Applications that store their own set of user credentials. Application-specific credential stores can block efforts to integrate the application with technologies to enable single sign-on and identity management.

While many legacy applications have been discarded, quite a few have been carried forward to the present time. The surviving legacy applications will usually be both vital to the enterprise and considered impossibly difficult and expensive to replace.

This was Canaxia's situation. Much of its IT department involved legacy applications. Several mainframe applications controlled the car manufacturing process. The enterprise resource planning (ERP) was from the early 1990s. The inventory and order system, a mainframe system, was first created in 1985. The customer relationship management (CRM) application was recently deployed and built on modular principles. The legacy financials application for Canaxia was of more immediate concern.

Canaxia was one of the 945 companies that fell under Securities and Exchange Commission (SEC) Order 4–460, so the architecture team knew it had to produce financial reports that were much more detailed than the system currently produced.

The existing financials would not support these requirements. The architecture team knew that it could take one of the following approaches:

- It could replace the legacy financial application.
- It could perform extractions from the legacy application into a data warehouse of the data necessary to satisfy the new reporting requirements.

Replacing the existing financial application was looked at long and hard. Considerable risk was associated with that course. The team knew that if it decided to go the replace route, it would have to reduce the risk of failure by costing it out at a high level. However, the team had other areas that were going to require substantial resources, and it did not want to spend all its capital on the financial reporting situation.

The data extraction solution would allow the legacy application to do what it is used to doing when it is used to doing it. The data mining approach buys Canaxia the following:

- Much greater reporting responsiveness. Using a data warehouse, it is possible to produce an accurate view of the company's financials on a weekly basis.
- More granular level of detail. Granular access to data is one of the prime functions of data warehouses. Reconciliation of the chart of

accounts according to the accounting principles of the enterprise is the prime function of legacy financial applications, not granular access to data.

- Ad hoc querying. The data in the warehouse will be available in multidimensional cubes that users can drill into according to their needs. This greatly lightens the burden of producing reports.

- Accordance with agile principles of only doing what is necessary. You only have to worry about implementing the data warehouse and creating the applications necessary to produce the desired reports. You can rest assured that the financial reports that the user community is accustomed to will appear when needed and in the form to which they are accustomed.

In terms of the legacy applications that Myles found at Canaxia, he concurred with the decision to leave them intact. In particular, he was 100 percent behind the plan to leave the legacy financial application intact, and he moved to implement a data warehouse for Canaxia's financial information.

The data warehouse was not a popular option with management. It was clearly a defensive move and had a low, if not negative, ROI. At one point in the discussion of the cost of the data warehouse project, the architecture team in general and Myles in particular were accused of "being gullible and biased toward new technology." This is a valid area to explore any time new technology is being brought on board. However, the architecture team had done a good job of due diligence and could state the costs of the project with a high degree of confidence. The scope of the project was kept as small as possible, thereby substantially decreasing the risk of failure. The alternative move, replacing the legacy application, was substantially more expensive and carried a higher degree of risk. Also, it was true that bringing the financial data into the enterprise data model opened the possibility of future synergies that could substantially increase the ROI of the data warehouse. In general terms, the good news with legacy applications is that they are extremely stable and they do what they do very well. Physical and data security are usually excellent. Less satisfying is that they are extremely inflexible. They expect a very specific input and produce a very specific output. Modifications to their behavior usually are a major task. In many cases, the burden of legacy application support is one of the reasons that so little discretionary money is available in most IT budgets.

Most architects will have to work with legacy applications. They must concentrate on ways to exploit their strengths by modifying their behavior and focus on the contracts they fulfill and the interfaces they can expose.

Changes in any one application can have unexpected and unintended consequences to the other applications in an organization. Such situations mandate that you isolate legacy application functionality to a high degree. At some point, a function will have been decomposed to the point where you will understand all its inputs and outputs. This is the level at which to externalize legacy functionality.

Client/Server Architecture

Client/server architecture is based on dividing effort into a client application, which requests data or a service and a server application, which fulfills those requests. The client and the server can be on the same or different machines. Client/server architecture filled a definite hole and became popular for a variety of reasons.

Access to knowledge was the big driver in the rise of client/server. On the macro level, with mainframe applications, users were given the data, but they wanted knowledge. On the micro level, it came down to reports, which essentially are a particular view on paper of data. It was easy to get the standard set of reports from the mainframe. To get a different view of corporate data could take months for the preparation of the report. Also, reports were run on a standard schedule, not on the user's schedule.

Cost savings was another big factor in the initial popularity of client/server applications. Mainframe computers cost in the six- to seven-figure range, as do the applications that run on them. It is much cheaper to build or buy something that runs on the client's desktop.

The rise of fast, cheap network technology also was a factor. Normally the client and the server applications are on separate machines, connected by some sort of a network. Hence, to be useful, client/server requires a good network. Originally, businesses constructed local area networks (LANs) to enable file sharing. Client/server architecture was able to utilize these networks. Enterprise networking has grown to include wide area networks (WANs) and the Internet. Bandwidth has grown from 10 Mbs Ethernet and 3.4 Mbs token ring networks to 100 Mbs Ethernet with Gigabit Ethernet starting to make an appearance. While bandwidth has grown, so has the number of applications chatting on a given network. Network congestion is an ever-present issue for architects.

Client/server architecture led to the development and marketing of some very powerful desktop applications that have become an integral part of the corporate world. Spreadsheets and personal databases are two desktop applications that have become ubiquitous in the modern enterprise.

Client/server application development tapped the contributions of a large number of people who were not programmers. Corporate employees at all levels developed some rather sophisticated applications without burdening an IT staff.

The initial hype that surrounded client/server revolution has pretty much died down. It is now a very mature architecture. The following facts about it have emerged:

- The support costs involved in client/server architecture have turned out to be considerable. A large number of PCs had to be bought and supported. The cost of keeping client/server applications current and of physically distributing new releases or new applications to all the corporate desktops that required them came as a shock to many IT departments. Client/server applications are another one of the reasons that such a large portion of most IT budgets is devoted to fixed costs.

- Many of the user-built client/server applications were not well designed. In particular, the data models used in the personal databases were often completely unnormalized. In addition, in a significant number of cases, the data in the desktop data store were not 100 percent clean.

- The huge numbers of these applications and the past trend of decentralization made it extremely difficult for an architect to locate and inventory them.

The rapid penetration of client/server applications into corporations has been expedited by client/server helper applications, especially spreadsheets. At all levels of the corporate hierarchy, the spreadsheet is the premier data analysis tool. Client/server development tools allow the direct integration of spreadsheet functionality into the desktop client. The importance of spreadsheet functionality must be taken into account when architecting replacements for client/server applications. In most cases, if the user is expecting spreadsheet capabilities in an application, it will have to be in any replacement.

In regard to client/server applications, the Canaxia architecture team was in the same position as most architects of large corporations in the following ways:

- Canaxia had a large number of client/server applications to be supported. Furthermore, the applications would have to be supported for many years into the future.

- Canaxia was still doing significant amounts of client/server application development. Some were just enhancements to existing applications, but several proposals focused on developing entirely new client/server applications.

- One of the problems that Myles has with client/server architecture is that it is basically one–to–one: a particular application on a particular desktop talking to a particular server, usually a database server. This architecture does not provide for groups of corporate resources to access the same application at the same time. The architecture team wanted to move the corporation in the direction of distributed applications to gain the cost savings and scalability that they provided.

The architecture team knew that it had to get some sort of grip on Canaxia's client/server applications. It knew that several approaches could be taken:

- Ignore them. This is the recommended approach for those applications that have the following characteristics:
  - Are complex and would be difficult and/or expensive to move to thin-client architecture.
  - Have a small user base, usually meaning the application is not an IT priority.
  - Are stable, that is, don't require much maintenance or a steady stream of updates, usually meaning that support of this application is not a noticeable drain on the budget.

- Involves spreadsheet functionality. Attempting to produce even a small subset of a spreadsheet's power in a thin client would be a very difficult and expensive project. In this case, we suggest accepting the fact that the rich graphical user interface (GUI) benefits that the spreadsheet brings to the table are the optimal solution.

- Put the application on a server and turn the users' PCs into dumb terminals. Microsoft Windows Server, version 2000 and later, is capable of operating in multi-user mode. This allows the IT department to run Windows applications on the server by just providing screen updates to individual machines attached to it. Putting the application on a server makes the job of managing client/server applications several orders of magnitudes easier.

- Extract the functionality of the application into a series of interfaces. Turn the client/server application into a set of components. Some components can be incorporated into other applications. If the client/server application has been broken into pieces, it can be replaced a piece at a time, or the bits that are the biggest drain on your budget can be replaced, leaving the rest still functional.

Service-Oriented Architecture (SOA) is a formalized method of integrating applications into an enterprise architecture. For more information on SOA, see Chapter 3, Service-Oriented Architecture.

- Client/server applications are still the preferred solution in many situations. If the application requires a complex GUI, such as that produced by Visual Basic, PowerBuilder, or a Java Swing application or applet, many things can be done that are impossible to duplicate in a browser application, and they are faster and easier to produce than in HTML. Applications that perform intensive computation are excellent candidates. You do not want to burden your server with calculations or use up your network bandwidth pumping images to a client. It is far better to give access to the data and let the CPU on the desktop do the work. Applications that involve spreadsheet functionality are best done in client/server architecture. Excel exposes all its functionality in the form of Common Object Model (COM) components. These components can be transparently and easily incorporated into VB or Microsoft Foundation Classes (MFC) applications. In any case, all new client/server development should be done using interfaces to the functionality rather than monolithic applications.

- Move them to thin-client architecture. At this time, this usually means creating browser-based applications to replace them. This is the ideal approach to those client/server applications that have an important impact on the corporate data model. It has the important side effect of helping to centralize the data resources contained in the applications.

The Canaxia architecture team decided to take a multistepped approach to its library of client/server applications.

- About a third of the applications clearly fell in the "leave them be" category. They would be supported but not enhanced.
- Between 10 and 15 percent of the applications would no longer be supported.
- The remaining applications are candidates for replacement using a thin-client architecture.

One matter that is often overlooked in client/server discussions is the enterprise data sequestered in the desktop databases scattered throughout a business. One can choose among several approaches when dealing with the important corporate data contained in user data stores:

- Extract it from the desktop and move it into one of the corporate databases. Users then obtain access via Open Database Connectivity (ODBC) or (JDBC) supported applications.
- For the client/server applications that are moved into the browser, extraction may be necessary.

While client/server architecture is not a good fit for current distributed applications, it still has its place in the modern corporate IT world. We are staunch advocates of using interfaces rather than monolithic applications. As we have recommended before, concentrate on the biggest and most immediate of your problems.

Thin-Client Architecture

Thin-client architecture is one popular approach to decoupling presentation from business logic and data. Originally *thin clients* were a rehash of time-share computing with a browser replacing the dumb terminal. As the architecture has matured, in some cases the client has gained responsibility.

As noted, client/server applications have substantial hidden costs in the form of the effort involved to maintain and upgrade them. Dissatisfaction with these hidden costs was one of the motivating factors that led to the concept of a "thin client." With thin-client systems architecture, all work is performed on a server.

One of the really attractive parts of thin-client architectures is that the client software component is provided by a third party and requires no expense or effort on the part of the business. The server, in this case a Web server, serves up content to users' browsers and gathers responses from them. All applications run on either the Web server or on dedicated application servers. All the data are on machines on the business's network.

Thin-client architecture has several problematic areas:

- A thin-client architecture can produce a lot of network traffic. When the connection is over the Internet, particularly via a modem, round-trips from the client to the server can become unacceptably long.

- The architecture of the Web was initially designed to support static pages. When the next request for a static page comes in, the server doesn't care about the browsing history of the client.

- Control of which browser is used to access the thin-client application is sometimes outside the control of the team developing the application. If the application is only used within a corporation, the browser to be used can be mandated by the IT department. If the application is accessed by outside parties or over the Internet, a wide spectrum of browsers may have to be supported. Your choices in this situation are to give up functionality by programming to the lowest common denominator or to give up audience by developing only for modern browsers.

- Users demand rich, interactive applications. HTML is insufficient to build rich, interactive GUI applications. When developing thin-client applications, the development team must strive to provide just enough functionality for users to accomplish what they want and no more. Agile methods have the correct approach to this problem and do no more than what clients request.

- Data must be validated. The data input by the user can be validated on the client and, if there are problems with the page, the user is alerted by a pop-up. The data also can be sent to the server and validated there. If problems arise, the page is resent to the user with a message identifying where the problems are.

- The most common Web development tools are usually enhanced text editors. More advanced Web rapid application development (RAD) tools exist, such as DreamWeaver and FrontPage; however, they all fall short on some level, usually due to the facts that they only automate the production of HTML and they give little or no help with JavaScript or with the development of server-side HTML generators such as Java server pages (JSPs) and Java servlets.

- Server resources can be stretched thin. A single Web server can handle a surprising number of connections when all it is serving up are static Web pages. When the session becomes interactive, the resources consumed by a client can rise dramatically.

The keys to strong thin-client systems architecture lie in application design. For example, application issues such as the amount of information carried in session objects, the opening database connections, and the time spent in SQL queries can have a big impact on the performance of a thin-client architecture. If the Web browser is running on a desktop machine, it may be possible to greatly speed up performance by enlisting the computing power of the client machine.

Data analysis, especially the type that involves graphing, can heavily burden the network and the server. Each new request for analysis involves a network trip to send the request to the server. Then the server may have to get the data, usually from the machine hosting the database. Once the data are in hand, CPU-intensive processing steps are required to create the graph. All these operations take lots of server time and resources. Then the new graph has to be sent over the network, usually as a fairly bulky object, such as a GIF or JPEG. If the data and an application to analyze and display the data can be sent over the wire, the user can play with the data to his or her heart's content and the server can be left to service other client requests. This can be thought of as a "semithin-client" architecture.

Mobile phones and personal desktop assistants (PDAs) can be considered thin clients. They have browsers that you can use to allow interaction between these mobile devices and systems within the enterprise.

The rise of the browser client has created the ability and the expectation that businesses expose a single, unified face to external and internal users. Inevitably, this will mean bringing the business's legacy applications into the thin-client architecture. Integrating legacy applications into thin-client architecture can be easy or it can be very difficult. Those legacy applications that exhibit the problematic areas discussed previously can be quite challenging. Those that are fully transactional and are built on relational databases can often be an easier port than dealing with a client/server application.

Exposing the functionality of the legacy systems via interfaces and object wrappering is the essential first step. Adapting the asynchronous, batch-processing model of the mainframe to the attention span of the average Internet user can be difficult. We discuss this in greater detail later in this chapter.

Using Systems Architecture to Enhance System Value

As software and hardware systems age, they evolve as maintenance and enhancement activities change them. Maintenance and enhancement can be used as an opportunity to increase the value of a system to the enterprise. The key to enhancing the value of systems architecture via maintenance and enhancement is to use the changes as an opportunity to modify stovepipe applications into reusable applications and components. This will make your system more agile because you will then be free to modify and/or replace just a few components rather than the entire application. In addition, it will tend to "future proof" the application because the greater flexibility offered by components will greatly increase the chances that existing software will be able to fulfill business requirements as they change.

The best place to begin the process is by understanding all the contracts that the stovepipe fulfills. By *contracts*, we mean all the agreements that the stovepipe makes with applications that wish to use it. Then, as part of the enhancement or maintenance, the stovepipe externalizes the contract via an interface. As this process is repeated with a monolithic legacy application, it begins to function as a set of components. For example, some tools consume COBOL copy books and produce an "object wrapper" for the modules described in the copy books.

Messaging technology is a useful technology for integrating legacy functions into your systems architecture. With messaging, the information required for the function call is put on the wire and the calling application either waits for a reply (pseudosynchronous) or goes about its business (asynchronous). Messaging is very powerful in that it *completely* abstracts the caller from the called function. The language in which the server program is written, the actual data types it uses, and even the physical machine upon which it runs are immaterial to the client. With asynchronous messaging calls, the server program can even be offline when the request is made and it will fulfill it when it is returned to service. Asynchronous function calls are very attractive when accessing legacy applications. They can allow the legacy application to fulfill the requests in the mode with which it is most comfortable: batch mode.

To be of the greatest utility, object wrappers should expose a logical *set* of the underlying functions. We think you will find that exposing every function that a monolithic application has is a waste of time and effort. The functionality to be exposed should be grouped into logical units of work, and that unit of work is what should be exposed.

What is the best way to expose this functionality? When creating an object wrapper, the major consideration should be the manner in which your systems architecture plan indicates that this interface or contract will be utilized. The effort should be made to minimize the number of network trips.

Wrappering depends on distributed object technology for its effectiveness. Distributed objects are available under Common Object Request Broker Architecture (CORBA), Java, .Net, and by using Messaging Oriented Middleware (MOM) technology. Distributed objects rely upon an effective network (Internet, intranet, or WAN) to operate effectively.

In addition to increasing the value of a stovepipe application to other segments of the enterprise, exposing the components of that application provide the following opportunities:

- The possibility of sunsetting stagnant or obsolete routines and the incremental replacement of them by components that makes more economic sense to the enterprise.
- The possibility of plugging in an existing component that is cheaper to maintain in place of the legacy application routine.
- Outsourcing functionality to an application services provider (ASP).

If the interface is properly designed, any application accessing that interface will be kept totally ignorant of how the business contract is being carried out. Therefore, it is extremely important to design them properly. The Canaxia architecture group has an ongoing project to define interfaces for legacy applications and important client/server applications that were written in-house.

The best place to start when seeking an understanding of the interfaces that can be derived from an application is not the source code but the user manuals. Another good source of knowledge of a legacy application's contracts is the application's customers, its users, who usually know exactly what the application is supposed to do and the business rules surrounding its operation. Useful documentation for the application is occasionally available. Examining the source code has to be done at some point, but the more information gathered beforehand, the faster and easier will be the job of deciphering the source.

A network protocol is a set of agreements and specifications for sending data over a network. Many network protocols are in use today. Let's dive into a quick overview of protocols used to help you become familiar with this domain to allow you to make informed infrastructure decisions.

Network Protocols

TCP/IP

Transmission Control Protocol/Internet Protocol (TCP/IP) is the network protocol that has the widest use in industry:

- TCP/IP protocol stacks exist for all operating systems currently in use.
- It is an extremely robust and reliable protocol.
- It is routable, which means that it can be sent between disparate networks.
- It is available for free with all operating systems. Even Netware, the home of the once very popular network protocol SPX, offers TCP/IP in addition to its proprietary protocol.
- An extremely robust suite of security functionality has been developed for communication via TCP/IP.
- Internet communication by and large uses TCP/IP. Several other network protocols can be and are used over the Internet. They will be discussed later in this section. However, the Internet communication protocols HTTP, HTTPS, SMTP, and FTP all use IP.
- Web services use TCP/IP.
- Messaging protocols use TCP/IP.
- All remote object communication, such as DCOM, Java RMI, and CORBA, can use TCP/IP.

Subnets

Subnets are segments of a network that can communicate directly with each other. A person on a subnet can communicate directly with all the other computers on that subnet. Networks are split into subnets by the subnet mask part of the TCP/IP properties. Subnets simplify network administration and can be used to provide security.

Computers on different subnets require routers to communicate with computers on other subnets.

TCP/IP is a suite of protocols built on a four-layer model:

- The first layer is the network interface. These are the LAN technologies, such as Ethernet, Token Ring, and FDDI, or the WAN technologies, such as Frame Relay, Serial Lines, or ATM. This layer puts frames onto and gets them off the wire.

- The second layer is the IP protocol. This layer is tasked with encapsulating data into Internet datagrams. It also runs all the algorithms for routing packets between switches. Sub-protocols to IP are functions for Internet address mapping, communication between hosts, and multicasting support.

- Above the IP layer is the transport layer. This layer provides the actual communication. Two transport protocols are in the TCP/IP suite: TCP and User Datagram Protocol (UDP). These will be explained in greater detail in the next section.

- The topmost layer is the application layer. This is where any application that interacts with a network accesses the TCP/IP stack. Protocols such as HTTP and FTP reside in the application layer. Under the covers, all applications that use TCP/IP use the sockets protocol. Sockets can be thought of as the endpoints of the data pipe that connects applications. Sockets have been built into all flavors of UNIX and have been a part of Windows operating systems since Windows 3.1, see Figure 1–2.

The transmission protocol is the actual mechanism of data delivery between applications. TCP is the most widely used of the transmission protocols in the TCP/IP suite. It can be described as follows:

- TCP is a packet-oriented protocol. That means that the data are split into packets, a header is attached to the packet, and it is sent

Figure 1–2
TCP stack.

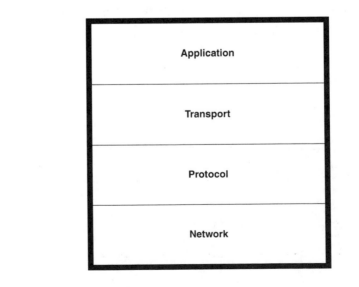

Application
Transport
Protocol
Network

off. This process is repeated until all the information has been put on the wire.

- TCP is a connection-oriented protocol in that a server requires the client to connect to it before it can transmit information.
- TCP attempts to offer guaranteed delivery. When a packet is sent, the sender keeps a copy. The sender then waits for an acknowledgement of receipt by the recipient machine. If that acknowledgement isn't received in a reasonable time, the packet is resent. After a certain number of attempts to transmit a packet, the sender will give up and report an error.
- TCP provides a means to properly sequence the packets once they have all arrived.
- TCP provides a simple checksum feature to give a basic level of validation to the packet header and the data.
- TCP guarantees that packets will be received in the order in which they were sent.

UDP is used much less than TCP/IP, yet it has an important place in IP communication because of the following:

- UDP broadcasts information. Servers do not require a connection to send data over the network via UDP. A UDP server can sit and broadcast information such as the date and time without regard to whether or not anyone is listening.
- UDP does not have the built-in facilities to recover from failure that TCP has. If a problem, such as a network failure, prevents a particular application from receiving the datagram, the sending application will never know that. If reliable delivery is necessary, TCP should be used or the sending application will have to provide mechanisms to overcome the inherently unreliable nature of UDP.
- UDP is faster and requires less overhead than TCP.
- Typically, UDP is used for small data packets and TCP for large data streams.

Other Protocols

ATM is a high-speed network technology like Ethernet. All data streamed over ATM are broken down into 53-byte cells. The constant size of the cells simplifies switching issues and can provide higher transmission capabilities than 10 or even 100 Mbs Ethernet. TCP/IP establishes a connection between sender and recipient machines, but it doesn't establish a circuit, a fixed set of machines through which all the traffic will go for the duration of the session. TCP/IP allows network conditions to modify the actual physical route that packets will take during a session. This makes TCP/IP robust and self-healing in the face of network problems. In the case of video or voice transmission, it is best to have a connection between the communicating parties, and ATM can provide that. TCP/IP can be sent over ATM.

Another protocol that has emerged is Multiprotocol Label Switching (MPLS). MPLS competes with ATM in that it allows the establishment of labeled paths between the sender and the receiver. This ability to establish paths has made MPLS of interest to the creators of virtual private networks. Unlike ATM, it is relatively easy with MPLS to establish paths across multiple layer 2 transports like Ethernet and FDDI. It also outperforms ATM and offers some very useful path control mechanisms. Like ATM, MPLS uses IP to send data over the Internet.

For further information, see the MPLS FAQ at *www.mplsrc.com/mplsfaq.shtml*.

The emergence of Gigabit Ethernet implementations has provided enough raw bandwidth to allow TCP/IP over Ethernet to compete with ATM for video and other bandwidth-intensive applications.

The big question to consider about TCP/IP is whether to utilize IPv4, which was released way back in 1980, or to move toward IPv6. IPv6 has many features of importance to the infrastructure of an enterprise:

- Virtually unlimited address space.
- A different addressing scheme that allows individual addresses for every device in an enterprise everywhere in the world.
- A fixed header length and improved header format that improves the efficiency of routing.
- Flow labeling of packets (Labeling packets allows routers to sort packets into streams, making TCP/IPv6 much more capable than TCP/IPv4 of handling stream-oriented traffic such as VOIP or video streams.)
- Improved security and privacy (Secure communications are compulsory with v6, meaning that all communications exist in a secure tunnel. This can be compelling in some circumstances. The increased security provided by IPv6 will go a long way toward providing a Secure Cyberspace.)

Secure Cyberspace

The Internet was designed with a highly distributed architecture to enable it to withstand such catastrophic events as a nuclear war. The infrastructure, the net part, is secure from attack. However, the structure of the Internet provides no security for a single node, router, or computer connected to the Internet.

Unprotected computers are the key to one of the greatest current threats to the Internet: denial-of-service attacks. The others are worms and email viruses that eat up bandwidth.

The U.S. government has outlined a national strategy to protect the Internet. For details, see the draft paper entitled "National Strategy to Secure Cyberspace" at www.whitehouse.gov/pcipb.

From a hardware and operating system point of view, converting to v6 can be very close to cost-free. This is based on the facts that all the major operating systems have v6 IP stacks built into them and that adding v6 support to devices such as routers only requires a software update.

The exhaustion of the IP namespace is another issue of concern. It is a fact that the current IP address space is facing exhaustion. Innovations such as network address translation (NAT) have postponed the day when the last address is assigned, buying time for an orderly transition from IPv4 to v6.

Network Address Translation

Network address translation is a technology that allows all computers inside a business to use one of the sets of IP addresses that are private and cannot be routed to the Internet. Since these addresses cannot be seen on the Internet, an address conflict is not possible. The machine that is acting as the network address translator is connected to the Internet with a normal, routable IP address and acts as a router to allow computers using the private IP addresses to connect to and use the Internet.

IPv6 contains numerous incremental improvements in connecting devices to the Internet. The enormous expansion of the naming space and the addressing changes that make it possible for every device on the planet to be connected to the Internet are truly revolutionary for most enterprises. For Canaxia, not only can every machine in every one of its plants be connected to a central location via the Internet, but every sub-component of that machine can have its own connection. All sections of all warehouses can be managed via the Internet. With a secure Internet connection, dealers selling Canaxia cars can connect their sales floors, their parts departments, and their service departments to a central Canaxia management facility.

The conversion of an existing enterprise to IPv6 is not going to be cost-free. Older versions of operating systems may not have an IPv6 protocol stack available, perhaps necessitating their replacement. In a large corporation, ascertaining that all existing applications will work seamlessly with v6 will probably be a substantial undertaking. In theory, IPv4 can coexist with v6. But we say that if you have to mix IPv4 with v6, you will have to prove that there are no coexistence problems.

We recommend the following be used as a template when contemplating conversion to IPv6:

- If you are a small or medium-sized firm without any international presence, wait until it is absolutely mandatory. In any case, you will be able to get by with just implementing v6 on the edge of the network, where you interface with the Internet.
- If you are a multinational corporation or a firm that has a large number of devices that need Internet addresses, you should formulate a v6 conversion plan. Start at the edge and always look for

application incompatibilities. Of course, you should have exhausted options such as using nonroutable IP addresses along with NAT.

- If you do decide to convert, start at the edge and try to practice just-in-time conversion techniques.

Because of its size and international reach, Canaxia has formulated a strategy to convert to IPv6. The effort will be spaced over a decade. It will start at the edge, where Canaxia interfaces with the Internet and with its WAN. New sites will be v6 from the very start. Existing sites will be slowly migrated, with this effort not due to begin for another five years. As applications are upgraded, replaced, or purchased, compatibility with IPv6 will be a requirement, as much as is economically feasible. Canaxia's architecture team is confident no crisis will occur anytime in the next 10 years due to lack of available Internet addresses.

Systems Architecture and Business Intelligence

If your enterprise runs on top of a distributed and heterogeneous infrastructure, the health of the infrastructure can be vital to the success of your business. In that case, the architect will need to provide visibility into the status of the enterprise systems. The ability to provide near real-time data on system performance to business customers is critical. Following is an example:

- The Web server was up 99 percent of the time, which means it was down 7.3 hours last month. What happened to sales or customer satisfaction during those hours? If the customers didn't seem to care, should we spend the money to go to 99.9 percent uptime?

- The Web server was up, but what was the average time to deliver a page? What did customer satisfaction look like when the page delivery time was the slowest?

- How about the network? Part of the system is still on 10 MBits/second wiring. How often is it afflicted with packet storms? With what other variables do those storm times correlate?

- Part of the service staff is experimenting with wireless devices to gather data on problem systems. What was their productivity last week?

In terms of quality attributes, the following figures for uptime relate to availability:

- *99 percent uptime per year equates to 3.65 days of downtime.*
- *99.9 percent uptime equates to .365 days or 8.76 hours down per year.*
- *99.99 percent uptime means that the system is down no more than 52 minutes in any given year.*

It should be possible for a manager in marketing, after receiving an angry complaint from an important client, to drill into the data stream from systems underpinning the enterprise and see if there is a correlation between the time it took to display the Web pages the customer needed to work with and the substance of his or her complaints. Perhaps several of the times that the Web server was down coincide with times when this customer was attempting to do business. Without data from all the possible trouble spots, it will be impossible to pin down the real source of the problem.

In most organizations, the tools to monitor the health of networks, databases, and the Web infrastructure are not plugged into the enterprise's overall BI system. They are usually stand-alone applications that either provide snapshots into the health of a particular system or dump everything into a log that is looked at on an irregular basis. Often they are little homegrown scripts or applications thrown together to solve a particular problem, or they are inherited from the past when the systems were much simpler and much less interdependent.

Start with the most important performance indicators for your system. Perhaps they are page hits per second or percent bandwidth utilization. Integrate this data into the BI system first. Perhaps the segment of your enterprise infrastructure architecture aligns with one of the company's business units. Fit the performance metrics to the unit's output and present it to the decision makers for your unit.

The planning stage for a new system is an excellent time to build performance metrics measurement into its architecture. New systems often are conceived using an optimistic set of assumptions regarding such metrics as performance and system uptime. When that new system comes online, you will be grateful for the ability to generate the data to quantify how accurate the initial assumptions were. If problems crop up when the system becomes operational, you will have the data necessary to identify when the problem lies at your fingertips.

Service Level Agreements

Service level agreements (SLAs) are a formalization of the quality attributes of availability and performance that have been externalized in a document. As infrastructure and applications become more vital to businesses, they are demanding that the providers of those assets guarantee, in writing, the levels of performance and stability that the business requires. SLAs are a manifestation of how important certain IT functionality has become to modern business processes.

The crucial part of dealing with an SLA is to think carefully about the metrics required to support it. If you are required to provide a page response time under 3 seconds, you will have to measure page response times, of course. But what happens when response times deteriorate and you can no longer meet your SLA? At that point you had better have gathered the data necessary to figure out why the problem occurred. Has the overall usage of the site increased to the point where the existing Web server architecture is overloaded? What does the memory usage on the server look like? For example, Java garbage collection is a very expensive operation. To reduce garbage collection on a site running Java programs, examine the Java code in the applications. If garbage collection is bogging down your system, the number of temporary objects created should be reduced.

The bottom line is this: When planning the systems architecture, you will have to think beyond the metric in the agreement to measuring all the variables that impact that metric. We suggest that the introduction of SLAs in your organization be looked upon as an opportunity rather than a threat and as an excellent tool to force the organization to update, rationalize, and above all integrate its infrastructure measurements. If a new project does not have an SLA, you might want to write up a private SLA of your own. The discipline will pay off in the future.

Systems Architecture and Storage

The vast majority of businesses data storage costs are increasing exponentially. The costs are both in the physical devices and the personnel costs associated with the individuals needed to manage, upgrade, and enhance the storage devices.

One problem with storage costs is that the real cost to the enterprise is hidden in hundreds or thousands of places. Most businesses upgrade storage a machine and a hard drive at a time. This results in scores or hundreds of small, low profile purchases that never show up as line items on the IT department's budget, see Figure 1–3.

The important point is not that you adopt a particular architecture but that you understand the benefits and trade-offs associated with the different architectures.

The conventional approach is to attach the storage devices, usually hard drives, directly to the machine. This is direct attached storage (DAS) and is an excellent choice for situations in which tight security must be maintained over the data in the storage device. Its downside is that it is expensive to upgrade and maintain. Upgrade costs arise more from the costs related to having personnel move applications and data from older, smaller storage devices to the newer, bigger device than from the costs related to the storage device itself. In addition, this storage mechanism makes it difficult to establish exactly what the storage costs of the organization are and to manage those costs.

Storage area networks (SANs) offer basically unlimited storage that is centrally located and maintained. Using extremely high-speed data transfer methods such as FDDI, it is possible to remove the storage media from direct connection to the computer's backplane without affecting performance. SANs offer economical enterprise-level storage that is easy to manage and to grow, but implementing a SAN is a large operation that requires thorough architectural analysis and substantial up-front costs. However, the ROI for most SAN enterprises is very compelling. SANs should not be considered unless it is possible to establish the very high-speed data connection that is required.

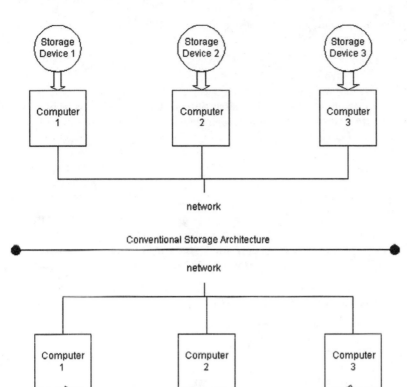

Conventional Storage Architecture

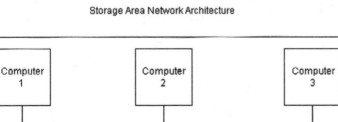

Storage Area Network Architecture

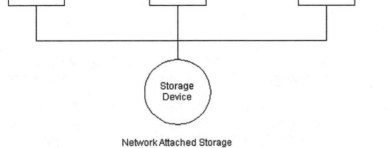

Network Attached Storage

Figure 1-3
The three storage
architectures.

If the machines to be connected are geographically remote, different storage architecture is required.

Network attached storage (NAS) devices are low-cost, very-low-maintenance devices that provide storage and do nothing else. You plug a NAS into the network, turn it on, and you have storage. Setup and maintenance costs are very low; the only cost is to relocate the existing, attached storage to the NAS. These devices are perfect for increasing storage to geographically distributed machines.

The major determinant for choosing between NAS and SAN should be the data storage architectural design. The following will help you choose between the two:

- Disaster recovery strongly favors SAN because of the ease with which it can be distributed over large distances. As of this writing, fiber can extend up to 150 kilometers (95 miles) without amplification. This means that data can be mirrored transparently between devices that are 300 kilometers (190 miles) apart.

- Distributed performance is better with SANs.

- The following functionality favors SANs:
  - Very large database applications
  - Application server duties

- File storage definitely favors NASs.

- Ease of administration is a tie. In their own ways, both storage solutions are easy to administer. With a NAS, you plug it into the wall and into the network and you have storage. The work lies in partitioning the storage, moving data onto the device, and pointing users to the device. SANs require quite a bit of up-front design and setup, but once online, adding storage is very simple and more transparent than with a NAS.

- High availability is pretty much a tie. The SAN can mirror data for recovery, and the NASs all have hot-swappable hard drives in a RAID 5 configuration.

- Cost favors NASs. Initial costs for an NAS storage installation are about one-fifth the cost of a similar-sized SAN storage installation. However, the ongoing costs of a SAN are usually less than for a similar NAS. This is due to the following factors:
  - Staffing costs are less due to the centralization of the storage devices. This makes the task of adding storage much quicker and easier.
  - Hardware costs are less. Less is spent on storage devices. Less disk space is needed with a SAN because they are more efficient in the utilization of storage. Normally, SAN storage will average 75 to 85 percent utilization, while utilization for some NASs storage devices will be 10 to 15 percent.
  - LAN infrastructure spending is less. NASs are accessed over the network, and backups are usually conducted over the network. This increase in network traffic can force costly network upgrades.

Canaxia has a SAN that hosts the company's mission-critical databases and data. Portions of that data are mirrored to data centers physically removed from the operation center itself. In addition, each company campus has a central file-storage facility that consists of large numbers of rack-mounted NAS arrays. Most application servers are connected to the SAN. Storage requirements continue to grow at a steady rate, but the cost of administrating this storage has actually dropped as the data have been centralized onto the SAN and various NASs.

Most of you will use a mix of the three architectures. It is important that this mix be planned by your architects and be easy for managers to cost and to justify.

While disaster recovery planning is not about providing backup of a company's data, the storage architecture chosen can make the task of protecting and recovering the enterprise data storage materially cheaper and easier. It will take significant effort to make direct attached storage (DAS) as robust in the face of disaster as distributed storage architecture, such as a SAN or a NAS with remote mirroring. Quick (a few hours) recovery is possible with a SAN architecture.

Disaster recovery is discussed in greater detail later in this chapter.

Systems Architecture Aspects of Security

Ensuring enterprise security is a wide-ranging operation that touches on almost every area of a business. As such, it has to grow out of extensive interactions between the company's management and the architecture team. One of the issues that has to be on the table first is how to build a security architecture that increases a company's competitive advantage. Since security is an enterprise-wide endeavor, the input of the entire architecture team is required. It is important to adopt a graduated approach and apply the proper security levels at the proper spots in the enterprise.

Effective enterprise security consists of the following:

- Effective, well thought out, clearly communicated security policies.
- Effective, consistent implementation of these policies by a company staff that is motivated to protect the business's security.
- A systems architecture that has the proper security considerations built in at every level.

When discussing enterprise security, one of the first matters to discuss is what needs to be protected and what level of protection is appropriate for that particular item. A useful rule of thumb can be borrowed from inventory management. Proper inventory management divides articles into three levels: A, B, and C. The A level items are the most valuable, and extensive security provisions are appropriate for them. Trade secrets, credit card numbers, and update and delete access to financial systems are just a few of the items that would be on an A list. B items need to be protected, but security considerations definitely need to be balanced against operational needs. C items require little or no security protection. As a rule of thumb, 5 percent of the list should be A items, 10 to 15 percent should be B items, and the rest should be C items. A similar analysis is appropriate for the security aspects of an enterprise's systems architecture. The data assets are located on machines that are part of its systems architecture. In addition, elements of the systems architecture, such as the network, will most often be used in attacks upon the business's vital data resources. The following is a list of the major classes of security attacks, in rough order of frequency, that must be considered when building the security part of the systems architecture:

- Viruses and worms
- Attacks by dishonest or malicious employees
- Destruction or compromise of the important data resources due to employee negligence or ignorance
- Attacks from the outside by hackers
- Denial-of-service attacks

Viruses and worms are the most common IT security problems. The vast majority of the viruses and worms that have appeared in the last few years do not actually damage data that are resident on the computer that has the virus. However, in the process of replicating themselves and sending a copy to everyone on a corporate mailing list, viruses and worms consume a large amount of network bandwidth and usually cause a noticeable impact on productivity. For the last couple of years, the most common viruses have been email viruses. They exploit extremely well-known psychological security vulnerabilities in a business's employees. In addition, some person or group of persons in corporate infrastructure support will be required to monitor computer news sites daily for the appearance of new email viruses and to immediately get and apply the proper antivirus updates to, hopefully, prevent the business from becoming infected by this new email virus. Unfortunately, the current state of antivirus technology is such that defenses for viruses can only be created after the virus appears.

The majority of attacks against corporate data and resources are perpetrated by employees. To protect your organization against inside attack, utilize the following:

- User groups and effective group-level permissions
- Effective password policies to protect access to system resources
- Thorough, regular security audits
- Effective security logging

Assigning users to the proper group and designing security policies that completely, totally restricts access to only the data and resources the group requires to perform its functions is the first line of defense against attacks by insiders. Don't forget to remove the accounts of users who have left the firm.

For those enterprises that still rely on passwords, another area for effective security intervention at the systems architecture level is effective password policies. In addition to mandating the use of effective passwords, make sure that no resources, such as databases, are left with default or well-known passwords in place. All passwords and user IDs that are used by applications to access systems resources should be kept in encrypted form, not as plain text in the source code. Passwords are the cheapest method of authentication and can be effective if strong passwords are assigned to users, the passwords are changed on a regular basis, and users don't write down their passwords. Users can reasonably be expected to remember one strong password if they use that password on at least a daily basis. Since a multitude of applications are password-protected in most enterprise environments, we recommend that enterprises standardize on Windows operating system logon user name and password as the standard for authentication and require every other application use the Windows authentication as its authentication. This can be via the application making a call to the Windows security service or by the application accepting a Kerberos ticket from the operating system.

Unfortunately, the vast majority of enterprises have a multitude of applications that require a user name and password. As a result, most users have five, ten, even fifteen passwords. Some passwords will be used several times a day, some will be used a couple of times a year. Often the corporation cannot even standardize on a single user name, so the user will have several of those, too. In a situation such as this, most users will maintain written username and password lists. The justification for this situation is always cost: The claim is made that it would cost too much to replace all the current password-protected programs with ones that could get authentication from the Windows operating system. When faced with this argument, it is useful to document the time and money spent on resetting passwords and the productivity lost by users who are locked out of an application that they need to do their job. We expect you will discover costs in the range of $10 to $20 per employee per year. Those figures, coupled with the knowledge of the damage that could occur if one of the password lists fell into the wrong hands, might get you the resources necessary to institute a single sign-on solution.

Devices such as smart card readers and biometric devices can authenticate using fingerprints and retina scans. These devices allow extremely strong authentication methods, such as changing of the password daily or even changing the user's password right after they have logged on. The cost of equipping an entire enterprise with such devices is considerable, and they only get you into the operating system. If the user has ten password-protected programs to deal with once he or she is logged in, the device has not bought you much. Protecting A-level assets with one of these devices makes excellent sense.

For the majority of employees and the majority of businesses, a single sign-on solution with the user expected to memorize one strong password every couple of months is adequate security and the most cost-effective solution.

You need to know where you are vulnerable and what attacks can exploit these vulnerabilities. If you have not run a security audit, make plans to do so. Large enterprises may want to engage outside consultants to audit the entire firm. As an alternative, some software packages can effectively probe your system for vulnerabilities. You might consider building up a security cadre of individuals in your organization. They would be tasked with knowing and understanding all the current hacker attacks that can be mounted against systems of your type and with running any security auditing software that you might purchase.

Finally, effective, tamperproof audit systems will allow you to detect that an attack has occurred and will provide you with the identity of the attacker. This is where scrupulously removing expired user accounts is important. If Bob Smith has left the company but his user account still exists, that account can be compromised and used in an attack with you having no clue as to who really perpetrated it.

In any case, the cost of implementing the patch to the vulnerability has to be balanced against the seriousness of the threat and the probability that someone in your organization would have the sophistication necessary to carry out such an assault. Lock the most important doors first.

Inadvertent damage to or compromise of business data by well-meaning or ignorant employees causes substantial business losses annually. While this type of damage has no malicious component, the results are the same as for a malicious attack. Inadvertent damage can be prevented in a variety of ways. Training is first and foremost. When new corporate applications are being brought online, it is crucial that people who will be using them are thoroughly trained. Effective training provides a positive ROI. After an application is in regular operation, it is important that experienced operators be given the time and resources to train and mentor new operators. However, even the best training programs are not 100 percent effective. It is also important to make sure that people are in the proper roles and that the security parameters of these roles are so crafted that people are given the least opportunity to do damage without restricting their ability to carry out their assigned functions. Audit trails are useful for establishing exactly what was damaged or compromised. After that has been ascertained, it is the role of the backups that have been applied to this data that will allow you to recover from the situation.

Hacker attacks are high-profile events that invariably become news items when discovered. It is difficult to accurately judge the size of business losses caused by hacker attacks from the Internet. In any case, you have to take them seriously. All companies can expect to experience hundreds of low-level "doorknob rattling" attacks, such as port scans run against them, in the course of a year. On the positive side, the vast majority of technical hacker exploits are wellknown, and the measures necessary to defeat them are standard parts of all companies' Internet defense systems. The major response that hacker attacks will prompt is you keeping all your machines both inside the firewall and in the DMZ 100 percent up to date on security patches. Any stratagem that you can devise to streamline the application of security patches will give your company a strategic advantage over a company that does it all by hand or ignores the problem completely.

Of the attacks that can occur from the outside—from the Internet— denial-of-service (DOS) attacks are the least common but potentially the most destructive. DOS attacks involve the recruitment of large numbers of outside computer systems and the synchronization of them to flood your system with such a large number of requests that it either crashes or becomes unable to respond to legitimate service requests by your customers. Fortunately, due to the large-scale effort involved on the part of the attackers, DOS attacks are rare and are normally directed against high-profile targets. DOS attacks are extremely difficult to combat, and it is beyond the scope of this book to discuss methods to deal with them. It is important, though, that if your company is large enough and important enough to be a possible target for a DOS attack, you begin now to research and to put into place countermeasures to fend off a DOS attack.

All security mechanisms, such as encryption and applying security policies, will have an impact on system performance. Providing certificate services costs money. By applying agile architecture principles to the design of this security part of your systems architecture, you can substantially mitigate these impacts. To be agile in the area of systems architecture security design means applying just the right level of security at just the right time. It means being realistic about your company's security needs and limiting the intrusion of security provisions into the applications and machines that make up your systems architecture. Just enough security should be applied to give the maximum ROI and no more.

As a final note, do not forget physical security for any machine that hosts sensitive business data. There are programs that allow anyone with access to a computer and its boot device to grant themselves administrator rights. Once more, we recommend the A-, B-, and C-level paradigm. C-level data and resources have no special physical security. B-level data and resources have a minimal level of security applied. For A-level data and resources, we suggest you set up security containment that also audits exactly who is in the room with the resource at any time.

Systems Architecture and Disaster Recovery

Disaster recovery planning is sometimes referred to as "business continuity planning." DRP for the enterprise system infrastructure is a major systems architect responsibility.

The purpose of DRP is to produce a set of plans to deal with a severe disruption of a company's operations. DRP is independent of the modality of the disaster (flood, fire, earthquake, terrorist attack, and so on). It involves the following:

- Identification of the functions that are essential for the continuity of the enterprise's business.
- Identification of resources that are key to the operation of those functions, such as:
  - Manufacturing facilities
  - Data
  - Voice and data communications

- ○ People
- ○ Suppliers
- ○ Etc.
- Prioritization of those key resources
- Enumeration of the assumptions that have been made during the DRP process
- Creation of procedures to deal with loss of key resources
- Testing of those procedures
- Maintenance of the plan

DRP is normally a large project that involves input from every unit in the company. The sheer size of the effort can make it seem prohibitively expensive. DRP is largely about money. Perfect disaster protection will cost an enormous amount of it. A disaster coupled with inadequate DRP can destroy a company. However, the DRP process will be like any other company process in that the size and cost of the DRP effort will be adjusted to fit available company resources. To provide the best DRP for the available resources, it is vital that the analysis phase correctly do the following:

- Identifies all the key resources
- Accurately prioritizes the key resources
- That it provide accurate costing for protection of those resources
- That it provide accurate estimates of the probability of the destruction of the key resources

Given an accurate resource analysis, the IT/business team can work together to build an affordable DRP. When costing the DRP program, do not neglect the maintenance of the plan.

DRP planning for most enterprises will involve the coordination of individual DRP plans from a variety of departments. We focus on Canaxia's DRP and the process of its creation.

Initially, the disaster planning team (DPT) was created and tasked with creating a DRP process. Canaxia's architecture group was a core part of that team. It quickly became obvious that Canaxia required a permanent group to maintain and administer its DRP. As a result, the Department of Business Continuity (DBC) was created.

Following are some of the critical Canaxia resources that the DRP identified:

- Engine manufacturing facilities. All engines for the Canaxia line of vehicles were manufactured in one facility.
- Brake assemblies. Canaxia used a unique brake system available from a single supplier. That supplier was located in a politically unstable region of the world.
- Data. Of the mountain of data that Canaxia maintained, 10 percent was absolutely critical to daily functioning. Furthermore, 45 percent of the data was deemed irreplaceable.

- Voice and data communications. Canaxia depended on the Internet for the communication necessary to knit together its far-flung departments.
- The enterprise resource planning (ERP) system that totally automated all of Canaxia's manufacturing and supply activities.
- A core group of IT employees that had done the installation of the ERP system. Loss of the manager and two of the developers would have a severe negative impact on the functioning of the ERP system.

Once critical resources had been identified, they were divided into three categories:

- Survival critical. Survival critical resources are those absolutely required for the survival of the company. Normally, survival critical activities must be restored within 24 hours. Data, applications, infrastructure, and physical facilities required for the acceptance of orders and the movement of completed vehicles from manufacturing plants are examples of survival critical resources for Canaxia.
- Mission critical. Mission critical resources are resources that are absolutely required for the continued functioning of the enterprise. However, the company can live without these resources for days or weeks.
- Other. This category contained all the resources that could be destroyed in a disaster but were not deemed to be survival or mission critical. If they were replaced, it would be months or years after the disaster.

Within each category, the team attached a probability that the resource would become unavailable and a cost to protect it. All the assumptions used in the analysis phase were detailed to allow the individuals tasked with funding the DRP to do a reality check on the numbers given them.

Documenting existing procedures so that others could take on the functioning of key Canaxia employees was a substantial part of the DRP. Canaxia, like many other enterprises, had neglected documentation for a long time. That neglect would have to be rectified as part of the DRP. In many cases, producing documentation decades after a system was built would be an expensive task.

Every DRP will have to enumerate a set of tests that will allow the company to have confidence in the DRP. Running some of the tests will be expensive. Once more, the test scenarios have to be rated as to cost, probability of resource loss, and criticality of the resource. Testing is a good place to examine the assumptions from the analysis phase for accuracy.

A DRP will have to be maintained. As systems and business needs change, the DRP will have to be revised. In some cases, the DRP needs can drive business decisions. Canaxia made the decision to move to a generic brake assembly that could be obtained from a variety of sources. Canaxia's brake performance was one of its technical selling points, and management knew that moving to a generic brake would not help sales. Canaxia also established a company rule that strongly discouraged getting into single-source supplier relationships in the future.

We recommend an iterative approach to DRP. First do the top of the survival critical list all the way through the testing phase. Use the experience gained in that process to make the next increment more focused and efficient. Trying to do the entire job in one big effort risks cost and time overruns that can cause the process to be abandoned before anything is protected.

Conclusion

There are three important aspects to emphasize about systems architecture:

1. It must align with the business goals of the organization.
2. It must provide what the stakeholders need to perform their functions. This is a two-way street. The architecture team should take responsibility to establish communication with systems architecture stakeholders and to understand their issues.
3. The software and hardware infrastructure of an enterprise is a major asset that must be managed to provide the greatest return on that investment.

The following should be considered as systems architecture best practices:

1. Know the business processes that the systems architecture is supporting. Know them inside and out.
2. Keep support of those business processes first and foremost on your agenda. Know what the business needs and keep the business side aware of your accomplishments.
3. Know the components in your systems architecture: all the machines, applications, network connections, and so on.
4. Instrument, your system. That is, install monitoring and measurement systems that allow you to find the problem areas and the bottlenecks.
5. Attack the cheap and easy problems first. That will build and help maintain credibility and trust with the business side of your company.
6. Prioritize and be proactive. If you are not constrained to produce immediate results, identify the most important systems architecture problems and attack them first, even before they become problems. Good system measurements are key to being able to identify problem areas in your systems architecture and to establish the most effective means to deal with them.
7. Know all your stakeholders. The people aspects of your systems architecture are at least as important as the machines.
8. Only buy as much security as you need. Give up on the idea of becoming invulnerable. Prioritize your security issues into A, B, and C lists.

As architects team with the business side to align systems with business processes and keep them aligned as business needs evolve, they will get the opportunity to develop skills in understanding the business and working with financial algorithms and calculations.

chapter 2

Software Architecture

Maps encourage boldness. They're like cryptic love letters.
They make anything seem possible.

Mark Jenkins, "To Timbuktu"

The software architecture of a system or a family of systems has one of the most significant impacts on the quality of an organization's enterprise architecture. While the design of software systems concentrates on satisfying the functional requirements for a system, the design of the software architecture for systems concentrates on the nonfunctional or quality requirements for systems. These quality requirements are concerns at the enterprise level. The better an organization specifies and characterizes the software architecture for its systems, the better it can characterize and manage its enterprise architecture. By explicitly defining the systems software architectures, an organization will be better able to reflect the priorities and trade-offs that are important to the organization in the software that it builds.

The software architecture of a system supports the most critical requirements for the system. For example, if a system must be accessible from a wireless device, or if the business rules for a system change on a daily basis, then these requirements drastically affect the software architecture for the system. It is necessary for an organization to characterize software architectures and the level of qualities that their systems support to fully understand the implications of these systems on the overall enterprise architecture.

Since this book has a focus on agile methodologies, it is important to discuss the relationship between software architecture and agile methodologies. The recent push in software development toward agile methodologies, such as eXtreme Programming (XP) (Beck 1999), in some ways counters the belief in an explicit and formal definition of software architecture. Many agile methodologists assert that software design is the result of iterative refactoring of a system by developers until a sufficiently workable design emerges. However, in XP these iterative refactorings are done in a small, easily understandable, conceptual framework for the system called the *system metaphor*. The system metaphor is a simple shared story for how the system works. It consists of the core concepts, classes, patterns, and external metaphors that shape the system being built. The system metaphor plays the same role in the development of a system as conceptual software architecture. It provides a vision for the development of the software, and it is the goal that each system stakeholder must strive toward. A formal definition of the software architecture is more technical than the system metaphor, but both play the same role in providing a central concept for system development. The extent to which an organization needs to provide a formal technical description of the architectures of its systems depends on many factors. Clearly, it would not be cost-effective to formally define the software architecture for a small noncritical departmental software application, and it would be unacceptable to not formally define the software architecture of a highly available telecommunications software system. Each organization is different and has a different need for detailed software architecture. The agile principle of "If you don't need it, then don't do it" applies to software architecture as well as to all the other parts of an organization's enterprise architecture. For more on agile methods and architecture, see Chapter 9, Agile Enterprise Architecture.

What Is Software Architecture?

No single standard definition of software architecture exists. However, many authors and researchers have attempted to define the term *software architecture*. Following are some of the most notable definitions:

"The software architecture of a program or computing system is the structure or structures of the system, which comprise software components, the externally visible properties of those components, and the relationships among them." *Software Architecture in Practice*, Len Bass, Paul Clements, and Rick Kazman, Addison-Wesley, 1997.

"An architecture is the set of significant decisions about the organization of a software system, the selection of the structural elements and their interfaces by which the system is composed, together with their behavior as specified in the collaborations among those elements, the composition of these structural and behavioral elements into progressively larger subsystems, and the architectural style that guides this organization— these elements and their interfaces, their collaborations, and their composition." *The UML Modeling Language User Guide*, Booch, Jacobsen, Rumbaugh, Addison-Wesley, 1999.

"Software architecture is a set of concepts and design decisions about the structure and texture of software that must be made prior to concurrent engineering to enable effective satisfaction of architecturally significant explicit functional and quality requirements and implicit requirements of the product family, the problem, and the solution domains." *Software Architecture for Product Families: Principles and Practice*, Mehdi Jazayeri, Alexander Ran, Frank van der Linden, Addison-Wesley, 2000.

These definitions are a bit academic, and a practical guide must include a practical definition of software architecture and the reasons for having one. Mountains of research have been done on the subject, but why exactly would a project need to define the software architecture of the system it is building? With this practical guide in mind, we offer our definition of software architecture:

The software architecture of a system or a collection of systems consists of the important design decisions about the software structures and the interactions between those structures that comprise the systems. These design decisions support a desired set of qualities that the system should support to be successful. The design decisions provide a conceptual basis for system development, support, and maintenance.

The Role of a Software Architect

Creating software architecture is a difficult endeavor, and the software architect has one of the most difficult jobs in a software project. He or she must have the confidence of all the stakeholders. This confidence is based on a track record of successful projects and the respect of the developers who regard him or her as a technical leader. The architect must be able to communicate with varied constituencies. He or she must have excellent design skills, technology skills, and an understanding of software engineering best practices. He or she must be able to navigate through organizational politics to get the project done correctly and on time. The software architect must be a leader, a mentor, and a courageous decision maker.

Architecture, like life, is all about the people. Great people deliver great architecture, and the reverse is true. The techniques outlined in this chapter will give an architect some concepts and tips for delivering great architecture, but the best way to truly deliver great architecture is to start with truly great architects.

Why We Need Software Architecture

In cartography, a single map cannot fully characterize a place. There are many kinds of maps, such as highway maps, bike trail maps, and elevation maps. Each type explains and describes different aspects of the same physical place. Each map is relevant to a different user or stakeholder. The family on vacation is interested in having a highway map in its glove compartment. The cyclist needs the bike trail map, and a mountain climber needs the elevation map. In addition, a map doesn't have to be perfectly accurate to be useful. If a perfect scale map of rides and paths were given to visitors to Walt Disney World, it would be accurate and somewhat useful. However, the map that is actually handed out at Walt Disney World contains pretty pictures of the interesting rides and the paths are not to scale. For the Disney World visitor, this map is more interesting, though useful, and it imparts a better understanding of the layout of the park than a cartographer's map would. The same holds true in software architecture. The architecture that is presented to the end-user contains less information and is more interesting, but focuses on the critical aspects of the system that the particular stakeholder community should understand. The software architecture that is needed by developers can be more like a cartographer's depiction of the software architecture, with multiple maps outlining the multiple aspects of the system in more detail.

Just like maps, the purpose of software architecture is to impart an understanding of the design of the system to the reader. The point of software architecture is to communicate an idea. It takes the reader into the software and explains the important concepts. It helps them understand the important aspects of the system and gives them a feeling for a system without actually having to see inside it.

Despite the invention of satellite imagery, maps are still important. We can now get an exact picture of Earth at any level of detail we need. The pictures show rivers, oceans, and more, as well as the layout of Walt Disney World in their exacting detail.

"Maps have the character of being textual in that they have words associated with them, that they employ a system of symbols within their own syntax, that they function as a form of writing (inscription), and that they are discursively embedded within broader contexts of social action and power." John Pickles, "Text, Hermeneutics and Propaganda Maps," in Trevor J. Barnes and James S. Duncan, eds., *Writing Worlds: Discourse and Metaphor in the Representation of Landscape*, London: Routledge, 1992, 193.

Maps and architecture don't describe reality. They are representations of reality within a chronological and cultural context. They also have a distinct perspective on the place they describe. In other words, reverse engineering a Unified Modeling Language (UML) diagram from the source code of the system does not create an architectural model. The architectural model communicates the important design decisions that were made at a particular time and that were important to a particular group of people.

The cartography metaphor works, except for the fact that architecture is an upfront activity. In cartography, maps are created for existing places. They are meant to describe something that has already been created. In software architecture, the maps or models depict software that is yet to be created. The models embody the important design decisions that have been made about the system. By creating and contrasting different models of software that fulfill the same purpose, intelligent decisions can be made about which designs are better than others. This is the second purpose of software architecture.

The Two Extremes

Software development approaches vary between two extremes. The first method involves little or no upfront modeling or design. This is the "shanty town" method of system development in which a few developers code without a mental picture in their heads about the system they are building. Also, some managers believe that if developers aren't coding, they aren't working. These project managers also believe that the sooner developers begin coding, the sooner they will be done. This stems from the incorrect belief that a constant amount of time is involved in the coding of the system no matter what upfront process is used. In this type of environment, developers don't fully understand the requirements for the system. Some of these environments deliver decent software through heroics by developers and frequent rewrites, although this approach is not repeatable, and it is extremely risky.

The other extreme in software development is "ivory tower" software architecture in which a design team or a single architect design a system in every detail, down to the class and method level. The architect has a clear picture in his or her head about the design of the system but has not left many of the implementation details to the developers. The belief in these environments is that the architects are the most experienced developers and thus can design the best possible system from start to finish. No one person or small team can possibly understand all the requirements, predict every change in requirements, and have expertise in every technology that the project is built upon. Developers in these environments also suffer from low morale because they are perceived as somehow inferior to the designers of the system. Morale is also poor because the developers must implement the design in a prescriptive way with little or no input into the design of the system.

The Middle of the Road

So what does all this have to do with software architecture? Software architecture is the middle road between no design and complete design. It is a view of the system design that shows how the design satisfies the critical requirements of the system. It is the role of the software architect to design the structures of the software such that those critical requirements are satisfied. It is also the goal of the software architecture to facilitate the development of the system by multiple teams in parallel. In addition, if multiple teams or departments within an organization will support and maintain the software, the software architecture will allow those parts of the system to be managed and maintained separately. The most important role that the software architecture has is that of an organizing concept for the system. The software architect has an idea how the system should work. The software architecture is the communication of that idea to other system stakeholders so that everyone understands what the system does and how it does it.

In a practical sense, two rules determine whether or not a design detail should be included in the software architecture:

1. The design detail must support a quality requirement.
2. The design detail must not detract from stakeholder understanding of the software architecture.

If the design detail does not somehow improve on a quality requirement of the system, it should be left out. For example, the architect might not choose XML due to performance concerns. However, the system might benefit more from the modifiability of XML. Without an elicitation of the quality requirements for the system, these types of decisions might be made based on personal preference instead of quality requirements. Also, if a design detail is complex and cannot be described in a simple way that stakeholders can understand, it should not be included in the architecture. A design detail that is not understandable is also a sign of a bad design.

The System Stakeholders

Many people believe that the software architecture is meant only for developers to use as an overall guide for system design and construction. While this may be the software architecture's primary purpose, other system stakeholders can use the architecture as a basis to guide their activities as well. The following are some of the system stakeholders:

- Developers
- Managers
- Software architects
- Data administrators
- System customers
- Operations
- Marketing
- Finance
- End-users

- General management
- Subcontractors
- Testing and quality assurance
- UI designers
- Infrastructure administrators
- Process administrators
- Documentation specialists
- Enterprise architects
- Data administrators

The software architect must elicit input from all the system stakeholders to fully understand the requirements for the architecture. This is important because the requirements are built from the perspective of what the system should do. However, the architecture must reflect how the system will perform those functions.

The system's customers want the system to be of high quality. They want the system to be delivered in a timely manner. And they want it to be developed as inexpensively as possible.

The development organization is looking for a vision for the system it is going to design and develop. It wants to know that the architecture is easy to implement. It has hard deadlines that it must meet, so reusability is important. The developers are going to be looking for technologies in the architecture that they currently understand. They want the architecture to match their desired platforms, development tools, libraries, and frameworks. They need to meet dates, so the architecture should ease their development effort. Most of all, they want an architecture that they have participated in developing and evolving throughout the lifetime of the product.

The operations group wants a product that is supportable and maintainable. The product must not fail. It has to meet service level agreements that it can only meet if the product is reliable. If the system goes down, this group is on the front lines trying to get it back up. When it does fail, the operators need to find out why so that the problems can be fixed. Therefore, the system should provide some traceability for system transactions so that what went wrong can be tracked down. The operations group also has the responsibility for installing new machines and upgrading software platforms on a schedule. It needs the software to be flexible and portable so that moving it to a new machine or onto a new version of the operating system is fast and easy.

The marketing people are looking for an architecture that can deliver the greatest number of features in the shortest amount of time. An architecture that is flexible and can integrate off-the-shelf packages will win their hearts. In addition, if the product is a commercial product, the architecture may be a key selling point. Savvy customers of commercial products will recognize a good architecture from a bad one.

End-users need great performance from the system. It must help them get their jobs done more quickly and easily. The system must be usable. The interfaces must be designed with end-user tasks in mind and, ideally, the system should be customizable so that end-users can choose how they wish to use it.

Every stakeholder has his or her perspective on what is important for the system to do. It is up to the architect to mediate among these individual concerns. Not all stakeholders can get everything they want all the time. Sometimes, a requirement can be easily met without detracting from another requirement. Sometimes trade-offs have to be made among the various requirements. These are the decisions that the architect must facilitate within the constraints that the project sponsor places on time and money.

Our fictitious automobile manufacturer Canaxia was losing sales to other manufacturers because it relied completely on its dealer network to sell its cars. Other auto manufacturers created Web sites that allow customers to customize and order their car online. The other auto manufacturers ship the cars from their manufacturing facilities directly to the customers through local dealerships. This resulted in greater customer service and reduced the hassle of buying a car from a dealership and struggling with the sales process.

Canaxia was about two years behind their competition. The management of the company has decided to fund a project for twelve months to create a Web site and related infrastructure that exceed the capability of their competition.

Canaxia has a mainframe system for orders, inventory, and financials. Its inventory and order system was written in the 1980s. The system functions, but it is very expensive to change. The financial system was purchased and customized in the late 1990s. The infrastructure architects have decided that IBM MQSeries will be used to integrate all the enterprise systems. The standard for Web development in the company is Java and J2EE.

The architects on the project faced a difficult job. They realized that the software architecture is implemented at the beginning, middle, and end of every project. However, much more emphasis is on it at the beginning of every project. Before the architects started, they created a checklist of principles they would strive to follow while they created the architecture:

1. The architecture should be thin.
2. The architecture should be approachable.
3. The architecture should be readable.
4. The architecture should be understandable.
5. The architecture should be credible.
6. The architecture doesn't have to be perfect.
7. Don't do big upfront design. If given a choice between making the model perfect or implementing it, implement it.
8. Do the simplest thing that could possibly work without precluding future requirements.
9. The architecture is a shared asset.
10. Involve all stakeholders but maintain control.
11. The architecture team should be small.
12. Remember the difference between a pig and a chicken.

The Pig and the Chicken

One day on a farm near Canaxia, a pig and a chicken decided to open a restaurant.

The pig turned to the chicken and asked him, "So what should we call this restaurant?"

The chicken replied, "How about Ham 'n' Eggs?"

The pig thought for a moment and said, "I don't think that's a very good idea. You would be involved, but I would be committed."

The Scrum (Schwaber et al. 2001) development methodology uses this story as the central theme for distinguishing between those people who are pigs (assigned work) and those who are chickens (interested, but not working).

When creating software architecture, chickens can wreck the process in two ways. If chickens are on the architecture team, you should just give up and open a restaurant. Assuming that the architecture team consists of all pigs, make sure that the architecture addresses the concerns of the pigs in the organization. Don't let the chickens sneak in an egg or two and make you design for something that isn't really important.

The following sections describe the steps that the architects at Canaxia performed to create their architecture (Bass, Clements, and Kazman 1997).

The Business Case

Canaxia was lucky; it involved the architecture team when it created the business case for the system. Many organizations do not involve an architect at project conception. The architecture team was involved from the start of the project. The business customers needed to understand the relative costs of the various solutions they were contemplating. The architecture team understood the current technical environment and the tools, processes, and personnel required to implement the various options presented by the business community. The business customers realized that a great solution that is late is sometimes worse than a mediocre solution that is delivered quickly. Only the architecture team can evaluate the various options and provide input into the time required to create each one.

At Canaxia, the architect was involved up front with auto dealers, management at the company, system end-users, and the development team. The business case took into consideration the timeframe and the technical complexity involved in creating a Web site for the automobile business.

Understanding the Requirements

Canaxia realized that an architect couldn't build architecture for a system that he or she didn't understand. The requirements of the stakeholders provide the architect with a context from which to create a design. A use case is a common way of capturing a requirement. The use case describes some action that the system must perform. A use case describes in detail every input/output interaction that the system performs with a user or another system. These are known as *functional requirements*. In addition, the use cases specify how the interaction will occur. These are modifying clauses known as "nonfunctional requirements." For example, the *use case*, "User enters amount, presses enter, and system displays the invoice" is a functional requirement. A nonfunctional requirement modifies this phrase, such as "User enters amount, presses enter, and system displays the invoice within 5 seconds." The "within 5 seconds" is a nonfunctional or quality requirement of the system.

The architect must document how the system will accept the amount described in the use case by using a user interface, validating the request, storing the data in a database, and generating an invoice for the user. There is no architecture for the use case, but the architecture must satisfy all the use cases, including the nonfunctional or quality requirements. The architecture should address each pattern of interaction, such as "User enters data, data are saved to database, a result or an error is displayed."

At Canaxia, the requirements were well documented, but even more importantly, user representatives were involved in every stage of the project and provided daily input into the architecture and development of the system.

Creating or Selecting the Architecture

The requirements gathering process delivers a set of functional requirements with qualities identified with each requirement. At Canaxia, these requirements were a set of use cases or user stories. Each use case had a set of qualities that needed to be supported by the use case. The architecture that Canaxia selected needed to support all these requirements and qualities. Some of the requirements were easily met using techniques, technologies, and practices with which the developers and architects were familiar. The difficult part of selecting the architecture was satisfying those qualities using techniques and technologies that were risky and unknown.

To address and reduce the technical risks in the project, the architects created an *architecture baseline*. This was the main milestone in the development of the architecture (Jacobsson, Booch, Rumbaugh 1998). The architecture baseline is the first fully executable portion of the system. A small thread of execution through all system layers was completed to prove that the system could be built. To create an architecture baseline, the architecture team followed the steps described in the following paragraphs. These steps were performed in an iterative manner with the architects working toward an architecture baseline that satisfied the functional and quality requirements for the system:

Select Use Cases

Select a small number of use cases from the requirements for the system. These are selected to address the most technically risky areas of the system. This subset of use cases is the *architecturally significant* use cases. For example, Canaxia chose a new software package for printing documents from the system. It included the use cases for printing documents in the architecture baseline to demonstrate that the interface to the new software package was going to work.

Identify Important Qualities

Software architecture requires trade-offs. Canaxia could not get the architecture to satisfy every requirement in the best possible way. Therefore, the qualities that the architecture should support were prioritized. For example, Canaxia valued performance over modifiability. When decisions required a trade-off between quality attributes, it was helpful to understand what quality attributes were desired more than others in the system.

Design the Architecture

Canaxia designed an architecture that was able to implement the use cases that were chosen for the system. This involved adopting one or more *architectural styles* (described later in this chapter) and fleshing out those styles into a more detailed design. Canaxia decided to use the most well-known architectural style, the model-view-controller architectural style. Canaxia knew it was done with this step when the decisions it was making became harder and harder because less tangible information on which to rely was available.

Set Up a Development Environment

Canaxia then set up a development environment that included:

- Servers and space on servers such as file servers, application servers, and database servers
- Modeling and drawing tools
- Whiteboards
- Digital camera for taking pictures of whiteboards
- Project Web site and file subfolder
- Software with which they needed to integrate
- Integrated development environment (IDE)
- Unit testing framework (XUnit)
- Version control software
- Automated build process

Implement the Design

Canaxia started implementing the design. This was done by first implementing the tests for the design. Writing the tests fleshed out the contracts in the modules. When Canaxia began implementing the design, it learned what did and didn't work. Implementation will prove what was just theory in the design and will provide a concrete understanding of the architecture being developed. Canaxia stopped implementing when it exhausted the initial designs. When this happened, Canaxia improved the design and implemented more of the architecture in several more iterations until they were happy with it.

Know When You Are Happy with the Design

The architecture team tried to establish how to know whether or not the architecture was a good one. It adopted the following checklist of early warning signs when things might be going astray (Abowd et al. 1996):

1. The architecture is forced to match the current organization. Sometimes a good architecture is changed because someone says, "We just don't do that here." Architecture can be polluted because the practices and technical infrastructure of the organization don't mesh with the architecture for the project. Many times, compromises in the architecture are necessary to ensure enterprise consistency, but the conceptual integrity of the architecture should be maintained as much as possible.

2. There are too many top-level architectural components (too much complexity). If the number of components reaches a level (usually more than 25), the architecture becomes too complex for it to have conceptual integrity. The roles and responsibilities of each component must be clear. When the system consists of too many components, the responsibilities of the component tend to blend into each other.

3. One requirement drives the rest of the design. Some projects are built with a single overriding goal in mind that is sometimes the pet requirement of the project sponsor, project manager, or project architect. When the system is built around a single overriding requirement, other requirements may not be addressed.

4. The architecture depends on the alternatives presented by the operating platform. Sometimes the platform chosen is the wrong one for the project. For example, a project that requires a high level of usability might not be possible if the platform chosen for the user display is a 3270 terminal.

5. Proprietary components are used instead of equally good standard ones. Architects and developers are often lured by the latest cool technology or interesting designs that may have alternative standard technology available. For example, projects should take advantage of the capabilities of application server technology. When developers begin creating load balancing schemes or persistence frameworks, it is usually an indication that there is a problem. It would be better to use the standard capabilities of an application server and spend time developing software to solve the business problem rather than creating new technical features.

6. The component division definition comes from the hardware division. The components should be designed without regard for the physical topology of the system, except to recognize that a network is involved in transmitting data between components. The components should map to a discrete business or technical function of the application that is being built. These components should take advantage of the scalability features of modern computing systems.

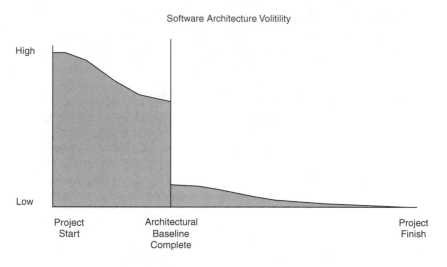

Figure 2–1
Software architecture volatility throughout a software development project.

Software Architecture Volitility

High

Low

Project
Start

Architectural
Baseline
Complete

Project
Finish

7. The design is exception driven; the emphasis is on the extensibility of the system rather than on the core requirements for the system. By "exception driven," we do not mean exception handling but rather that the system should not be designed exclusively with the requirements that someday might be necessary in mind. It should be designed to solve the more immediate requirements.

The architecture team finished the baseline architecture and felt good about it. It was careful to notice "code smells" during the creation of the baseline. These were aspects of the code that just didn't feel right. When the team saw something sneak in that didn't really belong or required extensive refactoring, it had the courage to rip it out and start over.

As shown in Figure 2–1, the architecture is volatile until the architecture baseline is complete. During the period of time that the architecture baseline is worked out, major design decisions will change. During this period, the overall design is proven. When the architectural baseline is complete, the architecture for the system should settle down so that full development can be done based on the stable baseline. If the architecture is volatile throughout the development process, the project will likely fail.

Representing and Communicating the Architecture

The architects at Canaxia knew for the architecture to be effective, it needed to be effectively communicated to all the stakeholders of the system. After all, architecture really has no other purpose than to provide a concept for the system about to be built. The architecture needed to be clear, concise, and understandable so that the important concepts within the architecture could be implemented and supported by the stakeholders. The architects understood that it was these important concepts that in many ways determined the success or failure of the project at every stage of its lifecycle.

To effectively communicate the architecture to the various stakeholders, the team created targeted material for each stakeholder community. For example, the user community was very interested in the usability of the system and how the architecture would support their needs. Therefore, the architects provided a storyboard and a prototype to describe that. This was a very effective means of conveying those aspects of the architecture to this community. The support organization wanted to know how to maintain the system, so a discussion of the software design using UML and data models was an appropriate means of conveying this information to them.

Analyzing and Evaluating the Architecture

Throughout the development of the system, Canaxia was careful to continuously evaluate the architecture to make sure that it met the needs of the project. It knew that the architecture really isn't finished until the project is delivered, and perhaps not even until the system is retired. It used an iterative process of evaluating and evolving the architecture to improve it as necessary throughout the system life cycle. The architecture evaluation process in the initial phases of a project was done through scenario-based techniques. To evaluate software architecture, Canaxia identified the architecturally significant scenarios for the architecture to support. Some methodologies, such as XP, call these scenarios *user stories*. These scenarios provided a context from which the quality attributes of the architecture could be estimated. As the project developed, the estimates became measurements and test cases for verifying that the desired quality attributes were actually supported by the software that was being created. For example, when the architecture was created, the team estimated the level of performance that the architecture should support based on the number of computations and network hops. Once the architecture baseline was completed, the estimates became measurements of performance for the set of scenarios that were implemented. If the performance requirement was not met or exceeded, the architecture was redesigned to support the requirement.

At each stage of the development process, the architecture was evaluated. At later stages in the project, some estimates were very precise because they were based on real working code. However, some of the quality attributes were difficult to measure and were somewhat subjective. For example, it was easy to use a stopwatch to measure the performance of a transaction through the system, however estimating the maintainability of the system was much more difficult. The maintainability estimation was based on many criteria that included the technology that was used, whether or not the system was sufficiently modular, and how much configuration data were used to configure the system at run-time, as well as many other criteria particular to the system that was built. Estimating this even after the system was built was difficult and still somewhat subjective. Canaxia had to rely on the architecture team's skill and experience within the organization and with software designs to deliver the right level of maintainability for the project.

Canaxia considered three popular methodologies for evaluating software architectures (Clements, Kazman, and Klein 2002):

1. Architecture Trade-off Analysis Method (ATAM)
2. Software Architecture Analysis Method (SAAM)
3. Active Reviews for Intermediate Designs (ARID)

Canaxia understood that for critical projects that require a large amount of rigor during the development process, formal methods help to formally evaluate the software architecture of a system. The ATAM and SAAM methods for evaluating software architectures are comprehensive, while the ARID method is meant for intermediate design reviews to ensure that the architecture is on track throughout the project. Canaxia purchased the book *Evaluating Software Architecture* (Clements, Kazman, and Klein 2002) to learn about each method in depth. In the end, Canaxia created its own ad hoc method to evaluate the software architecture that was partially based on the three methods presented in the book.

Ensuring Conformance

The architecture team realized that even with the best architecture, development teams don't always implement an architecture correctly. Usually, this is the fault of a poor architecture or poor communication of the architecture to developers. In order for the architecture to matter, the architecture in concept must become executing code in a system. At Canaxia, the architecture was implemented correctly in the final system. All the desired system qualities were met and the system was delivered on time and under budget.

In addition, the architects and developers realized that the architecture is an ongoing effort in refinement, even after the project is completed. The architects understood they needed to be involved not only during design and construction but also during maintenance of the system.

At Canaxia and at every other company that is developing software, the question of how software architecture should be represented is a difficult one. Stakeholders of the system need targeted material that speaks to them because, above all else, stakeholders must understand the architecture in order to implement it correctly. For technical stakeholders or those who understand software development, UML is the most popular notation to describe the design of software systems. On the surface, UML appears to be well suited as a notation for describing software architectures. UML has a large set of elements that can be used to describe software designs. The Rational Unified Process (RUP) best represents the viewpoint that UML is adequate for representing software architectures.

RUP is an "architecture-centric" process that promotes the use of UML for depicting software architecture. However, academics have questioned UML as a means of depicting software architecture (Medvidovic 2002). This is mostly because early versions of UML did not contain notations for components and connectors as first-class elements. Other constructs are important when describing software architecture, such as ports or points of interaction with a component and roles or points of interaction with a connector. In UML 1.5, components are expected to be concrete, executable software that consumes a machine's resources and memory. Although some parts of software architecture are concrete components, not all architectural components are concrete software entities. They may be an entire system or a federation of systems that need to be depicted as a single component that provides a single function.

In addition, a connector is an architectural notion that describes something that provides a conduit from one or many components to one or many components. The connector may also adapt the protocol and format of the message from one component to another. UML 1.5 does not provide a similar concept, although one could get around this by depicting a connector as a set of cooperating classes or as a component.

UML 2.0 was released in June 2003 and addresses many of these issues in the language. In UML 2.0, a component can be depicted to use an interface and provide a port. A port can be a complex port that provides and consumes multiple interfaces. Each interface can be designated with attribution that indicates the visibility of the interface, whether or not it is a service and has asynchronous capability or not. UML 2.0 is making strides toward becoming the standard notation for depicting architectures.

Using UML has the distinct advantage of being a standard notation for software design. It is desirable to use UML for describing software architecture because it is standard. To use earlier versions of UML for this purpose, readers of the UML architecture description must be willing to suspend their disbelief. For example, an architectural component could be described by a UML component in a UML diagram. Another popular approach is to use a stereotyped class. This will work as long as the reader does not take this to mean that the component is an actual software entity and that it describes a conceptual component, not a physical one.

In addition, researchers have created several architecture description languages that have a small set of core elements that allow for the first-class representation of architectural concerns. These languages focus on a precise description of software architecture. They argue that the only way to assess the completeness and correctness of the software architecture is to precisely describe the software architecture. These methods and languages suffer from the fact that there are dozens of them, and they all have the goal of precision over understandability.

The bottom line is that there is no standard notation for documenting software architecture. The key criteria when choosing a modeling language—whether it is UML, an ADL, or your own notation—is that it should further the understanding of the architecture by those who read it. The model should accomplish this primary goal regardless of the notation used to document it.

Quality Attributes

The software architecture of a system promotes, enforces, and predicts the quality attributes that the system will support. Quality attributes are those system properties over and above the functionality of the system that make the system a good one or a bad one from a technical perspective. There are two types of quality attributes: those that are measured at run-time and those that can only be estimated through inspection. Since the software architecture of a system is a partial design of a system before it is built, it is the responsibility of the software architect to identify those quality attributes that are most important and then attempt to design an architecture that reflects those attributes. The quality attributes that most architects should be concerned with are (Bass, Clements, Kazman 1997; Clements, Kazman, Klein 2002):

1. **Performance**—a measurement of the system response time for a functional requirement.

2. **Availability**—the amount of time that the system is up and running. It is measured by the length of time between failures, as well as by how quickly the system is able to restart operations after a failure. For example, if the system was down for one day out of the last twenty, the availability of the system for the twenty days is 19/19+1 or 95 percent availability. This quality attribute is closely related to reliability. The more reliable a system is, the more available the system will be.

3. **Reliability**—the ability of the system to operate over time. Reliability is measured by the mean-time-to-failure of the system.

4. **Functionality**—the ability of the system to perform the task it was created to do.

5. **Usability**—how easy it is for the user to understand and operate the system.

6. **Security**—the ability of the system to resist unauthorized attempts to access the system and denial-of-service attacks while still providing services to authorized users.

7. **Modifiability**—the measurement of how easy it is to change the system to incorporate new requirements. The two aspects of modifiability are cost and time. If a system uses an obscure technology that requires high-priced consultants, even though it may be quick to change, its modifiability can still be low.

8. **Portability**—measures the ease with which the system can be moved to different platforms. The platform may consist of hardware, operating system, application server software, or database server software.

9. **Reusability**—the ability to reuse portions of the system in other applications. Reusability comes in many forms. The run-time platform, source code, libraries, components, operations, and processes are all candidates for reuse in other applications.

10. **Integrability**—the ability of the system to integrate with other systems. The integrability of a system depends on the extent to which the system uses open integration standards and how well the API is designed such that other systems can use the components of the system being built.

11. **Testability**—how easily the system can be tested using human effort, automated testing tools, inspections, and other means of testing system quality. Good testability is related to the modularity of the system. If the system is composed of components with well-defined interfaces, its testability should be good.

12. Variability—how well the architecture can handle new requirements. Variability comes in several forms. New requirements may be planned or unplanned. At development time, the system source code might be easy to extend to perform new functions. At run-time, the system might allow pluggable components that modify system behavior on the fly. This quality attribute is closely related to modifiability.

13. Subsetability—the ability of the system to support a subset of the features required by the system. For incremental development, it is important that a system can execute some functionality to demonstrate small iterations during product development. It is the property of the system that allows it to build and execute a small set of features and to add features over time until the entire system is built. This is an important property if the time or resources on the project are cut. If the subsetability of the architecture is high, a subset of features may still make it into production.

14. Conceptual integrity—the ability of the architecture to communicate a clear, concise vision for the system. Fred Brooks writes, "I am more convinced than ever. Conceptual integrity is central to product quality. Having a system architect is the most important single step toward conceptual integrity. . . . After teaching a software engineering laboratory more than 20 times, I came to insist that student teams as small as four people choose a manager and a separate architect" (Brooks 1995). Kent Beck believes that metaphors are the most important part of the eXtreme Programming methodology (Beck 1999). The metaphor is a powerful means of providing one or more central concepts for a system. The metaphor provides a common vision and a shared vocabulary for all system stakeholders. The metaphor provides a means to enforce conceptual integrity. When the design of the system goes outside the bounds of the metaphor, the metaphor must change or new metaphors must be added; otherwise, the design is going in the wrong direction. If any of these design decisions are made without the concept feeling right, the conceptual integrity of the system will be lost. Sometimes the system metaphor is an architectural pattern, such as MVC or Blackboard (discussed later in this chapter). These architectural patterns provide a common metaphor for system developers or others who understand the patterns. However, they don't help the stakeholders who aren't familiar with the patterns. One good thing about using architectural patterns for the system is that they describe the structures of the software in more detail; on the downside, not all stakeholders will understand the references.

15. Buildability—whether or not the architecture can reasonably be built using the budget, staff, and time available for delivery of the project. Buildability is an often-overlooked quality attribute. Sometimes, the best architects are simply too ambitious for a project team to complete given project constraints.

Is Agility a Quality Attribute?

Some architects use the term agile *to describe their architecture. While flexibility and agility are important, these words have many dimensions. If the architecture is agile, does that mean that it is easily changed? Is it easy to integrate it into the enterprise? Is it portable, reusable, testable? The answer to all these questions is probably "yes." Agility is a composite quality that includes many of the base quality attributes. If the levels of maintainability, portability, testability, and integrability are high, the architecture is most likely an agile one.*

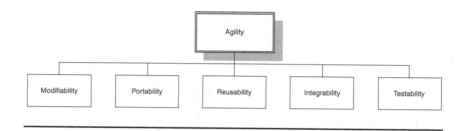

It is important for the system and enterprise architecture designers to understand the desired qualities that the systems must exhibit. To do so, the architects should encourage as precise a specification of the desired quality attributes as possible. A checklist provides a way of ensuring the completeness of the specification. Following are some of the questions to ask in order to fully characterize the desired quality attributes for a system (Clements, Kazman, and Klein 2002; McGovern, Tyagi, Stevens, and Mathew 2003):

Performance

What is the expected response time for each use case?

What is the average/max/min expected response time?

What resources are being used (CPU, LAN, etc.)?

What is the resource consumption?

What is the resource arbitration policy?

What is the expected number of concurrent sessions?

Are there any particularly long computations that occur when a certain state is true?

Are server processes single or multithreaded?

Is there sufficient network bandwidth to all nodes on the network?

Are there multiple threads or processes accessing a shared resource? How is access managed?

Will bad performance dramatically affect usability?

Is the response time synchronous or asynchronous?

What is the expected batch cycle time?

How much can performance vary based on the time of day, week, month, or system load?

What is the expected growth of system load?

Availability

What is the impact of a failure?

How are hardware and software failures identified?

How quickly must the system be operational after a system failure?

Are there redundant systems that can take over in case of a failure?

How do you know that all critical functions have been replicated?

Are backups done? How long does it take to back up and restore the system?

What are the expected hours of operation?

What is the expected up-time per month?

How available is the current system? Is this acceptable?

Rellability

What is the impact of a software or hardware failure?

Will bad performance impact reliability?

What is the impact of an unreliable system on the business?

Can the integrity of the data be compromised?

Functionality

Does the system meet all the functional requirements specified by the users?

How well can the system respond and adapt to unanticipated requirements?

Usability

Is the user interface understandable?

Is the interface adaptable to support the needs of people with disabilities?

Do the developers find the tools provided for creating the system usable and understandable?

Security

How critical is the system?

What is the expected impact of a security failure?

How are security failures identified?

If there have been any security failures in the past, what was there impact?

Are they any known vulnerabilities?

Have users been trained in security issues?

Are there a process and a response team in place to handle a security breach

Modifiability/Variability

How often will a change be required to the system?

What new functionality do you anticipate adding in future versions of the system?

How will you handle new releases of the execution platform?

Do any components have access to the implementation details of global variables?

Do you use indirection mechanisms such as publish/subscribe?

How do you handle changes in message formats?

Were design compromises made to enhance performance?

How many interfaces must change as a result of a change in a piece of functionality?

Does the software use meta data to configure itself using declarations rather than code?

Can the user interface change independently of logic components?

What changes result from adding a new data input source?

Is the system prepared to move from a single processor to a multiprocessor execution platform? How much will it cost?

How long does it take to deploy a change?

Who is expected to make the change?

Portability

Do the benefits of a proprietary platform outweigh the drawbacks?

Can the expense of creating a separation layer be justified?

At what level should system portability be provided? At the application, application server, operating system, or hardware level?

Reusability

Is this system the start of a new product line?

Will other systems be built that more or less match the characteristics of the system under construction? If so, what components will be reused in those systems?

What existing components are available for reuse?

Are there existing frameworks or other code assets that can be reused?

Will other applications reuse the technical infrastructure that is created for this application?

Is there existing technical infrastructure that this application can use?

What are the associated costs, risks, and benefits of building reusable components?

Integrability

Are the technologies used to communicate with other systems based on standards?

Are the component interfaces consistent and understandable?

Is there a process in place to version component interfaces?

Testability

Are there tools, processes, and techniques in place to test language classes, components, and services?

Are there hooks in the frameworks to perform unit tests?

Can automated testing tools be used to test the system?

Can the system run in a debugger?

Subsetability

Is the system modular?

Are there many dependencies between modules?

Does a change in one module require a change in other modules?

Conceptual Integrity

Do people understand the architecture? Are there too many basic questions being asked?

Is there a central metaphor for the system? If so, how many?

Was an architectural style used? How many?

Were contradictory decisions made about the architecture?

Do new requirements fit into the architecture easily, or do new features require "code smells"? If the software starts to "stink," the conceptual integrity has probably been lost.

Buildability

Are enough time, money, and resources available to build an architecture baseline and the project?

Is the architecture too complex?

Is the architecture sufficiently modular to promote parallel development?

Are there too many technical risks?

This is by no means an exhaustive list of questions to ask about architecture or a design. On every project, there are specific questions to ask about the domain of that project and organization. For example, if an organization uses messaging middleware, there is a list of very specific questions about how that middleware system is used and whether or not the architecture uses it effectively and correctly. If the organization has an in-house framework for creating components and services, there is a list of questions about the design of a component or service that uses that framework. The questions that must be asked on each project vary. It is important that the architecture team understand the intricacies of the organization's domain, the architecture that supports it, and, especially, the obstacles that may be encountered so that they can be avoided. Only if a design team is aware of the details of particular organization can it properly design a system that runs in that organization.

Nonfunctional Requirements and Quality Attributes

Nonfunctional requirements are almost the same as quality attributes. Nonfunctional requirements are defined as the nonobservable properties of the system. A classical functional requirement can be stated as a noun–verb phrase, such as "The system displays the report." A nonfunctional requirement can be thought of as a modifying clause, such as "The system displays the report within 5 seconds."

In other words, a functional requirement is stated in mathematical terms. An input is given to a function, and the function returns an output. The nonfunctional requirements state how the functions of the system will be performed.

The big problem with nonfunctional requirements is that most requirements gathering teams tend to leave these requirements out, or they do not fully state the nonfunctional requirements of the system. They do this because they focus only on the business case for the system. They concentrate on the business stakeholders and not on the technical stakeholders of the system. Requirements such as modifiability, security, and so on are usually overlooked because they are not perceived as directly impacting the cost-benefit for the system. These requirements are perceived as being only technically related requirements. This is not true. Nonfunctional requirements are critically important to the success of any project. They are technical risks that, if not addressed, can make or break a system. For example, if a report displays correctly but it does so in thirty minutes instead of a more reasonable thirty seconds, the functional requirement is met but the system is not usable because it does not meet the user's performance expectation. If a hacker is able to retrieve credit card information for the businesses customers, for example, the future of the company may be in jeopardy.

Nonfunctional requirements are not only within the jurisdiction of the project under development. The quality attributes of a system are supported at the enterprise level. Typically, the reliability, availability, performance, and other quality attributes are supported by the platform on which the project is deployed.

Architectural Viewpoints

Once the quality attributes of the system have been characterized, how do you document how they will be fulfilled? Creating the software architecture of a system can be a large endeavor, depending on the size and complexity of the system. The software architecture should be partitioned into multiple views so that it is more understandable. When we describe any entity—be it an architecture, a process, or an object—there are many different perspectives or viewpoints to describe. For example, if you were to describe an orange to someone, would you talk about its color, weight, sweetness, skin thickness, or some other attribute of the orange? The attributes that you would choose to describe would depend on the role, the needs and the perspective of the person to whom you are describing the orange. If the person is a purchaser at a grocery store, the purchaser would be more interested in the color of the orange so that customers would buy the orange. A consumer of oranges would be more interested in the taste of the orange than the color. A chemist that is considering using oranges in a cleaning solution product would be interested in the chemical properties of oranges that could be applied to cleaning solutions. The point is that every stakeholder in oranges has a different need and a different perspective, and thus the orange must be described to them in different ways.

The same goes for architecture. All stakeholders in the architecture hold viewpoints that speak to their different perspectives on the project and within the organization. It is also important to separate the architecture description into different viewpoints so that a single stakeholder can understand different aspects of the architecture.

4+1 View Model of Software Architecture

No single standard set of viewpoints must be described for software architecture. In fact, we discuss two popular models to illustrate the point that multiple views are necessary. Philippe Krutchen from Rational software divides architecture into the 4+1 view model (Kruchten 1995) discussed in the following sections.

Logical View

The logical view, or logical architecture, is the object model for the design. It describes the structures of the software that solve the functional requirements for the system. It is a subset of all the classes of the system. The logical view is strictly a structural view of the software, including the important classes and class relationships in the architecture.

Process View

The process view, or process architecture, describes the view of the architecture that includes running processes and instantiated objects that exist in the system. It describes important concurrency and synchronization issues.

Development View

The development architecture view focuses on the module organization of the software. It shows how classes are organized into packages, and it outlines the dependencies between packages of software. This is the view of the design that shows the layered structures of the software and what the responsibilities of each layer in the system are.

Physical View

The physical view describes the machines that run the software and how components, objects, and processes are deployed onto those machines and their configurations at run-time, see Figure 2–2.

+1

The +1 in the 4+1 view model describes the scenarios that the architecture is meant to satisfy. The scenarios represent the important requirements that the system must satisfy. The scenarios that are chosen are those that are the most important to solve because they are either the most frequently executed or they pose some technical risk or unknown that must be proven out by the architecture baseline. The other four views are centered on the set of scenarios that are chosen for the creation of the architecture.

Figure 2–2
4+1 view.

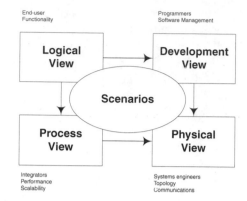

Krutchen, P. *The 4 + 1 View Model of Architecture*. IEEE Software, pp. 42–50, November 1995.

Applied Software Architecture Viewpoints

The 4+1 view model is only one of several suggestions for the viewpoints that should be included in software architecture. Hofmeister, Nord, and Soni (1999) propose a different set of viewpoints.

Conceptual Architecture View

The conceptual architecture view is similar to the logical view in the 4+1 view model. However, the conceptual architecture view is more conceptual and broader in scope. It takes into account existing software and hardware integration issues. This view is closely tied to the application domain. The functionality of the system is mapped to architectural elements called *conceptual components*. These conceptual components are not mapped directly to hardware, but they are mapped to a function that the system performs. This view provides an overview of the software architecture. It is the first place that people will go to find out how the system does what it is supposed to do. The concerns addressed in the conceptual view include the following:

1. How does the system fulfill the requirements?
2. How are the commercial off-the-shelf (COTS) components to be integrated, and how do they interact (at a functional level) with the rest of the system?
3. How are domain-specific hardware and/or software incorporated into the system?
4. How is functionality partitioned into product releases?
5. How does the system incorporate portions of prior generations of the product, and how will it support future generations?
6. How are product lines supported?
7. How can the impact of changes in the requirements domain be minimized?

Module View

The module view of software architecture shows how the elements of the software are mapped into modules and subsystems. The module architecture view shows how the system will be partitioned into separate run-time components. Some of the questions that are answered by this view are as follows:

1. How is the product mapped to the software platform?
2. What system support/services does it use and where?
3. How can testing be supported?
4. How can dependencies between modules be minimized?
5. How can reuse of modules and subsystems be maximized?
6. What techniques can be used to insulate the product from changes in third-party software, changes in the software platform, or changes to standards?

Execution View

The execution view of software architecture shows how modules are mapped onto the hardware of the system. This view shows the run-time entities and their attributes and how these entities are assigned to machines and networks. It shows the memory usage, processor usage, and network usage expectations. This view shows the flow of control between hardware systems that execute the software of the system. Some questions that this view answers are the following:

1. How does the system meet its performance, recovery, and reconfiguration requirements?
2. How is resource usage balanced?
3. How are concurrency, replication, and distribution handled in the system?
4. How can the impact of changes in the run-time platform be minimized?

Code View

The code view shows how the source code and configuration are organized into packages, including package dependencies. It also shows how the executable portions of the system are built from the source code and configuration. This view answers the following questions:

1. How are the builds done? How long do they take?
2. How are versions and releases managed?
3. What tools are needed to support the development and configuration management environments?
4. How are integration and testing supported?

How important is it to define your architecture using one of these standard sets of views? The answer is: not at all. These views are presented here to give you an idea of the kinds of questions that need to be answered when you define your software architecture. When you are on a big project and you don't have a lot of experience with software architecture, it might be a good idea to download the 4+1 view model or purchase *Applied Software Architecture* (Hofmeister, Nord, and Soni 1999) book to get started. Both provide appropriate guidelines for the kinds of things to keep in mind, but every project and every organization are different. The best way to develop sound software architectures is to have the best software architects and developers. People who understand the intricacies of the technology, processes, and politics of your organization and who can apply some of the fundamental concepts outlined in this chapter will succeed in creating the best possible software architectures. If the method for capturing the architecture is completely ad-hoc or loosely based on the above methods, that is fine. Again, the most important issue is that the important questions get answered and that everyone knows what the answers are. What is not important is the particular format or style of the answers.

Architectural Styles, Patterns, and Metaphors

What is the difference between an architectural style, an architectural pattern, and a system metaphor? The answer is not much. An architectural style (Bass et al. 1997) and an architectural pattern (Buschmann et al. 1996) are essentially synonymous. A system metaphor is similar but more conceptual than an architecture pattern or an architectural style, and it relates more to a real-world concept than to a software engineering concept. An architectural style and an architectural pattern are similar to a design pattern in that they both describe a solution to a problem in a particular context. The only difference is the granularity at which they describe the solution. In a design pattern, the solution is relatively fine grained and is depicted at the level of language classes. In an architectural pattern, the solution is coarser grained and is described at the level of subsystems or modules and their relationships and collaborations. Each subsystem or module within an architectural pattern consists of many language classes that are designed using design patterns.

Every system needs a central, organizing concept. The conceptual integrity of the system depends on how strong this organizing concept is for the system. So what is an organizing concept? Some examples of architectural styles and patterns (Buschmann et al. 1996) include the following:

1. Model-View-Controller (MVC) architecture pattern. The MVC architectural style is a popular organizing concept for systems. The model represents the data for the system, the view represents the way the data are presented to the user, and the controller handles the logic for the system.

2. Publish-subscribe. The publish-subscribe architecture pattern is a system in which a publisher publishes data on a bus. Subscribers subscribe to portions of the data that are published by publishers on the bus. They register for various topics. When a message appears on the bus that matches the topic in which a subscriber is interested, the bus notifies the subscriber. The subscriber can then read the message from the bus.

3. Pipes and filters. Anyone who is familiar with UNIX systems will recognize this architectural pattern. The pipe and filter pattern allows a system to be assembled from small programs called *filters*. A filter has an input and an output. The filters are assembled into a chain in which each filter gets data from the previous filter in the chain, processes the data, and passes the data to the next filter in the chain. The best example of a pipe and filter system is a compiler. The lexical analysis, syntax analysis, semantic analysis, intermediate code generation, and optimization occur in a pipe and filter style chain.

4. Layers. A layered system is one in which different layers of the system take care of a specific function of the system. Each layer in a layered architectural style is a package of software that has a well-defined interface and a few well-known dependencies with other layers. Each layer implements one technical function within the application. For example, a data access layer is responsible for encapsulating the technical means for accessing a database. All data access requests to a database go through the data access layer for that database. The data access layer has the responsibility of hiding the data access mechanism from upstream layers. In a closed layer system, a layer may only access adjacent layers. In an open layer system, layers may access any other layer in the system, not just the ones to which they are adjacent.

Many other popular architectural patterns are used to provide a conceptual basis for software architecture. An application can use one or more architectural patterns in its development. Different subsystems can be built using different patterns. Also, the methods for component interaction can follow one pattern, while the internal implementations of the components could use a different pattern.

Architectural patterns are meant for software people to use and understand. One must study the pattern and understand the concept. MVC or pipes and filters have little or no basis in real life. The difference between an architectural pattern and a system metaphor is that a system metaphor is understandable by software people and customers alike. For example, a publish-subscribe pattern is also a system metaphor. In a publish-subscribe system, a publisher provides the data like a newspaper publisher or a book publisher. Each newspaper article or book relates to a particular topic. Consumers subscribe to various topics. When a magazine article or a book in which suscribers are interested comes out, they buy the book or magazine article. As you can imagine, system metaphors are not always pure. Magazine subscribers subscribe to the entire magazine, not just articles within the magazine. In addition, consumers don't subscribe to books, they purchase them. A system metaphor usually starts out with "The system is designed like a. . . ."

Many products and concepts in software development come from metaphors. Following are a few examples:

- Library
- Stack

- Queue
- Desktop
- Account
- Directory
- Window
- Scheduler
- Dispatcher

A system can have many metaphors, but the metaphors have to make sense within the system to maintain its conceptual integrity. For example, Microsoft Windows has a desktop that contains windows. Would it have been better for windows to be placed on a wall? Are windows meant to move around on the wall? By combining multiple metaphors, some aspects of the metaphors must be forgotten and other must be emphasized. With time, the system itself can become a metaphor. We no longer think about the Windows desktop relating to a physical desktop or a window relating to an actual window. Products can become metaphors in themselves. For example, a new system could say that the user interface is like the Windows desktop.

Conclusion

There is no magic when it comes to creating software architecture. Software architecture captures what is important about the design and communicates those concepts to the stakeholders on the project. Enterprise architecture is in many ways a product of the combined software architectures of the systems in the organization. Therefore, it is important to get the architecture right. To be credible, the architecture should be thin, approachable, readable, and understandable. With an intense focus on the architecture baseline and a quality attribute-based analysis of the software architecture as it is being built, it is likely that the architecture will suit the needs of the project.

In Chapter 4, we look at software product lines. Software product lines will allow an organization to leverage great architecture across multiple projects that have similar characteristics. Using great architecture and a product-line approach to delivering it, an organization can achieve great enterprise architecture.

chapter 3

Service-Oriented Architecture

Opportunity is missed by most people because it is dressed in overalls and looks like work.

Thomas Edison

Service-Oriented architecture (SOA) is an architectural style that formally separates services, which are the functionality that a system can provide, from service consumers, which are systems that need that functionality. This separation is accomplished by a mechanism known as a *service contract*, coupled with a mechanism for providers to publish contracts and consumers to locate the contracts that provide the service that they desire. Rather than coupling the consumer with the service in terms of technical aspects of invoking the service, SOA separates the contract from the component or implementation of that contract. This separation produces an architecture in which the coupling between the consumer of the service and the modules that produce the work is extremely loose and easily reconfigured.

In a preceding chapter, Systems Architecture, we discussed integrating legacy and client/server applications by encapsulating their functionality in objects and publishing that object's interface. That is just the first step in the process. This chapter explores the next step, integrating functionality into an SOA.

SOA should not be equated with Web services. Web services are a realization of SOA, but SOA implementations can and have been created that have nothing to do with Web services.

SOA can be of enormous benefit to the modern enterprise. It provides an important new avenue for integration of applications. Creating new applications under an SOA offers a significant increase in the qualities of availability, interoperability, maintainability, and reliability for those applications. For the enterprise as a whole, the SOA translates into lower operating costs, lower development costs, higher quality, and greater corporate agility.

Benefits of an SOA

SOA benefits flow primarily from breaking applications into modules with a well-defined interface contract that leads to very loose coupling between services and applications. Loose coupling between consumer and provider benefits the consumer because consumer applications are effectively protected from changes in service provider implementations and the consumer has a greater choice of providers. It benefits the provider because from an implementation of loosely coupled systems come applications that map much more closely to the business processes that represent a company's value proposition. In addition, these applications increase the enterprises' competitiveness because they are easier to modify to satisfy changing business conditions. In addition, applications and work processes assembled using an SOA are cheaper to maintain. Organizations that adopt a service-oriented philosophy of development will be able to handle change more quickly and cheaply. SOA can provide a major increase in the value of the data and application resources of a company by enabling a major new mode of integration of these assets.

The benefits a Service-Oriented Architecture lie in the following areas:

- Decreased application development costs
- Decreased maintenance costs
- Increased corporate agility
- Increasing overall reliability by producing systems that are more resistant to application and equipment failure and disruption.
- Providing an application upgrade path that is considerably cheaper and less disruptive than the total application replacement that is the norm using monolithic applications.

Let's examine these areas in detail. Application development costs are reduced for the following reasons:

- Code reuse is extensive.
- Most of the code has been thoroughly tested.
- The presentation layer is the only layer requiring customization for different clients.
- RAD development via automated code generation becomes a possibility.

Once the infrastructure of an SOA has been built, and the application development staff has been educated in its use, you'll see extensive reuse of the SOA infrastructure's code. Building new applications becomes close to a plug-and-play operation. This plug-and-play ability derives from the manner in which application functionality has been factored into components and from the loose coupling between these components.

Reuse will also substantially reduce the time and expense involved in testing new applications and certifying them ready for production. Since the bulk of the code and logic lies in components that have already been extensively tested, the testing effort will probably only be regression testing. Even more important than reducing the quantity of code that must be tested is the fact that the really difficult stuff—the transport, resource access, and business logic—has not been changed and hence needs little attention from your quality assurance (QA) team.

A solid, well-tested SOA implementation also substantially reduces the risks involved in developing new applications. That reduction in risk stems from the fact that the application will be largely assembled from a palette of well-tested components. The parts that are new will be isolated from the rest of the application by loose couplings. This will have the effect of limiting and controlling dependencies between what is new and what is well tested. This will allow application development to proceed with a significantly higher level of confidence.

In practical terms, when the business side of Canaxia asked for access to a set of information that resides partially in CRM and partially in the financial systems, the application development team was able to quickly respond. It could state that the GUI layer was going to take 3 person weeks for development and QA; the service to access the information in the financials would take 4 person weeks; and the component to access the CRM would take only 1 week because an existing module could be modified easily. Integration would take another week. The business customers were very pleased with the speed that the design generated and the quick development that was provided. They were even more pleased when it was discovered that the functionality of the application could be greatly enhanced by accessing a different section of data from the financials and that the application development team was able to satisfy that new requirement by developing and plugging in another data-gathering module.

Development of user interfaces, particularly browser-based GUIs, is only minimally enhanced by an SOA. An SOA does insulate the GUI code from all the back-end details, and that makes GUI development much faster and maintenance much easier. The GUI needs only to capture the data in some form and pass it to the transport component. If the application is browser-based, the transport will be HTTP/S, SMTP, or FTP/S. If it is a Java Swing or Microsoft Foundation Classes GUI, the transport layer could be any of the transports mentioned, plus Java RMI, DCOM, or CORBA IIOP. It has been our experience that separation of the transport functionality into its own layer means that it takes only a few lines of code to select the proper transport and pass the data to the correct service.

SOA designs are amenable to the development of RAD tools to speed the development of new services. Since the service contract is published in a directory and easily accessible it can be used by a modern integrated development environment (IDE) to generate code that will connect to the service at run-time. Many service frameworks can also configure a dynamic proxy using the contract to connect to the service at run-time over various transports. RAD development is made possible by the modular, layered architecture of the SOA and the lack of dependencies among the various layers.

A good SOA implementation reduces maintenance costs due to the tested nature of the code and the fact that the production support staff is more familiar with the back end code. Due to the modular nature of the components in the various layers, once they have been tested and debugged, they can be plugged in with confidence where needed. The lack of dependencies among the various components in the different layers is also very important in reducing the cost of maintenance of applications developed under an SOA framework. The fact that the dependencies are so few and are well known makes it easy to state with confidence that a given change will have no unexpected side effects. New application development carries a maintenance risk as well as a development risk. Building applications using an SOA will reduce the maintenance risk as well as the development risk. Production support staff will soon become familiar with and confident in the SOA code. Since this code is well tested and debugged, the production support people must comb through much less when a defect appears in a new application.

> Instituting an SOA framework is an important step in the direction of building a product line development system. See Chapter 4, Software Product Lines, for further details.

We're talking about a measurable and significant reduction in recurring IT costs. This is not a one-time reduction in costs but savings that will persist.

For most enterprises, a major value added for an SOA is that it greatly increases the agility of the corporation. This increase in agility is due to the way in which SOA makes it easier to respond to new conditions and opportunities. It is possible to build an adapter layer that allows easy access to the services from all clients who are known now, which makes it easy to open the service layer to client access modalities that haven't yet been imagined. The fact that the services themselves are loosely coupled to the service consumer makes it easy to change the implementation of the service without affecting the client. This provides a relatively simple and painless evolutionary pathway for the applications that satisfy the business needs of the organization. In addition to allowing evolutionary growth and change, the SOA makes the possibility of revolutionary change much simpler.

SOAs can be used as a method to integrate legacy applications by exposing sets of their functionality as services. Once legacy application functionality has been externalized as a service, modifying, replacing, or outsourcing that function becomes a much more manageable proposition. The reduction in IT costs brought about by the cheaper application development and maintenance that come from an SOA also helps to make a corporation more agile.

SOA is one of the most effective tools to use for incremental integration of legacy application functionality. Once an interface (contract) has been defined for some part of a legacy application's services, plugging that interface into an SOA is relatively straightforward.

We have examined the benefits of an SOA; let's now take an abstract look at Service-Oriented Architecture.

In general, SOAs have the following characteristics:

- Services have well-defined interfaces (contract) and policies.
- Services usually represent a business function or domain.
- Services have a modular design.
- Services are loosely coupled.
- Services are discoverable and support introspection.
- The location of services is transparent to the client.
- Services are transport independent.
- Services are platform independent.

SOA can be implemented in many different ways. Currently the most common and visible SOA is Web services. In fact, many articles equate SOA and Web services, but that is incorrect. Web services have specialized the SOA to fit an Internet implementation. The purpose of this chapter is to acquaint the reader with the full definition of Service-Oriented Architecture.

Services Have Well-Defined Interfaces and Policies

Well-defined interfaces (contract) are a central concept for SOAs. All services publish a contract. This contract encapsulates the agreement between the client of the service and the service. Contracts are what the consumer peruses when searching for a service. The contract contains all the information necessary to create an application that is capable of accessing the service. Using the information in the contract to access and utilize the service is called *binding*.

Contracts are a new concept to many IT professionals. The old paradigm, carried over from procedural programming days from object-oriented development (OOD), is that applications are a set of classes that provide the desired functionality. Classes are organized into inheritance hierarchies with subclasses inheriting both data members and functionality from their chain of parent classes. Applications are built from a collection of classes that interact with each other via their functions. These functions consist of a (hopefully) descriptive name and a function signature. The function signature states what data type the class will return and what data it requires as input. Function signatures imply synchronous, tightly coupled, procedures called *interactions*. Classes provide a type to which to bind during the compile.

This system of classes and subclasses has several limitations. Tight coupling introduces rigidity and makes future enhancements harder to implement, which is undesirable in a software system of any size. If changes are made in the parent, it can affect the functionality of the children. Incorporating functionality from more than one superclass involves multiple inheritance, which introduced even more fragility. Some object-oriented (OO) languages, Java being one of them, do not support multiple inheritance.

To answer some of the problems with straight inheritance, interfaces were developed. Interfaces allow the specification of an interface contract (method signature and return type) without implementing any functionality. Interfaces outline the design for the object in pure terms, devoid of any implementation details. In OOD, a class that subclasses another inherits data and functionality from its parent. Interfaces, on the other hand, have no associated implementation. This places an important level of indirection between the consumer and the provider. Any class can declare that it implements an interface, making it much easier to change the subunit that is providing the service. Another way of thinking about interfaces is that they specify an interface contract, not an object. An interface is moving in the direction of the SOA concept of a contract. Interfaces provide the following to the consumer:

- A data type
- Expected output
- Required inputs
- Error messages (usually exceptions that can be thrown)

Systems of distributed objects, such as CORBA and DOM, make extensive use of interfaces. Interface Definition Language (IDL), a standard language to allow different programming languages to specify interfaces and their characteristics, has been created.

SOA is built on the idea of a consumer and a service being tied by a contract. SOA contracts considerably extend the idea of interfaces. The SOA contract specifies the following:

- Functionality provided
- Required inputs and expected outputs
- Preconditions
- Post-conditions
- Error handling
- Quality of service guarantees and SLAs (optional)

A service ideally should have two interfaces. The technical interface was discussed previously. We refer to the second interface as the business policy interface. The producers and consumers of a service both define policies around reliability, availability, security, and exception policies.

Functionality

The functionality provided specifies exactly what the service agrees to accomplish. For Canaxia, examples of functionality are transfer vehicles to dealers, get inventory status, and get current financial balance sheet. Functionality will normally map to a business process or a subunit of a business process. Occasionally it will be a technical service that is provided, such as authentication and authorization.

Expected Inputs and Outputs

What the service expects as input and what it agrees to provide as output are important additional considerations for a client. It is better to think in terms of interfaces when thinking of inputs and outputs rather than the traditional semantics of function calls.

Pre- and Post-Conditions

Preconditions are inputs or application states that must exist prior to a service being invoked. A common precondition is that the client has been authorized through a security mechanism. This could be represented as a requirement for a security token to be part of the input or for information required for the service to authenticate a user and obtain authorizations.

Post-conditions are the state of the service after the request has been processed. If the service has been called as part of a transaction, that state could be that the service should not commit the transaction until notified to do so by a transaction coordinator. Post-conditions that are absolutely vital to nail down are how the service will respond to errors. The state of the system after an error is encountered could well depend on the exact error encountered, so it is extremely important that all this be spelled out in the post-conditions section of the contract.

Error Handling

Error handling is another area that should be established in the contract. From a modeling point of view, an error is an alternate use case or path through the process. All error paths do not return the product of value that the actor desires. If an error condition is encountered in the operation of the service, the client will most likely expect to receive some structure that contains a useful description of the error or errors encountered. Usually that error structure will consist of an XML string or document.

Quality of Service Agreements and SLAs

Quality of service (QoS) agreements and SLAs are optional but very important components of an SOA contract. These are specifications on matters such as performance, multithreading, fault–tolerance, and so on. A consumer could well base his or her choice of a provider on the service levels and guarantees that the provider can offer. The ability to provide QoS or SLA information for a consumer to browse is an important aspect of SOA.

The registry ties everything together. It is a place where the service deposits or registers and where the consumers go to look for a contract that fulfills their needs. The term *registry* has many meanings. A registry provides a mechanism for consumers to find contracts based on specified search criteria. Consumers then will bind to the service, as shown in Figure 3–1.

Contracts do not contain any information on the location of the service (endpoint). This is an important point. To tie endpoint information to the contract would introduce implementation details into the contract that do

Figure 3-1

SOA contract
mechanism.

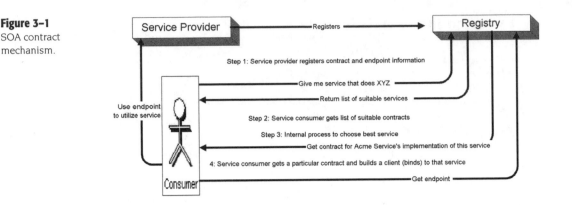

not belong there. The information necessary to locate to the desired service is in another part of the registry. For example, a Canaxia service consumer gets a list of services from the Canaxia registry. When it has made its choice of services, it passes the fully qualified service name to the service lookup function of the registry, and that part of the registry returns an endpoint to use to actually locate and use the service.

Contracts are not just a way station on the path to accessing a service; they contain information that can be a significant part of the run-time relationship between consumer and provider:

- The interface information that contracts contain also can be used as part of a process that dynamically builds the client's proxy layer.
- Contracts can contain XML specifications for the format of the data coming in and out of the service.

Registry

The concept of a registry is central to the SOA. A registry provides a catalog of available service providers, a mechanism to iterate through and examine what a service provider has to offer, and a facility to provide an object (an endpoint) to which the consumer of the service can bind. All these functions can be combined in the same object, or they can be split into a registry that deals exclusively with contracts and a run-time registry that provides endpoints. This registry can be maintained and provided by the enterprise, by independent sources, or by other businesses that have services to provide. All registries must implement an application programming interface (API) that allows services to be registered and consumers to discover service providers and bind to them. If you expect outside entities to use your services, the registry API should conform to open standards.

Registry Coordinator

Leaving the task of publishing the service's contract to the developer or architect of the service could produce duplicate services (functionally equivalent services with different interfaces) or services that offer less than the best business functionality. If your company is setting up its own registry, you should consider creating a coordinator position to control the contents of the directory. Ideally this person will be someone with broad exposure to business concepts.

Registries are the central mechanism for separating consumers and providers. This separation allows an SOA to increase capacity on demand and to provide continuous availability of services. It can also allow contextual routing, if desired.

Registries don't have to contain the contracts. They can contain descriptions of what the service provider offers and pointers to the location of the actual contract. This allows the service provider to maintain the contract information locally, where it is easier to update.

Services Represent a Business Domain

Services can be established to represent a variety of problem domains. A service can represent either a business domain or a technical domain. One of the most common types of services are ones that provide technical functionality. Registries, security providers, and logging are a few of the infrastructure and technical applications that make excellent services.

However, the real power of an SOA lies in its ability to model a business domain. Business services are normally more difficult to implement than technical services but more valuable internally and externally. Producing services that represent a significant business process is the real lasting value of an SOA.

Ideally, the architecture team would sit down with the business customer and produce a business model of the business process that is slated to become a service in an SOA. Output of this process could be UML: use cases, class, sequence, and activity diagrams coupled with a business-process-model workflow diagram.

As part of employing modular design, all the services should completely encapsulate a business domain or problem. Once more, the object of this exercise is to reduce or eliminate dependencies among different services. If your services are dependent on other services, changes in the other service can potentially cascade to your service. This could force you to redesign some of the modules in your service. At the very least, it will force you to perform a complete regression test on your service. Beyond the practical considerations of application maintenance, forcing services to represent a business domain greatly facilitates the mapping of application architecture to business architecture (McGovern et al. 2003).

The process of mapping of business processes into services is the beginning of the process of the company defining its business architecture. This synergistic interplay of better definition of business architecture leading to a better definition of the service can be a major impetus to the company's further pursuit of business modeling.

As the business domains that are realized in your SOA become larger and more complex, you will find yourself building the totality of a business process from a multitude of smaller services. These services will be tied together by messages and operate in a sequence or a flow. The concept of service composition is being developed in the Web services space to allow for the enumeration and description of the component services that are combined to form the whole. Orchestration defines the message linkages and the workflow among component services. A business process execution language (BPEL) is being developed for Web services to allow the description of the orchestration of a complex business service. This will allow for the dynamic assembly of small services into complex business processes. In addition, work is being done to allow orchestration and compositions to be generated from BPELs. The end result of this is to allow an SOA to speed the realization of business processes considerably and to make the modification of the business process assemblage dynamic and almost painless.

> For choreography, please see *lists.w3.org/archives/public/www-ws-arch/2003Feb/att-0212/02-wd-wsa-arch-review.htm*.
>
> For the Web service initiatives to BPEL4WS (*www.oasis-open.org/cover/bpel4ws.html*).

Services Have a Modular Design

Services are composed of modules (Parnas 1972). Modular design is important to SOAs. A module can be thought of as a software subunit or subsystem that performs a specific, well-defined function. For the purposes of our discussion, a module is a set of software units that provides value to a service consumer. A module should perform only one function, but it should perform that function completely. That is, the module should contain all the subunits or sub-modules necessary to completely perform required functions. In other words, modules should exhibit high internal cohesiveness.

Application of this rule brings up questions of granularity, the measurement of size of the functionality that a module performs. Fine-grained modules perform a single, small function. Coarse-grained components perform a multitude of functions. For example, a transfer of money in a banking system involves withdrawal from one account and deposit into another account. A fine-grained module would be one that only performs the withdrawal functionality. A coarser-grained module would be one that indivisibly combines both the withdrawal and the deposit functions. Keeping modules fine-grained promotes flexibility and reuse at the expense of performance. Coarse-grained modules are difficult to mix and match with other modules to produce new services. Modules should be fine-grained components. Use cases will most often be translated into modules.

For example, the movement of a vehicle from Canaxia's inventory to a dealer involves a series of interconnected steps. The data manipulation involved in each step is encapsulated into a fine-grained object. Then the appropriate fine-grained objects are aggregated into a single function. This is the process:

1. On a weekly basis, orders from dealers are queried to ascertain what makes and models have been ordered.

2. The vehicles destined for particular geographic areas are put together, and the transport company is notified that *x* numbers of cars are going to, for example, the Northwest.

3. The transport company responds with a date and time that the car-transport trucks will be at the Canaxia plant.

4. The day of shipment, pick lists are generated and assembly points for all the cars going on a particular truck are identified.

5. When the cars have been successfully loaded on the transports, they are taken off Canaxia's inventory.

6. All dealers receiving vehicles in this shipment are then notified of the makes and models that have been shipped, along with other shipping details.

7. When the vehicles have arrived, dealers notify Canaxia and receipt is recorded in the proper database.

The individual steps should be encapsulated into fine-grained components. Then the fine-grained components should be aggregated into a single process. If, in the future, changes are made to any of the components, the rest of the module and any client accessing that module will remain unaffected.

Keeping these rules in mind will make it easier to design modules or to work with existing applications to prepare them to fit into an SOA environment. Putting too many functions into a module will make it awkward and difficult to replace or modify. If a module does not have all the functionality required to completely fulfill its purpose, other modules may be linked in to add the missing capabilities. That could introduce dependencies into the environment that will make it difficult to modify the module at a later date. We suggest keeping subunits fine-grained and using use cases to help specify the functionality of the module and those subunits that should be included within it.

Breaking functionality into modules allows for tremendous freedom in swapping modules in and out of a service. Being able to swap modules freely without requiring any changes to any of the other modules in the application or even a recompile of the other modules, is one of the things that gives an environment built on SOA principles a tremendous amount of reusability and room for growth.

Services Are Loosely Coupled

Service clients and service providers should be loosely coupled. Loose coupling means that there are no static, compile-time dependencies between clients and providers. Consumers dynamically find providers at run-time. Dynamic location of providers allows details of the service, such as physical location, clustering, and fail-over, to be completely hidden from the consumer. A proxy object is an effective mechanism to hide the details of the physical network location from the consumer. The consumer asks a proxy object for a handle to a service. The proxy object performs a lookup to ascertain the current physical location of that service and passes the request to that service, then returns the results to the client.

Having the service hide the internal details of how it functions to fulfill its duties also provides loose coupling. Knowledge of internal implementation details can lead to unnecessary dependencies between client and service. One very effective way to manage the exposure to clients of internal service details is by using the Façade or the Composite pattern (Gamma 1995). Façades and composites are particularly useful in providing the correct granularity for the service. As indicated previously, providing the correct granularity can be difficult. Forcing the user to interact with a myriad of fine-grained services is poor design and can lead to poor performance due to the many network calls required to complete a unit of work. Coarse-grained design, by aggregating too much functionality in a single service, reduces the flexibility and adaptability of an architecture. The use of a design pattern such as Façade or Composite allows the flexible aggregation of fine-grained components into what appears to be a coarse-grained component of just the right functionality.

We have previously discussed Canaxia's process of moving a vehicle from the factory inventory to the dealer. The modules that are involved in each step can be aggregated into a single service and put behind a contract that says a press of the button will prompt all orders to be filled. What you would have in this case is a stovepipe type of service. This is not a good design. Many steps in this process should be open to input and intervention. If the current factory inventory is insufficient to fill the orders, it should be possible to plug a prioritization system between step one and step two. Or, suppose that a big promotion event is being generated around the creation of the 1,000,000th Canaxia vehicle. A picture of the vehicle rolling off the assembly line would be produced, but the marketing department needs to get information from the components responsible for step 4 so that a picture of the 1,000,000th vehicle being loaded on the transport can be taken. Marketing may even want to intervene in the choice of which area gets the 1,000,000th vehicle. Multigrained service interfaces require proper support for the range of requests that might be made on the service. By keeping the actual modules that carry out the vehicle distribution fine grained, the architecture gains flexibility and modifiability. By putting an object that amalgamates all the functionality into a single operation, the service creates ease of use.

> Another way to resolve the issue of granularity is the concept of multi-grain. Multigrained services combine fine-grained components to produce a coarse-grained result. See *Java Web Services Architecture* (McGovern, Tyagi, Stevens, and Mathew 2003) for a full discussion of multigrained services.

By adding access to some of the subassemblies that encapsulate the steps in the process, the service adds all the additional functionality that the business requires without sacrificing ease of use. The key to making all this possible is modularization and loose coupling.

Façade is one design pattern in which a single object provides a unified, high-level interface to a subsystem of components.

The Composite pattern composes objects into tree structures. Composites allow clients to treat individual objects in the composition uniformly.

We refer you to the seminal book on software design patterns, Design Patterns: Elements of Reusable Object-Oriented Software *(Gamma 1995), for a more detailed discussion of the Façade and Composite patterns.*

Services are meant to be loosely coupled. Therefore, there should be a preference for the service to leverage other services for common, clearly defined tasks such as authentication/authorization, reporting, and so on. This will enable support for orchestration.

Services Are Discoverable and Support Introspection

Another key to the flexibility and reusability of an SOA is the concept of dynamic discovery and binding. When the modules of the client are compiled, they have no static linkages with the service. Similarly, when the modules of the service are compiled, they have no static linkages with any clients. Rather than use static linkages built in at compile time, clients of an SOA use a registry to look up the functionality they desire. Then, using the access pointer obtained from the registry, the client gets the endpoint from the service and uses that information to access the service. Thus, the service is completely free to modify or move the module that fulfills the contract. Conversely, if the needs of the client change or a service provider withdraws its service offering, the client is completely free to choose another service. As long as both sides are using the same contract, the consumer can change service providers without having to make any changes in its internal workings. It is incumbent upon the service provider not to change its contract. Contracts, once published, must not be changed. To do so creates a risk of breaking any clients that are counting on using that service. Contracts can be versioned, and a graceful upgrade path from version to version can be designed and implemented.

Services can be provided on a time-limited basis, that is, they can be leased. Either the consumer or the provider can specify a time limit on the contract. When the lease on the contract expires, the consumer is forced to go back to the registry and rebind to the contract or choose a different one. This allows the consumer to avoid an unlimited lock into a particular contract without having to explicitly code for it. It also allows the provider of the contract a graceful way to revisit the service and decide if it wants to continue to provide the service and, if it is still interested in providing the service, to decide if it wants to change the conditions of the contract.

The scheme of going to a registry every time you wish to access a service can impose a substantial performance penalty on SOAs. The concept of a lease can be extended to allow the consumer to cache a connection and call it directly without having to go through a registry. In this situation, the lease is a guarantee on a reference, and while the lease is in force, the consumer can rely on being able to access it through this connection.

Services Are Independent of the Transport Mechanism

Clients access and utilize services using a network connection. SOAs are independent of the kind of network connection used to access services. Services are independent of the transport mechanism used to access them. In practice, this usually means that an adapter is created to allow access to the service via the various transports. Normally, adapters are created as needed. If clients wish to access the service via HTTP, an HTTP adapter is created. If another set of clients comes along that needs to access this service via RMI, the necessary RMI adapter is created. The same adapter can be used with multiple services, allowing reuse of this component. In addition, this architecture allows the service to transparently utilize new connection protocols as they are developed. In Web services, this is known as *transport binding*. The service client may choose to bind to a number of transport protocols that the service supports, as described by the Web Service Description Language (WSDL) contract definition for the service.

Ideally, adapters should be created that are not language specific, like RMI, as they break the notion of introspection.

Location of Service Is Transparent to Client

Making the location of the service transparent to the client allows tremendous flexibility in the implementation of an SOA. Since the client doesn't know or care where the service is located, the group tasked with providing the service can be located wherever it is most convenient. Instances of the service can be spread across several machines in a cluster. Enterprise reorganizations can move hosting of the service to a third-party provider. Outages and disruptions to one location can be concealed from the client by forwarding service requests to instances of the service running in entirely different locations. Making it unnecessary for the client to know the location of the service allows for an architecture that is much more flexible, maintainable, cheaper, and resistant to failure.

A Service Should be Platform Independent

For the greatest flexibility, a service shouldn't care upon which platform it is running. Therefore, the ideal service should theoretically be operating system independent.

In the real world, by making services independent of the transport, having an SOA that is platform independent is much less important. A .NET service running on Windows can, in theory, have access to clients running on any operating system via Web services.

The subject of interoperability of Java and .NET Web services is complex. Theoretically, since both sides are using transports that are very platform independent (HTTP, FTP, and SMTP) and they are communicating data via a relatively standard message (SOAP), no problems should arise when having a .NET consumer access a Java Web service and vice versa. Due to vague and undefined areas in the SOAP specification, there can be problems with appli-

Many enterprises run on a variety of platforms. Services developed for these corporations should be platform independent to provide the flexibility in hosting that is required for maximum business functionality. Services developed for smaller organizations, as well as businesses that are utilizing a single operating system, will not find being platform independence particularly important.

Web services have been chosen for in-depth discussion because they are a well known and extremely important example of an SOA implementation. Many enterprises have already started to implement Web services, and most others have plans to implement them in the future.

Web Services

Web services are an example of an SOA. One very important thing that Web services have over most other SOA implementations is that they adhere to open standards. The open standards that form the basis of Web services theoretically allow any Web service to interact with any other Web service. Proprietary protocols, data translation, and vendor lock-in become a thing of the past. The menu of solutions for your IT problems grows enormously.

The open standards behind Web services have gained allegiance from all the big players—IBM, Microsoft, Sun, BEA, and Oracle to name a few. These normally warring entities are in bed together on open standards because they realize it is vital for the future of their respective businesses that they be able to talk to anyone via Web services.

Following are the open standards utilized by Web services:

- The transport protocols HTTP, FTP, and SMTP
- The messaging protocol SOAP (Simple Object Access Protocol)
- The interface description language WSDL
- Registry protocols such as UDDI and repositories such as ebXML

Let's examine how Web services implements an SOA. One of the SOA principles is that services should be independent of the means of transport. Currently, all Web services communicate using a single transport: HTTP. FTP and SMTP are listed as alternate Web services transport modalities, but they are not particularly popular because they preclude carrying on a conversation between applications. However, HTTP will continue to be the most popular transport for Web services messages for some time to come. HTTP is popular for Web services because HTTP messages can pass readily through firewalls. When you are contemplating connecting to a service physically located in a different enterprise, or even in a different location within the same enterprise, firewall transparency is attractive. Difficulties in traversing firewalls are one of the reasons that Java applets and CORBA are not popular in Internet scenarios. Web services notwithstanding, it remains our recommendation that, when building internal SOA environments, time and attention be devoted to making the service transport independent.

To say that FTP and SMTP are incapable of supporting request-response Web services oper-ations is inaccurate. See www.w3.org/TR/2002/WD-soap12-part0-20020626/#SMTP for an example of an SMTP SOAP message. Theoretically, you could have an application that could open the email, ingest the SOAP message, generate a reply SOAP message, and email it back to the sending application. However, email is designed for human ingestion, and that, plus the fact that issues such as delivery and reply operations are totally defined by the SMTP pro-tocol, will keep Web services interactions with email on the level of sending a message to a human. FTP, and in particular FTPs, has some real potential as a Web services transport pro-tocol to automate interactions with batch-processing systems.

Web services utilize the SOAP messaging protocol to transmit data. This protocol is central to Web services. The SOAP protocol, among other uses, defines how to represent a message in a standard manner. In addition, it defines data types to be used when using remote procedure calls (RPC) via Web services. XML is the language used to compose SOAP messages. A SOAP message consists of three parts:

- Envelope, which basically identifies this XML as a SOAP message
- Header, which contains information for activities such as transaction management, routing and security, processing directives, and so on for a system
- Body, which contains the actual data

The SOAP protocol also demonstrates the difficulties of producing a completely unambiguous data communications vehicle. The original SOAP protocol left many key areas undefined or poorly defined. As a result, inter-operability between Web services proved difficult to obtain. SOAP v1.2 has addressed some of those issues, but interoperability is still an elusive goal. Interoperability is discussed in detail later in this chapter.

Handling of the SOA contract requirements by Web services is very well developed and deserves detailed study by any organization implementing an SOA. As stated previously, the SOA contract must clearly state the service that is provided and what is required of the Web service consumer. This con-tract is in the form of WSDL. WSDL has been developed for the purpose of discovering Web services that suit the consumer's criteria. Using WSDL, the provider of the service describes that service. That description consists of the following:

- The functionality that the service provides
- A description of the messages that are acceptable to the service and their format
- The protocol that the consumer must use to utilize the service

In conjunction with the WSDL contract specified by the service, Web services provide a mechanism to dynamically build the proxy that allows con-nection to the service using WSDL.

Web services offer two methods of establishing connections between modules: One is dynamic, the other static. It is possible to provide to the consumer of the Web service an object, a "stub," to which it can bind at compile time. Changes in binding information or the contract may require a recompile. Any static method of connecting Web Service consumer and supplier is limited and inflexible and puts the service outside an SOA. Of much more interest is the fact that Web services have evolved dynamic methods of service discovery via interaction with a registry.

The future world of Web services is certain to contain many different registries, each with its own API. Small consumer-oriented Web services will probably be concentrated in one or a few registries. However, the location of business services will most likely be much more diffuse. Many enterprises may choose to implement their own registry. Having a registry of their own provides corporations the level of control and security that most of them need to feel comfortable with Web services. Having a plethora of Web services registries is not a problem. Having a plethora of APIs to interact with a plethora of registries is a problem. Standardization on a small set of Web service registry APIs is important for the widespread adoption of Web services. Having to change the registry access code when changing a Web service from one provider to the other greatly reduces the agility that Web services offer.

Web services actually are beginning to deliver on the promise of a simple, universal, effective method to allow application-to-application communication between disparate entities. This versatility is achieved by the universal nature of the HTTP transport mechanism and the universal nature of the XML message format. We believe that an effective Web services strategy should be a part of every business's enterprise architecture.

Web Services Issues

Web services have some serious flaws, some temporary and some fundamental.

One concern is Web services are typically slower when compared to many proprietary approaches. XML is verbose and hence tends to produce messages that are larger than more optimized approaches. XML parsing tends to be a slow process. Asynchronous communication is sufficient in some circumstances, but sometimes the speed of RPC operations is necessary. Specifications for passing binary data in SOAP messages, reliable Web services, nailing down the SOAP specification to enhance interoperability, and more are still in flux.

For a detailed discussion of architectural considerations for Web services, see *Java Web Services Architecture* (McGovern, Tyagi, Stevens, and Mathew 2003).

The following is a description of how Canaxia moved into Web services. The functionality that they chose to turn into Web services and the thought processes behind the choices.

Canaxia's SOA Analysis

The system architecture analysis done by Myles Standish indicated that several areas would benefit greatly from an SOA. The business drivers for the SOA implementation would be these:

- Save money by creating components from existing legacy applications and client/server functionality so that they can be integrated into the enterprise architecture.
- Make Canaxia agile by increasing architectural flexibility and by increasing the choices of how to provide a given functionality.
- Produce shared components for the software product line that Canaxia is building.

Given this architectural analysis, it was decided to implement a generic SOA internally and to begin the process of externalizing selected functionality as Web services.

Internal Services

The architecture team at Canaxia recognized the potential of SOAs and has implemented a generic SOA. As part of that SOA, the following services were developed:

- A set of technical services (including logging, reference, and the registry that is used to locate services)
- Security/trust service
- Financial reporting service

For these internal services, UDDI was overkill, so Canaxia has developed a simpler registry system. The registry operates as a service. Consumers connect to the service via a proxy object. The proxy object can be accessed via HTTP/S or by RMI/IIOP (EJB access). The proxy acts as a front to the actual service locating functionality. This registry functionality is implemented using the command pattern. The user creates a Canaxia data transfer object (CanData), builds the XML message that the CanData object will carry, and passes the CanData object and the fully qualified command name (package name plus name of service interface) to the registry service. The service interface that handles that particular command is located in the Canaxia command catalog, and the CanData object is passed to the module that is listed as implementing that interface. The consumer is now directly connected to the service and receives the data returned by it in the form of a CanData or a CanError object.

The Command pattern allows the consumer to issue a request and have the command inter-
preter locate the proper receiver of this request and pass the request to it. All details of how
the command is executed and who executes it are hidden from the requestor (Gamma 1995).

The Canaxia registry implementation allows the dynamic linkage of service consumer with service provider, as is required for an SOA. When it is desirable to change the physical location of the service or the module that implements the service interface, the change is completely transparent to the consumer.

In addition to the registry service, a logging service was developed. Previously, each development area built its own logging mechanism, with varying levels of quality and functionality. This unruly set of logging solutions impeded the development of a software product line for Canaxia. In addition, the multitude of formats for log file entries made them useless as a systems monitoring resource. As a result, a logging service was developed and its use was mandated for all future development. Since quite a bit of effort was expended to make the new logging service easier to use than the existing logging objects, developers readily adopted the new service and even did some limited retrofitting of it to existing code. In several areas, being able to mine logging information was considered crucial, and these applications were rewritten to use the new logging service.

The registry service was created to provide in-memory access to configuration data. The configuration data are contained in a set of XML files, which are read at startup and reread when a change in them is detected.

A file system resource adapter was developed for the logging service. This resource adapter encapsulates all the details of writing the logging entry to the file system. The first-pass implementation of this service is multithreaded, formats the logging information into XML, and logs everything to a central server.

The security service encapsulates the existing set of Canaxia security applications. Access is via a proxy. The HTTP adapter allows external businesses to obtain credentials from the Canaxia security service. The beefed-up authentication of HTTP v1.1 is required by the security service, which is why the Canaxia HTTP adapter was developed for that version. Most Canaxia applications are J2EE and they use the RMI/IIOP adapter to access the security service.

The financial service encapsulates access to the data warehouse developed for financial reporting. As noted in Chapter 1, the data necessary for generating quick financial reports is mandated by SEC Order 4–460. It utilizes the existing transport adapters. On the back end, a JDBC resource adapter was created to extract data from the data warehouse, and database connection information is obtained from the Reference Service.

The choice of what functionality to move into the SOA came out of a matrix of the business priority, architecture priority, development risk, and effort. The business driver for moving the logging functionality to the SOA was to improve systems management by mining log files for error conditions and alerts. Because the security service touched so many other parts of Canaxia's application ensemble, it had a high business and architectural priority. The choice of the financial service for the first round of development was driven solely by the fact that this was a very high business priority.

Web Services at Canaxia

Canaxia has a long-range plan to integrate its supply chain via Web services. However, the current immature state of Web service standards precludes the publishing right now of any Web services by Canaxia.

Canaxia will be proceeding with a low level of Web service development. The initial plan calls for the creation of a Web service that allows visibility into Canaxia's vehicle inventory and that can produce figures outlining current vehicle consumption patterns.

The decision has been made that the Canaxia Web service registry will be UDDI compliant. It will be built and owned by Canaxia.

Internationalization

Canaxia is an international company with business units in many countries. The ability of different business units to operate in their native languages is vital to the smooth operation of Canaxia. Therefore, all Canaxia applications have to be internationalized, and any SOA for Canaxia must support effective internationalization. Internationalization is handled on several levels. For the presentation layer, Canaxia follows Java and J2EE standards in that all the messages and labels presented to the user are in resource bundles. The localization setting on the user's workstation brings up the proper language resource bundle to use for the UI.

The UDDI-compliant Web services registry that Canaxia will create for locating Web services takes advantage of the fact that consumers can specify a language when searching for a binding Template from the registry.

UDDI registries organize data pertaining to services, at least in part, with binding Templates. See McGovern et al. (2003) for more detail.

In addition, XML tags can have a language attribute. Therefore, the XML data generated from Canaxia locations in the Caribbean specifies Spanish as the language for the tags. If the locale specified for the computer displaying the data is not Spanish, a translation of the tags is performed.

Implementing an SOA environment will cost time and money. Some organizations have no budgetary process to finance infrastructure development. In such organizations, all information technology development projects are developed for and managed by a specific customer. This customer assumes all the costs associated with the development of the application. If it were decided, under this model, to develop an application for a customer using an SOA environment, the customer would have to assume the entire cost of developing the environment, as well as the cost of using it to build the application. This system of financing for IT projects punishes infrastructure development.

A better financial model is the one used by car manufacturers, such as Canaxia. Every four years, all of Canaxia's car models undergo a major rework. This rework requires an investment of several billion dollars. In spite of the size of the outlay required, it is accepted because it is known that expensive retooling is the cost of doing business. Therefore, the initial retooling outlay is amortized over the four years of the product run by adding a small amount to the cost of each car. Organizations that adopt a similar approach to financing IT infrastructure will have a competitive advantage in today's marketplace.

Applications built using an SOA will not only be cheaper to develop and have a faster time to market but will be significantly less expensive to maintain. Unfortunately, it is a common financial procedure in most enterprises to separate the cost of developing an application from the cost of maintaining it. It is well known to software engineers that the cost of maintaining an application is several times more than the cost of developing it. An effective method of financing application development is to have the customer pay for both development and maintenance costs. Using that financial model, what maintenance is really costing will become painfully evident to the business side of the enterprise. When cradle-to-grave financing is used, the lower maintenance costs of SOA applications will become quickly evident. Building an SOA and using it to develop applications will demonstrate a positive ROI that will more than justify the initial outlay required.

Architecture is a result of the organization's funding model (Stevens 2002).

You should be aware that as you build an SOA implementation and the system becomes more complex, maintenance or enhancements of the infrastructure components could carry considerable risk. We strongly recommend that you couple all development, maintenance, and enhancements with the generation of automated test scripts so that a thorough regression test can be quickly run. SLAs are a complex area. Certain architectures and applications make satisfying SLAs much easier.

It is relatively easy to write an SLA for a stovepipe application. Tightly self-contained, they are like watches. You know pretty well how they will perform. They are relatively immune to network issues. Database changes are one of the few things that can slow down or speed up a stovepipe application.

> See Chapter 1, Systems Architecture, and Chapter 11, Data Architecture, for a discussion of issues related to stovepipe applications.

Distributed architectures such as SOA are at the other end of the spectrum when it comes to specifying and satisfying SLAs. The plus side is as follows:

- The modular, layered nature of an SOA naturally lends itself to setting up parallel, redundant pathways of communication between the various components that are required for the functioning of the service. This can help make a server resistant to network problems.

- The simple, modular nature of the components in the service layer lends itself to achieving stated reliability levels through clustering of servers.

- Asynchronous communication can be much more tolerant of network disruption than synchronous communications.

- Since services are located and connected to at run-time, it is possible for system architects to easily change the location of components in response to systems architecture changes. Distributed architectures also provide the possibility of having applications recover from the unavailability of a component by binding to an alternative component, perhaps at an alternative location.

Following is the negative side:

- The distributed nature of SOAs makes them very vulnerable to network issues. Not just gross network failures that are easy to spot, but also slow, easy-to-overlook network slowdowns and intermittent congestion.

- SOAs are hosted on many machines. A seemingly innocuous change in the availability any one of a number of computers has the potential to disrupt a service.

- The complex nature of some systems built on an SOA makes it very difficult to mathematically derive SLA parameters. Unless you have an extremely thorough system to monitor the elements of your execution platform, initially any SLA numbers will be speculative.

- Yes, there are numerous ways to tune and tweak SOA systems. However, that tuning and tweaking will cost time and money.

In summary, SOAs live in a complex environment. The layered, modular nature of the systems, plus the fault-tolerant ability of the find-and-bind service location system, help SOAs satisfy SLAs.

SOA Management

An SOA will eventually become the backbone of your business. The business case for it is too compelling for it to be otherwise. The more central your SOA becomes to your business, the more you will require an effective set of management tools. The SOA attributes of loose coupling and decentralization of service modules mandate a centralized control structure. The ideal end result is for your SOA to be loosely coupled but tightly managed.

Existing network management tools that are not designed for SOA management are inadequate to manage an SOA for the following reasons:

- They are usually binary in nature; they can tell if an application is up or down. Applications are now composed of interacting modules; information about the health of the modules and of their connections is what is required.

- They have no awareness of business processes.

- They have no understanding of the concept of grouping modules into functional units.
- They have no way to effectively manage the security requirements between the modules in the SOA network.

To put it in perspective, the management needs of an environment of monolithic applications are simple and not survival–critical. The management needs of a client/server environment are more complex but still seldom critical to the survival of the business. Some N-Tier applications are mission–critical and, as a result, come under the control of a management system. Effective SOA management can be critical to the continued existence of the business.

SOA management is a complex issue. We suggest examining your needs around the following topics before examining SOA management solutions:

- Performance information
- Monitoring and management of running services
- Monitoring and management of network issues
- Dynamic method for a service to find and bind to its management agent or services
- Management of SOA security issues
- Management of SLAs
- Management of the evolution of services and the service life cycle
- Management having the capability to be extendable across enterprise boundaries

Performance monitoring, the ability to examine individual services, and good network monitoring and management are obvious needs. These are bottom-line, absolute, must haves.

> Vendors such as Confluent, Amberpoint, and Infravio provide offerings in the SOA management domain.

Your management solution should not require the static linking of your service modules to the application that it is monitoring and controlling. Rather, the linkage must be dynamic and discovered when the module starts up. On the complex end, this can mean a contract in a registry. On the simple end, it can mean building the ability to blindly send and possibly receive events and messages. Any management and monitoring scheme for an SOA must follow SOA principles.

Distributed service environments offer a plethora of points of attack. It is vital that proper security permissions be set among all the modules in your SOA. In a Windows environment, do all your services run with system privileges? On your J2EE application server, how accurately and precisely have you set the security descriptor? Managing all the permissions and roles is an error-prone process when done by hand.

Most of the services in your SOA will support SLA. In addition, the system as a whole will have a global SLA. Having a single point that can document how well you are performing against your SLAs is another strong reason for a services management tool.

Another very useful function that your SOA management tool can perform is to handle service life-cycle issues. You create and deploy this wonderful service. A few defects are surfaced and corrected, so your service modules start to have version numbers. You do a redesign but keep the contract. Initially, you only want to expose this service to a few trusted consumers, while keeping the rest on the old version. The beta run goes well, and the new component is deployed. A couple of the consumers are unable to utilize this new version because of obscure hardware issues, so they have to get the old version when they access the service. In theory, contracts and interfaces are supposed to be immutable for all time. In fact, in some cases you will have to change the contract and deprecate the old service. You should be able to turn to your SOA management tool to handle these issues.

Eventually, you will be consuming services from other enterprises and providing services to businesses other than your own. Ideally, your management tools will be able to manage and monitor not only your own services, but also the outside services upon which you depend. Also, in some cases your business should allow other enterprises to manage and monitor any of your services that they are utilizing. We realize this is a little like asking the lamb to lie down with the lion. If the service is being provided as part of how that business makes its money, you have a much stronger case when you ask the company that is selling you Web services to have visibility into their network and to the service you are utilizing. In the case of Canaxia, it is extremely unlikely that the company will grant any sort of monitoring to its suppliers when it puts up its supply-chain integration Web services. However, if the economic stakes were high enough, that could change.

On the other hand, the introduction of a management system into your SOA environment will bring the following benefits:

- Increased visibility into systems operations. In the Systems Architecture chapter we discussed the need to provide management with information about the functioning of the IT infrastructure. A good SOA management tool can help you realize that goal.

- Of much greater importance is that an SOA management tool has the possibility of allowing visibility into the performance and health of the business processes. An SOA isolates the business processes into discrete sets of modules, independent of transport or resource access functionality, so they can be looked at in isolation.

Everything said in this section applies to Web services as well. In fact, many of the existing SOA management tools are specific for Web services.

For those who want to buy, the best course would be to pick your SOA management platform early in the process of building your SOA and build it into your SOA as it evolves. Every store-bought management platform will have an approach to SOA. You will be allowed to do some things and not others.

Trying to force-fit a well-developed SOA into a management tool could be a painful and expensive process.

The following is a short and almost certainly incomplete list of SOA best practices. Feel free to write your own in the margins.

SOA Best Practices

1. Do your business architecture work first. Understand the major business processes and how they relate to each other. Map the business processes to the data and systems architectures. Use that knowledge to plan your SOA.

2. Start small: Build incrementally. Use the first project to build the component infrastructure for your SOA. Add to your SOA on an ad hoc basis, and document and share what you have learned from each SOA project.

3. When encapsulating existing legacy functionality, use the SOA.

4. Wire in what you have. Leverage the standards-based interoperability of the SOA to allow you to integrate your application infrastructure.

5. Architecture is as important to your Web services as to your SOA. Use architectural principles to set the contracts that your services offer to consumers. Get the grain—the size—of the service you expose in the contract correct. The contract should expose a relatively coarse-grained contract and fulfill the contract by aggregating several fine-grained components.

6. Think agile when building services. Make the creation of services an opportunity to increase the adaptability and efficiency of your organization.

7. Maximize reuse of components by making them small and cohesive.

8. Start building in your management tools early in your SOA effort. Do not allow yourself to get in the position of being forced to retrofit a management solution, at great cost to the business, when your SOA suddenly starts behaving poorly.

The following subsections explore some SOA thinking that should be avoided.

SOA Antipatterns

SOA Is Everything. Infrastructure Is Nothing.

An SOA of any sort—a generic SOA or Web services—runs on the network and is hosted on servers. For an SOA to work, you need the following:

- Sufficient network bandwidth to provide adequate throughput.
- Redundant network connections to increase availability.
- Dedicated machines (Hardware that is hosting mission–critical components should be used for that purpose and that purpose only. In addition, this hardware should be totally under the control

of the people responsible for the service SLA. If that is not possible, then the group providing the hardware should agree to SLAs that are at least as restrictive as the SLA that pertains to the service that is being run on those machines.

Every increase in the size and complexity of the SOA should come with the dollars to beef up the infrastructure.

Web Services Are All We Need to Know About SOA

Web services are a very important SOA implementation and will be the preferred method of business-to-business interoperability. However, as discussed previously, Web services have limitations and are, in many cases, a less-than-optimal method of providing services. In most cases, enterprises that take the time and make the effort to build their own SOAs on the plans laid down by the generic SOA implementation will have SOAs that are much better fits for the totality of their needs.

Web service RAD tools are a particular nuisance. Some maverick downloads a Web services development tool and suddenly a manager is informing the architecture team that the company already has Web services. The manager's group has built five and has eight more ready to come online. Rogue Web service development must be squashed quickly and ruthlessly.

> This is otherwise known as the service junk drawer.

SOA Is About Technology

UDDI and SOAP, HTTP and WSDL: This is what SOA is about. Wrong! SOA is about architecture. SOA incorporates many of the best practices of business and enterprise architecture and modeling.

Everything Is a Service

This stems from the concept that more is better. If one service is good, a hundred is better, and a thousand even better. Not exactly.

Development of an SOA should proceed from business priorities and fit into a well-thought-out architecture. As part of that thinking, you must ask the following questions:

- Can we stand the performance hit that will come from having this functionality accessed via a distributed connection? In the case of Web services, the performance issue will have to be looked at with particular care.
- What are the security implications of plugging this into the network? In the case of Web services, what are the security implications of opening this application to the world?

- Is our infrastructure capable of handling this extra load?
- How are we going to manage this service?

SOA strategies have a great advantage in that services can be brought online in a series of small, three- to six-month projects, rather than requiring one huge effort. The ease of adding services should not blind you to the fact that the architecture is everything. Every service development project should be based on sound business thinking, compliance to the desired future state of the enterprise architecture and leverage the best practices of software architecture.

Conclusion

Many years from now, it will be taken for granted that applications should be assembled from a collection of loosely coupled modules and that applications, and in some cases modules, should easily talk to each other using consistent, open standards-based protocols. In other words, SOA will become the architectural norm.

Starting today, an SOA offers solid ROI. SOAs make legacy application integration and EAI straightforward processes. New application development is made cheaper and faster using an SOA, and the resulting applications are more reliable and cheaper to maintain.

Having a large variety of choices that enable you to move quickly and inexpensively between those choices is a hallmark of an agile enterprise. Service-Oriented Architecture is an excellent architectural style to provide agility to business processes.

chapter 4

Software Product Lines

One of my primary objects is to form the tools so the tools themselves shall fashion the work and give to every part its just proportion.

Eli Whitney

Any organization that develops software creates multiple software applications that have some characteristics in common. Some software has the same application architecture, some run on the same execution platforms, and others support the same segment of the business. Whatever the commonalities are amongst the software applications, it is important that these commonalities be managed properly so that the organization can realize the highest economy of scale. The software product line practice was designed to manage software products, and their commonalities were designed to maximize the benefits to the organization.

These commonalities among software systems are embodied in artifacts called *core assets*. Core assets are reusable and can be any of the following:

- A component
- A framework
- A library
- A tool
- A development or execution platform

Each core asset shares an architecture that all products in the product line will have in common. In addition, a process is attached to each core asset and prescribes the optimal method of using the asset to build a product in the product line. Test cases, design documentation, and other documentation are also attached to the core asset to guide its use in products.

Why is this important? Every organization builds products that have aspects in common. Design patterns have been a method of describing design similarities in software artifacts for about a decade. Design patterns are an excellent means of documenting designs that work across multiple applications with the same or similar characteristics. Product lines take this concept further. A core asset documents not only a software design that works, but it also includes the software that implements that design. The asset is not just sample code that explains a design idea; it is working code, components, and systems that can be used directly in other applications. One of the great assets of design patterns is that they are applicable in a wide range of applications. Core assets are not as widely applicable, but they can provide enormous benefit to applications that have the desired characteristics. A product line also provides a means of characterizing products that have similar characteristics. They can take advantage of core assets that were built to provide benefit in the context of a particular product line.

What are these benefits? When an organization decides to fund a new project to deliver some benefit to the business, what is the state of the project at the moment of inception? Is there a technical infrastructure available to begin development? Can any existing software architectures, components, frameworks, or libraries be leveraged? In a typical organization, when a new project is started, one of the following is done to acquire these assets:

- Assets are copied from other projects and modified in the new project.
- Assets are acquired or built from scratch for the purpose of the new project.

Not only is it more expensive to acquire or build new assets for every new project, but it also produces yet another product to maintain that has little or nothing in common with the other products in the organization. An organization that continues this process over and over will find it extremely expensive to maintain all these applications.

A product line treats these core assets as separate from the products into which they are assembled. The product line core assets are acquired, created, and managed separately so that every product that is built in the product line can do the following:

- They can provide a jump-start for new development. The core assets provide an existing infrastructure, software assets, process, and expertise for new projects.
- They can reduce maintenance because there is simply less to maintain and the people who do the maintenance have knowledge about all applications in the product line because they all share core assets.

If managed correctly, the bottom line is that an organization that is oriented around a product line method of creating and maintaining software can dramatically reduce expense and dramatically decrease the time to market for new applications. The key phrase in the previous sentence, however, is "managed correctly." For example, creating a product line with a single product in it has a negative benefit. There is also a negative benefit if the core assets in the product line don't meet the needs of new applications. This chapter will give you some advice on implementing product lines that make sense and provide benefit to your organization.

Our favorite auto company, Canaxia, has a huge maintenance expense problem. Canaxia spends 90 percent of its IT budget on maintaining existing systems, leaving little to fund new projects. As a result, Canaxia is falling behind its competitors because it takes so long and costs so much to develop new software and add new features to its existing software.

For example, its Internet and intranet sites are a mess. It has six small intranet Web sites. Three of these sites use .NET, one uses J2EE, and the others use PHP. They all access different databases. Some access an Oracle database, some access a DB2 database, and the .NET sites access an SQL server database. Canaxia also has three Internet Web sites, one for corporate, one for sales, and one for dealerships. Each has a different user interface. Two are developed in J2EE, and the other was developed in .NET by an external consulting firm. Each project team used a different process to develop the sites. One team used RUP, one used eXtreme Programming, and the other used an ad-hoc process. In addition, each site has its own customer database and users must remember separate user IDs and passwords to access each site. Components were developed to support each site, such as a logging component and a component to store reference and configuration data. Of course, each project team also created different versions of these components.

The situation at Canaxia is probably familiar to most people who work in IT. Given this situation, how can Canaxia spend less on maintenance and improve the way it delivers new applications? How does an organization take advantage of the opportunities to reuse infrastructure, process, architecture, and software assets across applications?

It is surprising that Canaxia got itself into this mess because this is not how the company builds cars. When a car is ordered from Canaxia, Canaxia does not build a custom car from scratch. That would be too expensive. Canaxia has several product lines. It has a product line for compact cars, midsize cars, and sport utility vehicles. At Canaxia, each product line is based on four aspects of building cars within that line.

1. Shared process
2. Shared components
3. Shared infrastructure
4. Shared knowledge

However, each car goes through a different process during its manufacture. In the compact car product line, the seats are placed before the steering wheel. In the sport utility vehicle product line, the steering wheel goes in first. In addition, many of the components of a vehicle are similar within a product line. For example, the steering wheels, tires, visors, and other components are identical in every Canaxia midsize car. In addition, within a product line, a single infrastructure produces the cars. The midsize car line has a single assembly line consisting of robots and other machinery that builds a midsize car with minor variations, such as paint color and trim. All the workers on the assembly line understand the process, the components, and the infrastructure and have the skills necessary to build any type of midsize car within Canaxia. By having shared product line assets, Canaxia has the flexibility to build similar car models with the same people because they are familiar with the line, not just with a particular model. By applying these same concepts to software product lines, Canaxia can achieve a similar benefit in the way it develops and maintains its software products.

The idea of product lines is not new. Eli Whitney created interchangeable parts for rifles in the 1880s to fill an order for ten thousand muskets for the U.S. government. He did this because only a handful of skilled machinists were available in Connecticut at the time. A few decades later, Henry Ford perfected the assembly line to create Model T cars. Ford's process was instrumental in achieving orders-of-magnitude increases in automobile productivity. He was able to provide a complex product at a relatively inexpensive price to the American public through increases in productivity.

The Manufacturing Metaphor

Before dropping everything and setting up an assembly line for creating software products, it should be noted that the manufacturing metaphor for software development should be used with caution. The manufacturing metaphor for software development has been around for awhile. In some respects, the metaphor works. Shared components, process, and infrastructure will increase productivity and quality. However, a car designer has to work in the physical world. He or she is bound by physics. It is relatively easy to measure the roll-over potential of a vehicle based on its center of gravity and wheelbase. It is also obvious that a car with four wheels is better than a car with two wheels. These properties are easily tested, and quantitative evaluations can be used to compare different designs. Physical systems can be measured and compared using quantitative methods in an objective fashion.

In software, no universally accepted quantitative measurement states that a component that has four interfaces is better than one that has two interfaces. In software, it is often said that source code modules "should not be more than 1,000 lines of code" and the design should exhibit "loose coupling" or "high cohesion." Does this mean that a source code file that is over 1,000 lines is a bad one? While we know that a car with one tire will fall over, we cannot say that a source code module with more than 1,000 lines is always a bad one.

Software process and design are less quantitative (measurable with statistics) and more qualitative (measurable with descriptions). Qualitative analysis requires analysis and judgment based on contrasting and interpreting meaningful observable patterns or themes. Several key differences are notable when it comes to the process of manufacturing a product versus creating a software product:

1. Software development is much less predictable than manufacturing a physical product.
2. Software is not mass-produced on the same scale as a physical product.
3. Not all software faults result in failures.
4. Software doesn't wear out.
5. Software is not bound by physics.

The creation of software is an intellectual human endeavor. Creating good software relies on the personalities and the intellects of the members of the teams that create it. When applied to a different team of developers a process that delivers great software for one team of developers may fail to deliver anything at all for another team.

The three main goals of a software product line are to reduce cost, improve delivery time, and improve quality. A software product line is a "family of products designed to take advantage of their common aspects and predicted variabilities" (Weiss 1999).

Any organization that has many software systems will notice that many of those software systems have characteristics in common. When a set of systems has common characteristics, they are candidates to become part of a product family or product line. A product line has a set of core assets upon which a shared family of systems is built. Core assets include shared components, infrastructure, tools, process, documentation, and above all else, shared architecture.

A product line is a decomposition of the entire application portfolio of an organization according to these common characteristics. For example, Canaxia hired Scott Roman as its new CIO of Internet systems. Scott decided to create an Internet product line that included all Internet-based systems because they share a common architecture. Chapter 2 explored how software architecture is built to achieve the quality-attribute requirements of the project. In product line development, the software architecture that belongs to the product line is based on the common quality-attribute requirements for all the applications in the product line. Scott realized that all the Internet systems require 24 x 7 availability and have the same performance and scalability requirements and generally need the same software architecture. These requirements drove him to create a set of common core assets that met the quality-attribute requirements for all the Internet applications at Canaxia.

Figure 4–1 (From "Software Product Lines: Practices and Patterns" by Paul Clements and Linda Northrop, Addison Wesley 2002) illustrates that product line development consists of cooperation among three different constituencies: core asset development, product development, and management.

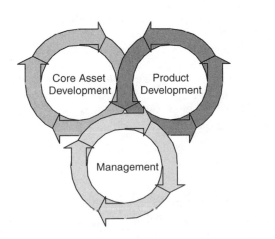

Figure 4–1
Product line development.

Core Asset Development

Core asset development is the creation and maintenance of the artifacts or core assets in the product line. These core assets are used to create systems that match the quality criteria of the product line. For example, if the types of products that are developed in the product line have a high maintainability requirement, then the core assets should reflect this requirement and account for the need for good maintainability. The goal of the core asset development activity is to create a capability within the organization to produce a particular type of application and will thus yield the same or similar software architecture.

Product Development

The second constituency is product development. Product development involves the creation of products or systems from the core assets of the product line. If a system requires an asset that is not included in the core assets, the core asset must be created if the asset can be shared across multiple products in the product line. It is a strategic decision whether or not to build a new core asset or to create a product-specific feature to the project under development. Also, if the core asset that exists in the product line does not match the quality requirements of the product under development, the core asset may be enhanced or modified. Later in this chapter, we talk about several models for organizing core asset and production development.

Management

Management must be involved to ensure that the two constituencies are interacting correctly. Instituting a product line practice at an organization requires a strong commitment from management. It is also important to identify which assets are part of the product line and which ones are part of the development of the individual products of the system. Management consists of the management of individual projects within the product line, as well as overall product line managers. The role of product line manager (Northrop 2002) is one of a product line champion. The champion is a strong, visionary leader who can keep the organization working toward the creation of core assets while limiting any negative impact on project development.

Product Line Benefits

There are many benefits to establishing a product line. Principally, the product line leads to reduced cost and faster time to market for new projects. Also, a product line approach to software development will lead to a more portable staff because the architecture is similar from project to project. Finally, risks are also reduced and quality is improved because the architecture has been proven on multiple projects.

Reduced Cost

Just as demonstrated by Eli Whitney and Henry Ford, adopting a product line approach to developing and maintaining applications can dramatically reduce costs through the specialization of roles and the reuse of core assets that otherwise would have needed to be developed or acquired and maintained separately for each application.

Improved Time to Market

For many organizations, cost is not the primary driver for product line adoption. Reusable components speed the time it takes to get a product out the door. Product lines allow organizations to take advantage of the shared features of their product lines and to add features particular to the products they are building.

Flexible Staffing and Productivity

There is much more flexibility when moving people around the organization since they become familiar with the set of shared tools, components, and processes of each product line. A critical product development effort can benefit from using people from other product development teams who are familiar with the product line's core assets. The learning curve is shortened because the shared assets of the product line are familiar to staff who work on the products in the product line.

Increased Predictability

In a shared product line, several products are developed using a set of common core assets, a shared architecture and production plan, and people with experience for creating products within the product line. These core assets and architecture are proven on several products. Project managers and other stakeholders will have more confidence in the success of new projects within the product line because of the proven set of core assets and people.

Higher Quality

Because core assets serve the needs of more than one project, they must be of higher quality. Also, multiple projects exercise the shared assets in more ways than a single project would, so the shared assets will have a much higher quality. In addition, the shared architecture of the product line is also proven through implementation by several projects.

Not only are core assets of higher quality, but the applications that are developed from them are of higher quality. This stems from the high quality of the core assets, staff that have higher expertise, more project predictability, and a proven quality assurance process at the product line level.

A product line has the following four aspects:

Related Business Benefit

The product line should support an established business benefit. At Canaxia, the Internet sites provide timely information and electronic business functionality to a variety of users. Tangible business benefits accrue from transacting business with customers, dealers, and sales agents via the Internet. The business benefit also drives the qualities that the product line must support. These qualities are embodied by the software architecture that is central to the product line.

Core Assets

Core assets are the basis for the creation of products in the software product line. They include the architecture that the products in the product line will share, as well as the components that are developed for systematic reuse across the product line or across multiple product lines. Core assets are the key components of a software product line. They include the infrastructure, tools, hardware, and other assets that enable the development, execution, and maintenance of the systems in the product line. Each core asset also has an attached process that describes how to use the asset to create a product.

Source Code Reuse

Software reuse is usually identified with the reuse of source code across software systems. Source code is extremely difficult to reuse on a large scale. The software development community has tried and mostly failed to reuse source code. Bob Frankston, a programmer from VisiCalc, the first spreadsheet program, had this to say (Wired 2002):

"You should have huge catalogs of code lying around. That was in the 70s; reusable code was the big thing. But reusing pieces of code is like picking off sentences from other people's stories and trying to make a magazine article."

While you can write a magazine article using sentences from other works, it is a little like creating a ransom note from newspaper clippings. You might make your point, but not very clearly. It is usually easier to just write the whole code yourself. Direct source code reuse is extremely difficult and, as a result, has mostly failed to materialize, even with the invention of OOP in the 1990s.

The core assets at Canaxia are grouped according to technology, with a central IT department. It makes the most sense to group the products together according to technology. At other organizations, it might make more sense to group the core assets and product lines differently. For example, a company that sells software might create product lines according to its business segment.

Figure 4–2 outlines the types of assets that can be included in a product line. Several categories of assets exist in the product line.

Shared Architecture

The shared architecture (Bosch 2000) for a family of systems is the main core asset for a product line. For example, Canaxia has three Internet sys-

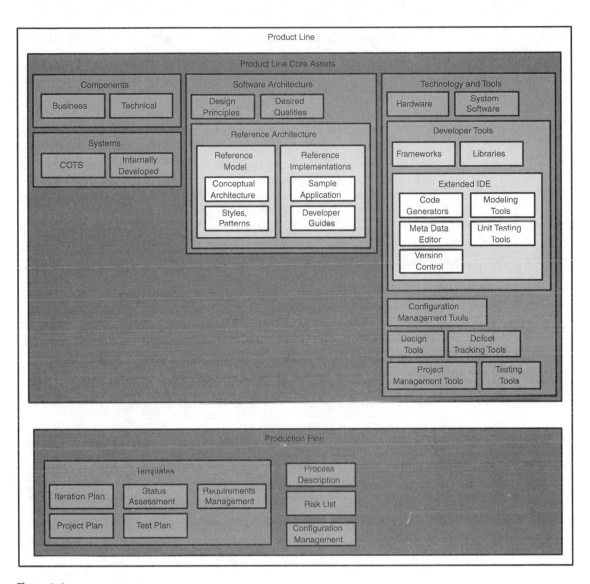

Figure 4–2
Product line decomposition.

tems. Each system uses a distributed model–view–controller architectural style. Each one is also a multilayered system, accesses a database, and sends markup to a browser client. All three systems also share the same quality attributes. For example, each one requires a similar level of performance, scalability, and security. By considering all three systems as part of a product line, an architect can construct a common conceptual architecture for all three systems. When new systems are developed that match the characteristics of this product line, the new system can reuse the architecture of the product line. If the new requirements do not exactly match the characteristics of the product line, a strategic decision must be made to either update or extend the product line or build product-unique assets.

The problem at Canaxia is that although each system has the same quality attributes, each one was developed separately. It is fairly obvious to Canaxia management now that all these projects should have been part of the same product line, been built on the same architecture, used the same tools, and used the same process during development. Now management has a problem. Should it continue with three separate systems or merge them together into a single product line? Canaxia spent millions on each project separately. To merge them into a single product line would take years and additional millions. For now, Canaxia is considering an evolutionary approach to merging the systems into a single product line.

This situation is familiar to anyone who works in IT. It is difficult to make the creation of a product line a big bang process. Product lines usually evolve over time, starting with one large project that becomes the basis for the product line. Canaxia has to figure out ways to synchronize its architectures over time. Perhaps this means that as enhancements are requested of each system, the company can migrate toward shared components. Web services and middleware play a role in sharing components across heterogeneous technology platforms. It might be time to move to the shared product line architecture when a major revision of each site is needed. This is a difficult decision to make, and if an organization has the courage to move to a shared architecture quickly and if it is successful at doing so, it will save time and money in the long run. Sometimes big change is necessary and an organization must recognize when it is best to do a wholesale move to a new architecture. However, the problem with legacy systems is that they work and usually work reliably. On the other hand, an organization must recognize when these assets become liabilities and should be replaced.

The architecture that is developed for the product line is built from the quality-attribute requirements that are known to the product line at the time it is created. New systems in the product line will require changes to the architecture because each new system has slightly (hopefully) different requirements. For example, if a new system must allow scalability to millions of users rather than the current thousands that the product line supports, the architecture must be changed to support that requirement. However, if the requirements are so different that the architecture must be overhauled, the new system is probably not a candidate for inclusion in the product line.

This is one of the negative aspects of product lines and reuse in general. When a core asset is updated to meet the requirement of a new system, any existing systems that use that asset might be impacted. For example, if a logging service must be updated to include asynchronous messaging, any system that uses the service might have to be updated. Even if the interface did not change, any system using the logging service would have to be thoroughly tested with the new version.

How should an organization document the architecture? The architecture artifacts that are relevant at the product line level are the reference architecture that consist of reference models and reference implementations.

The reference model is a conceptual model for the ideal system in the product line. It shows the layers of the system, the types of data that are transferred between the layers, the responsibilities of the major layers, and components in the system. It is the common starting point for products built in the product line. The model outlines all the commonalities of the products in the product line with as much detail as possible. Chapter 2, Software Architecture, presents additional information on documenting software architectures.

The ideal reference architecture is a sample application or examples that show how a working application is built using the architecture and the tools provided by the product line. A good example of a reference architecture is the Pet Store sample application that comes with the J2EE reference edition. The Pet Store application shows how an application should be constructed using the J2EE platform. In addition to working code, the reference architecture is built by people who are familiar with the architecture to help developers and others use the materials provided by the product line.

Shared Components

In the software industry, the term *component* is used in many different ways. Components come in many forms. Most people think of components as JavaBeans or ActiveX controls. Some people think of a component as any software artifact that can be reused. The term is used in the context of this book as a self-contained software module that has a well-defined interface or set of interfaces (Herzum and Sims 1999). A component has run-time and design-time interfaces. It is easily composed into an application to provide useful technical or business functions. A component is delivered and installed and used by connecting and executing an interface at run-time. It is also considered to be a software black box. No other process can view or change the internal state of the component except through the components' published interface. A component can be a shared run-time software entity, such as a logging component, a billing service, or an ActiveX control.

The two types of components are business components and technical components. The component types are differentiated because even the components themselves are part of their own product lines. They each serve a different purpose. A business component serves a business function such as a customer service (as we learned in Chapter 3, Service-Oriented Architecture, a service can be a service-enabled component or a CBS, a component based service). The customer service has a set of interfaces that manages customers for the company. A technical component has a technical purpose, such as logging or configuration. Both the business components and the technical components have a distinct set of quality attributes. Each component product line includes the core assets and production plans necessary to create and maintain components of each type.

At Canaxia, every Internet system has its own logging component, customer database, and configuration service. Rather than creating three separate versions of each of these components, Canaxia could create a single version of all three of these components and share them between systems. There are two ways to share components among different systems in a product line. Different instances of the components could be deployed into each application and used separately, or a single component or service could be used for the entire product line. The method of distributing the components will vary based on the needs of the project. Some product lines might even allow some systems within the product line to use a central component and also allow other systems to deploy and use an instance of the component within the system that needs it. For more on using component usage in product lines, see *Component-Based Product Line Engineering with* UML (Atkinson 2001).

Systems

The systems (Bosch 2000) that are constructed within the product line are also core assets. These systems are constructed using the architecture of the product line and the components that are part of the product line. The two types of systems are internally developed and commercial off-the-shelf systems (COTS). At Canaxia, the three Internet systems for corporate, sales, and dealerships are considered part of the same product line because they share similar characteristics. The characteristics they share are that they use the same software architecture and that they use the same components in their implementation.

COTS systems can share some aspects of architecture, components, and other core assets with internally developed systems within the product line. Some examples of core assets that a COTS can take advantage of may include a logging service, middleware, and infrastructure such as hardware, networks, and application servers.

Each system becomes part of the system portfolio for the product line. The product portfolio should be managed just like an investment portfolio. Determinations of buy, sell, and hold are relevant to products within the product line. Each system should exhibit some return on the investment made in its development and ongoing maintenance. Once the benefits are outweighed by the costs of maintaining the system, a sell decision should be made. By creating a product line mindset, the return on investment of systems in the portfolio should improve because the costs for shared assets are usually lower than the cost for multiple assets.

Shared Technology and Tools

A product line can share technology and tools for building and executing systems. The technology and tools that are selected have a dramatic effect on ensuring that the systems built within the product line conform to the architecture of the product line.

Technology includes hardware, system software, application servers, database servers, and other commercial products that are required to run the systems in the product line. The most obvious technology that can be reused within a product line is the execution platform for all the systems and components that run in the product line. Some obvious (and not so obvious) technologies that can be leveraged across projects include the following (McGovern et al. 2003):

- Application servers
- Database servers
- Security servers

- Networks and machines
- Modeling tools
- Traceability tools
- Compilers and code generators
- Editors
- Prototyping tools
- Integrated development environments
- Version control software
- Test generators
- Test execution software
- Performance analysis software
- Code inspection and static analysis software
- Configuration management software
- Defect tracking software
- Release management and versioning software
- Project planning and measurement software
- Frameworks and libraries

At Canaxia, one of the first steps toward creating a shared product line for Internet systems was to move all the applications onto a shared infrastructure. Each system separately used approximately 20 percent of the capacity of each of its servers. By pooling their servers, they shared their excess capacity for handling peak loads. Moving to a shared infrastructure also required each application to modify some of its systems and bring them into conformance with the product line. It also highlighted the areas in each application where commonalities existed.

In addition to hardware, frameworks, and libraries, an extended IDE provides the developers with a single development environment for the product line. The advantage to having a single development environment is that it gives the organization the flexibility to move developers from project to project without a steep learning curve before they become productive.

eXtended IDE (XIDE)

In *Business Component Factory*, Peter Herzum and Oliver Sims (1999) explain the concept of an extended IDE. The XIDE stands as an "eXtended integrated development environment." It is the set of tools, development environments, compilers, editors, testing tools, modeling tools, version control tools, and other software that developers need to perform their jobs. The concept of XIDE is to include all these tools in a single pluggable IDE, or at least to have a standard developer desktop environment that includes all the standard tools for the product line. Having a standard XIDE is crucial to providing developer portability from system to system within the product line.

An important role for core asset developers is to develop tools for product developers to use in their development of applications. These tools can be thought of as plug-ins for the XIDE. In addition to managing core assets that make their way into the systems within the product line, the core asset developers also create tools for other developers that can be plugged into their development environment, such as code generators, configuration tools, and other tools that are specific to the environment of the product line. These tools provide an excellent means of enabling and enforcing the product line architecture.

Supporting Organization

The product line has an organization to design, construct, support, and train developers and other users to utilize it. The organization that supports the product line is the domain engineering unit (Clements and Northrop 2001).

This group is responsible for the product line assets. Groups that use the product line assets rely on a group to handle upgrade, maintenance, and other reuse issues that arise when shared assets are employed on a project. Some organizations do not use a central group to maintain core assets. Core assets are developed along with the products. Project teams develop the core assets and have to coordinate the development of common core assets among several project groups. For example, Canaxia initially did not have a central domain engineering unit. They initially created the logging component for use in the corporate Internet site. When the dealer and sales Internet site projects were started, they called the corporate site developers and asked them if they had any components that they could use for their site. They installed and used the logging component from the corporate site and get periodic updates of the component from the corporate site team.

An organization can adopt several organizational structures to support the product line. In addition to domain engineering units, other forms of organizational structure may be adopted (Bosch 2000).

Development Department

This structure is one where both product and core asset software development is performed by a single department. This department creates products and core assets together. Staff can be assigned to work on any number of products or to develop and evolve core assets. This type of structure is common and most useful in small organizations (less than thirty staff members) that cannot justify the expense of specialized areas for core asset development.

These organizations benefit from good communication among staff members because all the members work for a single organization. There is also less administrative overhead.

The primary disadvantage of this structure is the scalability of the organization. When the number of members grows past thirty, specialized roles and groups should be created that focus on the different functional and technical areas of the project. This leads to the next type of organizational structure.

Business Unit

This structure specializes development around a type of product (Bosch 2000). Each business unit is responsible for one or several products in the product line (see Figure 4–3). The business unit is responsible for the development of the product, as well as for the development, evolution, and maintenance of core assets that are needed to create the product. Multiple business units share these core assets, and all business units are responsible for the development, maintenance, and evolution of the core assets.

Core assets can be managed in three ways. In an unconstrained model, all business units are responsible for all the core assets. With this type of structure, it is difficult to determine which group is responsible for which parts of the shared assets. Each business unit is responsible for funding the features required by its individual product. Features of the core assets that do not apply directly to the product under development usually fall to the business unit that needs the feature. A large amount of coordination is necessary for this model to work. Typically, components will suffer from an inconsistent evolution by multiple project teams with different feature goals. Components will become corrupted and eventually lose the initial benefit of becoming a shared asset.

A second type of structure within the business unit model is an asset-responsible structure in which a single developer or responsible party is tasked with the development, evolution, and maintenance of a single shared asset. In theory, this model should solve the problem, but the developer is part of a business area and subject to the management priorities of the project, not the shared assets.

A third type of business unit organizational model is mixed responsibility. In this model, a whole unit is responsible for different core assets. The other business units do not have the authority to implement changes in a shared component for which they are not responsible. This model has advantages over the other two. However, business priorities will still trump core asset priorities. The high-priority requests of one group for changes to a core asset will be less of a priority to a business unit that is responsible for the core asset and is attempting to deliver a product as well. The next model addresses these concerns for large organizations.

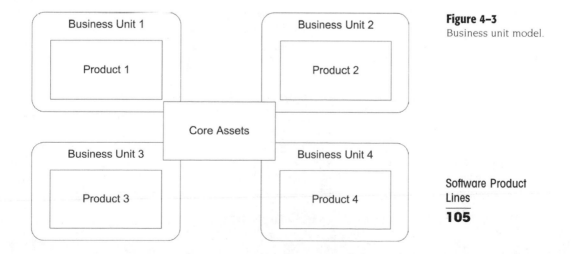

Figure 4–3
Business unit model.

Software Product
Lines

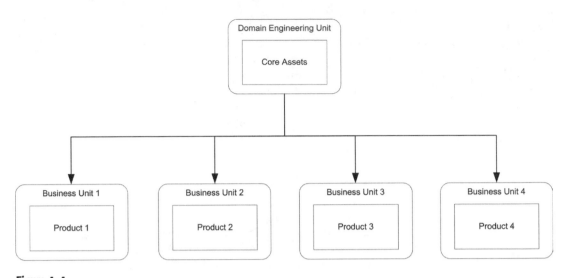

Figure 4–4
Domain engineering unit model.

Domain Engineering Unit

This structure contains several business units and a central domain engineering unit. The domain engineering unit is responsible for the development, maintenance, and evolution of the core assets. This model is the recommended structure for product line adoption in product line literature for large organizations. This structure benefits from a separate group that is focused on creating the core assets, process, and architecture for the product line. The group can focus on high-quality components that support multiple projects.

Many organizations are skeptical of this structure. It is believed that separate groups that perform core asset development will not be responsive to the business needs of an organization and will focus only on interesting technical problems. However, when the number of software developers reaches a level of about a hundred, a central domain engineering unit is the best way to scale the organization and take advantage of the benefits of shared core assets. It helps to improve communication, and core assets will be built to include requirements from multiple project teams instead of focusing on the requirements of a single project. However, it can be difficult to balance the requirements of multiple projects, and some project teams might feel that the domain engineering unit is less responsive than were the assets built as part of the project (see Figure 4–4).

Hierarchical Domain Engineering Unit

In extremely large organizations, it is likely that multiple domain engineering units are necessary to provide specialized core assets to projects. To accomplish this, each product line can have a separate domain engineering unit that is responsible for specialized core assets for the product line in addition to a single central domain engineering unit that is responsible for core assets that span product lines (see Figure 4–5).

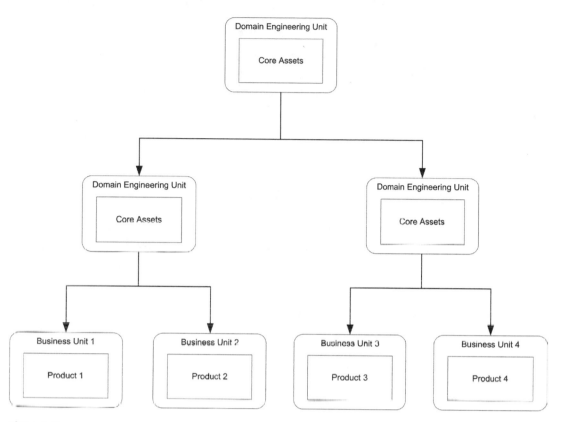

Figure 4–5
Hierarchical domain engineering unit model.

Since the characteristics of all the projects within the product line are similar, they will benefit by having a similar process for their development, maintenance, and evolution. Optimal processes can be created to use core assets in a new project. For example, at Canaxia the teams that use the customer database know that it is best to define the new attributes that have to be captured for a customer early in the elaboration phase of the project. The domain team has to be notified early in the process of the additional attributes that a new project team needs for a customer. That way, they can be factored into the schedule for the new system. Some processes that can be reused across projects include the following:

- Analysis
- Requirements gathering
- Design and development
- Software configuration management processes
- Software maintenance
- Release management
- Quality assurance

This shared process is a production plan. It contains all the necessary processes for building a project using the core assets. It outlines what groups should be involved, what their roles are, and when they should be involved. The project development is still up to the business units, but now that core assets may be out of the control of the business units, more coordination is necessary with the domain engineering units to make sure that core assets are updated for new projects in a timely manner.

When setting up product lines within an organization, figuring out how to scope the product lines is difficult. Should the product line support a particular architectural style, or should it map more to the business segment? A typical organization will already have many applications. Some of these will be related. They will have a common architecture or a shared infrastructure or be managed by a single organization. These applications will logically belong to a single product line. What about applications that belong to other organizations or have the same quality-attribute profile? What if they use different architectures, processes, and infrastructures? How does one decide how to group these applications into a set of product lines (see Figure 4–6)?

Two key factors determine how product lines are grouped: the business segment and the architectural style. A product line can be grouped according to business segment. For example, Canaxia could group its product lines by corporate or consumer sales groups. It can also further decompose its product lines according to architectural style. For example, the Internet systems and the mid-tier and mainframe systems could each become part of separate product lines.

To analyze how to group products into product lines, the existing inventory of the applications within the organization should be analyzed. One method of analysis is to create a grid with the business segments or organizations at the top and the existing architectural styles on the right. Business segments or organi-

Figure 4–6
Grouping existing systems into a product line.

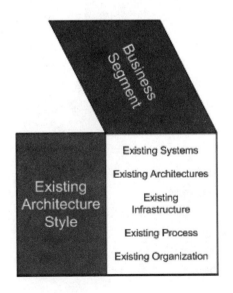

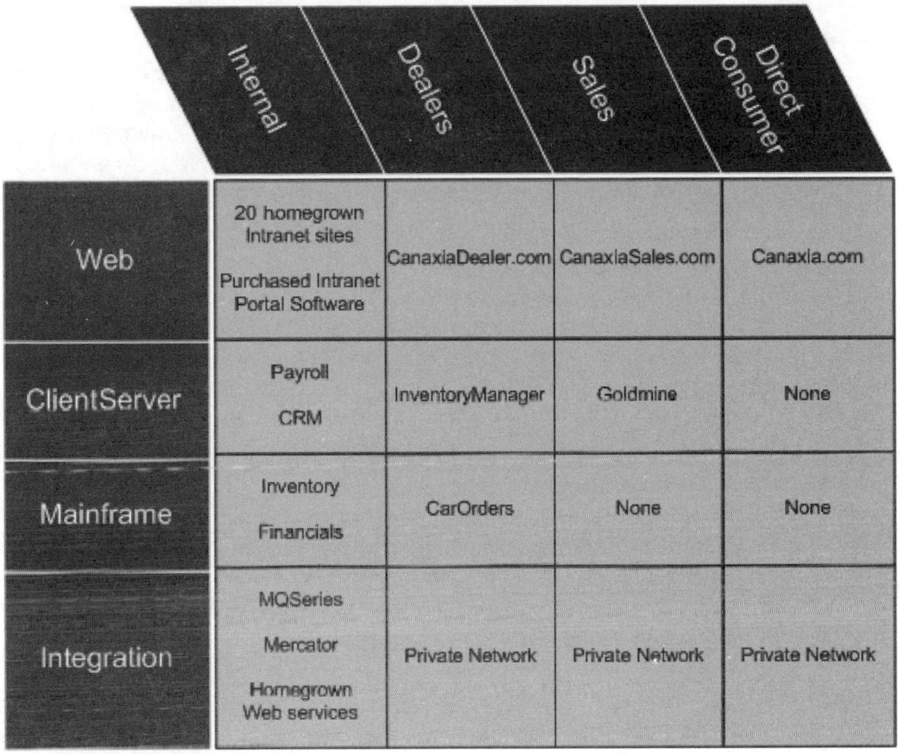

	Internal	Dealers	Sales	Direct Consumer
Web	20 homegrown Intranet sites Purchased Intranet Portal Software	CanaxiaDealer.com	CanaxiaSales.com	Canaxia.com
ClientServer	Payroll CRM	InventoryManager	Goldmine	None
Mainframe	Inventory Financials	CarOrders	None	None
Integration	MQSeries Mercator Homegrown Web services	Private Network	Private Network	Private Network

Figure 4–7
Grouping existing systems into a product line.

zations are aligned to the business need. The architectural styles are classes of technologies, such as Web, client/server, and so on. At Canaxia, Scott and his team went through this exercise and came up with a grid (see Figure 4–7).

After all the products within the organization were mapped, each application was grouped with other applications into a product line based on the business need and the architectural style of the application. For example, in the above grid, it was clear that the twenty homegrown intranet sites and the purchased intranet software should be grouped into a single product line. This may be reasonable if the organizations that maintain each of the homegrown sites are the same. If not, the organization must change or separate product lines that will align with each organization.

Once the products are grouped into their respective product lines, each product line must be managed by a single organization. The product line manager and his or her team should conduct a quality-attribute analysis to understand the needs of the architecture for the product line. Then they should work toward creating a shared architecture, infrastructure, and process for the product line and begin to work toward that common shared vision for the product line that supports the desired quality attributes.

Conclusion　　Every organization of any size has developed applications that have characteristics in common. Through informal means, many of these applications share common components, infrastructures, or processes. Product lines provide a way of formalizing the manner in which these applications are managed in an organization. The goal of a product line–oriented organization is to maximize the benefits that come from managing groups of applications together. Reuse in a product line is a byproduct of the structure of the organization. Reducing development, quality assurance, and maintenance costs and getting products to market faster are the real benefits of product lines.

chapter 5

Methodology Overview

I have not failed. I've just found 10,000 ways that won't work.
Thomas A. Edison (1847–1931)

Our protagonist, Myles Standish, understands today's technology projects are faced with steadily increasing expectations. Software has to be developed faster, better, and cheaper. Simultaneously, complexity of systems grows logarithmically as new technologies are introduced not only to extend the enterprise but also to bring legacy up to the foreground of company intelligence. In managing these conflicting factors, Myles relies on an armada of methodologies that can be used to reduce risk and deliver technology solutions on time and on budget.

Methodology is an amorphous term used in the technology industry that describes the processes and procedures used during the delivery of a technology effort. Over the past two decades, a number of formalized methodologies have evolved to assist in managing the processes associated with technology delivery in areas such as software architecture, software development, and systems management. This chapter covers the details of five popular methodologies that are used across the industry:

- eXtreme Programming
- SEI/CMM
- Zachman Framework
- Model-driven architecture
- Rational Unified Process

Each of these methodologies focuses on different aspects of technology processes, but all are similar in the vision of a flexible and disciplined approach to software and systems development. These methodologies are illustrated in practice through the experience of our faithful systems architect, Myles Standish, whose agenda is to create a consolidated and focused enterprise architecture approach to each of the technology efforts throughout the enterprise.

111

The discipline of software development by itself is an extremely complex process to manage. A great majority of corporate IT projects related to software development run over budget and beyond schedule. An estimated 50 percent of all corporate software development projects in 2000 were delivered over 180 percent above expected cost (Chaos Report, The Standish Group © 2002). Along with that, about a third of all software development projects are cancelled even before the first release of an application. This leaves a mere 25 percent of projects being delivered successfully and on time/budget. With dramatically poor industry statistics as this, it is obvious why processes and methodologies for mitigating the risks of project delivery is a primary concern for the enterprise architect.

Software methodologies trace processes and mitigate against risk areas that cause projects to fail. For architects, software development is a key part of their horizon of responsibilities and one of the most important for them to manage well. As the architect for Canaxia, Myles Standish understands that he needs to have exposure to all the software development projects throughout the enterprise. He's looking to provide the projects with processes, tools, and frameworks to more reliably deliver projects on time and on budget. At the same time, he's interested in building a set of enterprise services that leverage business intelligence and business applications across the various groups in Canaxia.

The Software Development Life Cycle

Before delving into the descriptions for each of the methodologies, it is important to understand the context of the problem that these process definitions are intended to solve. The software development life cycle (SDLC) is a standard definition of the phases involved in any software development project. Each methodology uses its own vocabulary to describe the following phases, but they are all consistent in purpose:

- *Concept Phase*: The concept phase is used to initially evaluate the size and scope of a potential software development task or project. This phase usually entails the definition of the problem the software product is to solve and the criteria for how to determine the success of the delivery.

- *Specification Phase*: This phase is used to spell out the detailed requirements for any new software development. This phase is used by the technology teams to intimately understand the nuances of the business processes and problems they intend to solve with the new product.

- *Design Phase*: The design phase is focused on mainly by the technology team to evaluate and plan the construction phase of the project. This phase is of particular interest to the enterprise architect who wants to make sure that technical design decisions for a project are in line with the direction of the entire enterprise architecture.

- *Construction Phase*: The construction phase of a project is where all the magic in code development occurs, from the definition of development environments to coding procedures to the compilation and construction of all the subcomponents for a project.

- *Quality Assurance Phase*: This phase is identified to manage the quality of the project prior to the launch of the product. Quality assurance encompasses multiple perspectives, from end-user usability, to requirements satisfaction, and overall system performance.

- *Deployment Phase*: The deployment phase of a project encompasses the launch and maintenance of a system. The majority of an application's life cycle is spent in deployment.

Anyone who has been responsible for the delivery of a software development project knows the two main criteria used to define successful delivery of a software project. The first is cost. The cost associated with a project is the allocated budget that is expected to be used during the phases of development. The second is the schedule. The schedule determines the calendar dates that are defined to track the progress of a project. Across the industry, projects have the bad reputation of usually running over budget and schedule.

Why is the practice of software development so complex? Why are there so many failed projects? In general, the factors that drive the success of a software development project are defined into three major categories of influence:

- *Business Drivers*: The business drivers are the conditions for which a software development project is intended. Business drivers are many and varied, but they are all generally aligned with either cost cutting and the bottom line or revenue generating and top-line solutions. Business drivers can be fickle where the conditions of business problems can change faster than technology can keep up.

- *People*: People will always be a complicating factor in software development. Different organizations have various roles with different personalities and varying levels of experience. The players involved in a project's delivery are a major factor in the complexity of a software project.

- *Technology*: Technology is a radically evolving facet of software development. Tools, APIs, standards, and products are all constantly evolving. In general, software product companies plan to release new versions of their software on a semiannual, if not quarterly, basis.

Methodologies are used to manage the complex influence of these factors in the development of a software product. First, in terms of business drivers, each methodology defines detailed means to understand the scope and horizon of effectiveness for business drivers. Second, in terms of people, each methodology defines in detail the exact roles and responsibilities for each of the players involved in the delivery of a project. Finally, in terms of technology, each methodology describes short-term iterative approaches to technology design and construction.

Variations on the SDLC

Recently, new variations of software delivery problems have gone beyond the three standard influences that affect the delivery of a software project. To understand the scope of these variations, it is important to understand how each of the methodologies described can encompass complexities caused by the following:

- SDLC *for Offshore Development*: In any enterprise's application development context, the use of offshore development has become more and more prevalent. The question is how does any methodology also encompass and mitigate against the complexity of the players in a project in different cultural, language, and physical contexts?

- SDLC *for Maintenance*: IT organizations are structured in various ways to handle the development and maintenance of applications in an enterprise. Many times, the people responsible for the maintenance of an application are not the people who actually develop the application. Each methodology can be judged on its flexibility to both describe the process for delivery technology and the process for maintaining it over time.

- SDLC *for Package Implementations*: Even though a company can standardize on methodologies to use in its software development life cycles, the integration of third-party products sometimes requires the incorporation of that product's particular implementation procedures.

The following sections describe various approaches to managing software development projects. Each of the methodologies takes a different approach to managing risk, tracking progress, and delivering for success, but they are all similar in that they look for to define the rules for successful software delivery.

eXtreme Programming

Myles Standish, in his tour around Canaxia's various software development groups, finds a small team of developers utilizing eXtreme Programming (XP) practices for their project delivery (Beck 2000). The group is extremely successful at rolling out small software releases quickly and on time, but friction has been identified with this development group working with other organizations in the enterprise, such as the data warehouse group and the data center facilities. Some business customers that have familiarity with agile software development principles appreciate accelerated delivery and increased customer focus. The customers that are not familiar struggle with agile approaches since they are used to highly process oriented approaches. Another key factor is that the development team has an extensive inventory of automated test scripts already defined for ongoing maintenance and enhancement of the system. eXtreme Programming has worked well for this group, but the key for Myles is to understand how this group and its methodology can be better integrated into his plans for the enterprise architecture.

eXtreme Programming has recently become one of the most attractive approaches to software development projects for developers. In its purest form, eXtreme Programming is based upon one simple tenet: "Find the essential elements of creating good software, do them all the time, and discard everything else." During their work at Chrysler Corporation in 1996, Kent Beck and Ward Cunningham developed a lightweight approach to the controlled delivery of software products. Their inspiration for the new software methodology was to develop a practice that took all the "good activities" associated with software development and to apply them all in an extreme manner. For example, designing as a project activity is good, so make sure your developers are designing all the time. Testing the project is good, so make sure the system is constantly being tested. Since coding is good for the project, make sure to code all the time. On the other hand, heavy documentation and designing for scenarios that do not exist does not contribute to the ultimate software product, so minimize or remove these activities from the project.

A lightweight approach was needed to develop a flexible framework to handle project risks associated with dynamically changing requirements and managing unsettled project expectations. Many times, the business—or customers, as they are referred to in XP—do not have a firm idea of the solution they are looking to create through a software solution. Without a clear understanding of all the requirements, the development team has virtually no chance of designing and constructing a successful software product. It became obvious that a flexible and adaptive methodology was necessary to handle ongoing changes in requirements without causing huge deviations in project delivery. XP defines a series of processes and practices to improve software delivery by four basic principles:

- *Feedback*: First, incorporate constant feedback in requirements and design while still managing the scope, schedule, and cost of a project's delivery.

- *Communication*: Second, facilitate communication throughout the team through quick and effective team meetings, abbreviated requirements-gathering processes, and constant peer feedback during development.

- *Simplicity*: Third, promote simplicity in the design of a system, thereby enabling a developer to effectively evaluate the design immediately upon the delivery of new or changing requirements.

- *Courage*: Fourth, all the members of an effective XP development team must have courage in their requirements, design, code, and testing procedures. It is only through courage and confidence in these areas that the team is able to quickly and effectively respond to deviations during the development cycle.

Three major roles are identified in this lightweight methodology. They are as follows:

- *Customers*: Customers are identified individuals who have an intimate understanding of the business for which the application is being developed. They are responsible for authoring the initial "user stories" or requirements specifications for the project. They are available constantly throughout the delivery of the project and continue to contribute during the project's delivery in feedback sessions.

Figure 5–1

Iterative XP process.

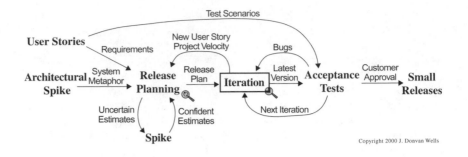

Copyright 2000 J. Donvan Wells

- *Developers*: The developer is really the central player in an XP project. They are all responsible for the design, coding, testing, and integration of the software product.
- *Coaches/Managers*: Coaches are the project leads who are responsible for coordinating the development activities and for ensuring that the practices of XP are followed throughout the team.

Figure 5–1 provides a detailed perspective on the structure of the iterative XP process.

The four main practices of XP require extreme attention in the delivery cycle. Each of the practices has a series of processes and procedures identified for the development of a project. The four main practices are the following:

- *Continuous Planning*: The planning phase for this project is synonymous with the concept and specification phase described in the SDLC process, but the approach defined in XP defines that this practice is constantly revisited.
- *Continuous Design*: Directly following any planning activity, the technology team responds with quick design sessions that are organized quickly both at the team level and at the developer level.
- *Continuous Coding*: Coding is conducted by pairs of developers who work together to satisfy the user stories defined in the planning practice of XP's methodology.
- *Continuous Testing*: The developers work immediately to develop automated test scripts to create a context through which new code is to be developed.

Continuous Planning

The crux of the planning activities for an XP development project is based around the user stories, which are descriptions of smaller parts of a project's delivery. User stories are usually identified as encompassing about 1 to 3 weeks of development activity. If a user story describes more than this amount of work, the story should be broken into multiple stories. If the stories identified are representative of less than this amount of work, they should be combined with other smaller stories. The user story is solely written by the customer and is generally about three to five sentences captured on an index card or a single-page document. User stories are found more often than not as handwritten notes describing particular behaviors of a system.

The stories themselves are used for three major purposes. First, they are descriptive of the portion of the product they are meant to describe. The level of detail in these user stories is recommended to be complete enough to create dependable estimates of the implementation time. Further details the developer may require will be reviewed between the developer and the authoring customer during the actual implementation. The second purpose for the user stories is to use them for user acceptance criteria. During the testing practices of XP, automated acceptance tests must be created to verify that the code satisfies the goals of the original user story. The third purpose of the user stories is for use during release planning. XP promotes smaller and more frequent releases of an application. Generally about twenty to thirty user stories are grouped together to describe particular releases for an application. For applications with more than this many defined stories, multiple releases are scheduled for the project.

As a metric for determining the timeframe for a release, XP defines a project's velocity. The velocity of a project is simply defined as the number of user stories completed during a release schedule. If, historically, a release of about twenty-five stories takes the development team about 6 weeks to react; this metric of twenty-five stories per 6 weeks can be used to plan the schedule for future releases.

Another major tenet of XP is that the developers of a team are to be moved around. As the project progresses, domains of expertise will evolve. A major risk that projects fall into is to continue assigning the same developers to the same areas of code development. This is because the developers who are familiar with particular areas of code will implement changes and enhancements to that area more quickly. The risk is that the team begins to develop pockets of knowledge that narrow the perspective of developers. It is important that the team members move around to different areas of the project's implementation to promote cross-training and reduce the risk of creating unintentional bottlenecks in the development cycle.

Continuous Design

eXtreme Programming champions the idea that a simple design is more flexible and faster to implement than a complex design. The technology team in an XP project takes the user stories and attempts to create the simplest design of technology to satisfy the stated requirements. The key factor is that these designs be defined to be adaptive and not predictive. Predictive designs try to incorporate anticipated changes in requirements and functionality. XP dictates that the developers must focus on designing for the requirements defined in the user story. The developers must have the confidence that as new requirements are defined, they can adapt their design or redevelop a new simple design to satisfy any future requirements.

During the design phase, the technology team will adapt a system metaphor in describing the components and behavior of a system. The system metaphor is the context and convention for naming classes and methods consistently. For example, a strong system metaphor for Canaxia could be to use terminology associated with the fabrication process for a car. For data access, the components can be defined in context to procuring raw materials. For object instantiation, the processes and classes can be context for an assembly line and workstations.

One of the key products of the design phase for an XP project is the Class, Responsibility and Collaboration (CRC) Card. Each CRC Card is usually a simple index card that defines an object or behavior in a system. These cards are used during team design sessions to describe message flow among CRC cards. The team members can then provide feedback during a design session based on the layout of the cards.

The next major portion of the designing during an XP project is to execute on spike solutions. At times, it is obvious that portions of the project are vastly more complex than other portions of the system. Rather than spending time in meetings or design sessions, the team will identify an area that requires a spike solution, where a pair of developers is assigned to quickly implement (keeping the scope to within a week or two) a plausible solution to the problem. The spike solution is geared toward gathering as much information as possible about a particular technology risk and is often simply thrown away once the information from the exercise has been synthesized into the team.

Refactoring is also an essential step in all design activities. Refactoring is the process of reevaluating and recoding portions of an application to simplify the design of the code. Developers and their managers must be trained to readily revisit and recode portions of an application as soon as the simplicity and the maintenance of that code are in jeopardy.

Continuous Coding

One of the central but most difficult practices to adopt in eXtreme Programming is pair programming. Pair programming dictates that all code that is to be incorporated into a release must be developed by two developers working together at a single computer. The premise is that two developers at a single computer are cable of generating as much functionality as two developers at separate computers; the difference being that the code created under paired development will be of higher quality because every line has been scrutinized from two perspectives. As one developer drives or keys in the lines of code, the other developer is able to retain a strategic perspective on how the methods fit into a class. The second developer can also provide feedback into how to keep the code as simple as possible and to make sure all the coding standards are continually satisfied. The paired developers are expected to switch off with the keyboard, each taking turns at driving versus strategizing the development.

Along with paired programming, another shift in the preconceptions of development in an XP project is coding the unit—an automated script that the developer can run to empirically observe whether a new piece of code satisfies the requirements for that component—first. Essentially, if done correctly, the combined time to create a unit test and then to create the code to satisfy that test is equivalent to the time required to simply create the code from scratch. This premise is based upon the fact that unit tests help the developer keep focused on creating only the essential functionality. The obvious benefit is that all the code in the system is created from the context of measurable test scripts that can be used to accurately describe the progress of development.

Along with generating unit test code for all new development, the developers must be integrating frequently. All code should be written and integrated on a daily basis, and even more frequently if it is possible. Constant integration provides the developers with immediate feedback about problems between the code components they are building. The difficulties of integrating code so frequently are reduced with the creation of the unit test scripts that must be satisfied before integration is allowed. What this constant integration and automated unit tests also allow is that developers are empowered to modify any code throughout the system. Too often, developers must rely on one another to make sure their piece of the development is working as expected. Using these practices enables developers to simply visit any pieces of code and make whatever changes they need for integration, and then, as long as the unit tests continue to be satisfied, developers can be confident that the systems will integrate properly. This also creates a culture of collective ownership of the code base. This collective ownership empowers all the developers to enhance, fix, and maintain any piece of code in the entire project.

The next major requirement during the coding practice is that the customer must always be available during the delivery cycle of a project. The customer or the author of the user stories has provided enough details for the development team to estimate and begin the coding activities, but, since the user stories are not meant to capture every detail of an implementation, the developers must have constant access to the user to hash through details of the implementation.

Continuous Testing

As stated, testing becomes an integral component of the coding cycle for an XP project. The unit tests instill a structure to the development activities to make sure that all the functionality is empirically tracked during development. These tests enable the developer to confidently enhance, refactor, or fix any area of code in an XP project. If a developer does integrate an area of code that causes a bug, the developer has an opportunity to enhance the unit tests and make the framework of tests even more comprehensive for future enhancements to the code base. The unit tests are also a great way for the manager of a project to track to the delivery of the project. Since the unit tests are to be automated, they can simply execute the battery of unit tests at any time and track the number of passed versus failed unit tests, thereby having an empirical view of what areas of functionality are complete versus incomplete.

Another activity during testing is the creation and execution of the acceptance tests. The acceptance tests are created from the context of the user stories. It is also good practice to automate these tests. The goal of each of these tests is to identify whether the requirements of the entire user story are satisfied by the implementation.

The Benefits and Shortcomings of XP

eXtreme Programming offers a variety of benefits to a company's enterprise software development capabilities. It is a methodology that empowers developers to interact intimately with business users, thereby increasing communication and effective feedback across the development teams and the business units. The methodology takes an aggressive stance in managing risk and creating a team of stakeholders for the successful delivery of a project. Developers tend to enjoy working in the context of the documentation light methodology of XP. They are empowered to make technical decisions at every level of an application delivery project. Many times other methodologies dictate that a project architect owns the overall architecture and design of the project. XP clashes with that premise by stating that every developer is an architect, developer, and quality assurance analyst.

Also from the company's perspective, XP projects are generally easier to maintain. The knowledge capital invested in any individual developer is distributed across a team and reduces the risk of losing a critical person with unique system knowledge. The business users—the customers—see releases of their new systems more quickly and more frequently, and they are encouraged to participate as team members for project delivery, which in turn means educating the customer better in the practice of software development.

On the other hand, XP as a methodology is difficult to integrate into the culture of many large corporations. Paired programming is a difficult concept to receive buy in from both existing development teams and corporate management. Development has historically been a single-person activity, and development professionals tend to have a hard time switching to a two-person-to-one-computer paradigm. Also, in budgeting and structuring a project in a corporation, a development staff must be available with the business to estimate the cost and schedule for new project developments. Because XP is defined to only provide estimates through feedback from a development team, it is more costly to the company to evaluate the initial cost and size of a project with this methodology. Finally, eXtreme Programming requires that a dedicated customer representative be on the team. This is inherently difficult because users with the proper business perspective for participating as a customer must be taken from their day-to-day responsibilities to support the development team.

SEI/CMM

The Capability Maturity Model (CMM) is a model for evaluating the maturity of a process within an organization. Originally conceived in 1987 through the inspiration of Watts Humphrey from IBM, CMM has evolved through the Software Engineering Institute (SEI) at Carnegie Mellon University. This model for evaluating the maturity of processes in organizations was a response to the dramatic percentage of software development projects that spiral beyond control-of-quality assurance, initial budgets, and schedules. The capability of a model defines the domain of possible results that are possible given a specified set of processes. The maturity of a process is described as the extent to which a specific process is defined, managed, measured, controlled, and made effective. In a defined mature and capable model, the processes therein are well understood throughout the organization and are reflective of richness and consistency. CMM does not directly compare to the other methodologies in this chapter. It is rather the definition of a framework for any repeatable, measurable, and consistent business process.

Over the years, CMM has evolved into a series of variations that deal with specific facets of evaluating the maturity of processes. The SEI at Carnegie Mellon has been coordinating the release and management of the following CMM variations.

- *Software Capability Maturity Model* (SW-CMM): The Capability Maturity Model for Software (CMM or SW-CMM) is a model for judging the maturity of the software processes of an organization and for identifying the key practices that are required to increase the maturity of these processes.

- *People Capability Maturity Model* (P-CMM): This is a framework that helps organizations successfully address critical people issues. Based on the best current practices in fields such as human resources, knowledge management, and organizational development, P-CMM provides the guidelines for organizations to improve their processes for managing and developing their workforces.

- *Software Acquisition Capability Maturity Model* (SA-CMM): This model is designed to benchmark and improve the software acquisition process for an organization.

- *Integrated Product Development Capability Maturity Model* (IPD-CMM): IPD is a systematic approach to product development that defines the necessary disciplines throughout the product life cycle to better satisfy customer needs.

- *Systems Engineering Capability Maturity Model* (SE-CMM): This model describes the essential elements of an organization's systems engineering process. Systems engineering is an interdisciplinary approach to managing the processes that involve people, technology, costing, and scheduling.

A recent development by the SEI is an attempt to create an Integrated Capability Maturity Model (CMMi) that encompasses software engineering (SW-CMM), systems engineering (SE-CMM), and integrated product and process development (IPD-CMM). The purpose of this integrated model is to create a consolidated process improvement framework suitable for software intensive systems. CMMi replaced SW-CMM in December 2003.

Because of the breadth and depth of the varieties of CMM framework definitions, this methodology overview will focus on the process definition improvements as described in SW-CMM. A CMM-certified organization benefits through improved understanding of the processes associated with software development, standardized and documented procedures, and defined metrics for measuring the performance of a process execution. CMM-SW provides direct impact to the performance of certified processes, thus reducing the delivery cycle of projects and reducing ongoing maintenance costs because of more effective quality-assurance measures.

Table 5–1 lists the five levels defined by the SW-CMM framework. Each level describes the next progressive step in a software development process's maturity.

Table 5–1

SW-CMM framework.

CMM Level	Name	Description
1	Initial	The software process is characterized as ad hoc and, occasionally, chaotic. Few processes are defined, and success depends on individual effort.
2	Repeatable	Basic project management processes are established to track cost, schedule, and functionality. The necessary process discipline is in place to repeat earlier successes on projects with similar applications.
3	Defined	The software process for both management and engineering activities is documented, standardized, and integrated into a standard software process for the organization. All projects use an approved, tailored version of the organization's standard software process for developing and maintaining software.
4	Managed	Detailed measures of the software process and product quality are collected. Both the software process and products are quantitatively understood and controlled.
5	Optimizing	Continuous process improvement is enabled by quantitative feedback from the process and from piloting innovative ideas and technologies.

At each level of maturity in CMM, a progression of processes must be defined. Past the first level of CMM, the processes characteristic for each level is described as a Key Process Area (KPA). A KPA describes the key processes that must exist in order for an organization to be promoted to the next level of CMM maturity. The following sections describe the criteria for each level of CMM.

Initial

Organizations identified at the initial level generally do not provide a stable environment for defining, developing, and deploying software. The nature of these types of organizations is very reactive to the conditions of a project delivery. The success of a project is usually dependent on an exceptional manager or a seasoned and effective software development team. Schedules, budgets, functionality, and product quality are unpredictable at this level of maturity, and performance depends on the capabilities of individuals and varies with their innate skills and knowledge.

This level of maturity is common among organizations that have no predefined processes for handling the various phases of a software development life cycle.

Repeatable

An organization described at the repeatable level will have policies for managing a software project and documented precedence that can be leveraged for future software development projects. At this level, organizations will have basic software management controls installed. This includes defined procedures for software development activities, such as project estimation, project tracking, change management, quality assurance, and so on. The definition of the procedures is the result of previous successful projects, and the information available is complete enough to facilitate repeatable results in these process areas. Also, at this level of maturity, the organization has defined standards for coding practices, architecture considerations, and specifications information. The organization must also have the process mechanisms to enforce the defined standards and procedures. Finally, for a level-2 CMM certification, an organization must have a process for establishing strong customer–supplier relationships with all its vendors.

In general, a level-2 repeatable-level organization for software development will have the following characteristics. There is a centrally available repository for process definitions and project documentation that is leverageable for new and ongoing software development projects. Next, some type of standards-enforcing group must be identified that has exposure to all projects. This group (usually referred to as a *program office*) is responsible for tracking the delivery of a project and verifying the compliance of projects to the existing standards. In addition, usually a vendor management group is created in the organization to centrally establish and manage customer–supplier relationships with vendors, subcontractors, and service providers.

Defined

At the defined level, an organization has thoroughly documented the standard processes for developing and maintaining software. These documented processes contain information regarding software development and project management practices, and they are readily integrated across the organization. The procedures for software development are permeated throughout the group and are ubiquitously understood as the *standard process* for software development. Next, a Software Engineering Process Group (SEPG) is identified in the organization and is responsible for maintaining the standards and documentation material for the software development process. This group is also responsible for keeping abreast of industry standards and incorporating recent developments effectively in the organization's processes. Finally, an organization-wide training program must be instated to ensure that both staff and managers have the skills and knowledge to participate effectively in the defined software project processes. Overall, the level-3 organization owns stable and repeatable standards and procedures for both software engineering and project management. Within these standards and procedures, project cost, schedule, functionality, and software quality are controllable. The capability of the organization is consistent across all members and roles in the organization.

The key differentiating factor for the level-3 CMM organization is that the SDLC is defined in detail for the full life cycle of a project delivery. Whereas in level 2, the processes for successful projects were documented, in level-3 organizations all processes must be well defined. Well-defined processes include all the following information:

- *Defined Readiness Criteria*: The process requires these conditions to be met before a process can begin.
- *Defined Inputs*: These are the inputs required for a process to start. For example, the process of designing a software solution requires that the requirements document be used as a primary input for this phase.
- *Standards and Procedures for Executing the Process*: This is the actual definition of the actual work that must be completed to satisfy the process. Design process procedures can include the creation of design documentation and a formal architecture review.
- *Verification Mechanism*: The verification mechanism is a means to verify that the work accomplished for the process is complete. This can be in the form of a review by the program office or some type of peer review.
- *Defined Outputs*: Outputs are deliverables that are defined by the process.
- *Defined Completion Criteria*: These final completion criteria are the conditions to verify that all the specifications of a process have been satisfied.

Managed

Organizations that have reached the managed level of process maturity set quantitative quality goals for software development applications and processes. The quality and productivity of the defined processes are measurable across all the software efforts in the organization. Finally, an organization-wide database is available to collect and analyze the metrics defined for software development projects.

The software processes in a level-4 managed organization are predictable and measurable. Also, these measured processes are used to establish a foundation for quantitatively evaluating a project's delivery performance. Projects with measured performance beyond the expected boundaries are reevaluated to understand the conditions of the metric deviations.

Optimizing

At the optimizing level of maturity, the entire organization is focused on continuous process improvement. The organization has identified groups that continually identify weaknesses, and they strengthen the processes proactively with the goal of preventing defects. Measurement captured to capture the performance of processes are used to create cost-benefit analyses of new technologies and proposed changes to the existing processes.

Level-5 organizations are capable of focusing on constant process improvement because the maturity of the established processes is already dependable, repeatable, and measurable. The risks of delivering software products are reduced dramatically by this point and the organization can continue to focus on optimizing existing processes.

The Benefits and Shortcomings of CMM

CMM-certified organizations are benefited in a variety of ways as they mature to a deeper level of process maturity. First, CMM is fully comprehensive for an organization's full software development life cycle definition. It describes all the process areas that are required to successfully budget, define, design, construct, and deploy software products. Where other software methodologies focus on the definition, construction, and deployment of software, CMM incorporates the procedures necessary to build organization-wide exposure to project estimation, project tracking, and standards compliance. The CMM framework is also generally compliant with any corporate procedures for project delivery. As a framework, it is up to the organization to fill in the detailed processes. For organizations that require proprietary steps in project sign-off and quality assurance, the CMM framework only identifies key areas that must be satisfied. This framework-based approach to process definition enables this methodology to be used in conjunction with other development methodologies as long as the key process areas are satisfied in the delivery. Next, CMM is developed in perspective to manage multiple projects across an organization. Where other methodologies generally focus on the delivery of the specified project, CMM defines the organizational and procedural requirements for managing multiple simultaneous projects. Finally, with the pervading practice of utilizing offshore-development vendors, organizations can utilize this standard framework to manage processes across disparate development teams while still being able to manage and evaluate project performance at a strategic level.

Implementing a CMM framework into an organization has a number of shortfalls as well. Because of the depth and breadth of the CMM framework, it is generally expensive to implement and maintain the levels of process maturity in an organization. To satisfy all the process areas, new groups must be identified to support the definition, evaluation, and tracking required of mature capability models in an organization. Also, CMM organizations tend to be documentation intensive and bureaucratically complex as projects navigate through the various procedures that must be followed for a software delivery. All the process definition required for CMM mature organizations adds overhead to projects. Until an organization reaches level 5—optimizing—many process procedures may not be applicable to a project's delivery but must be followed to adhere to the framework. This creates a scenario in which, regardless of a project's size, a sunk cost in the delivery of any project just complies with all the process requirements. For example, in a CMM level-3 organization, to develop even the simplest software project requires that every defined process and procedure be satisfied. Finally, a CMM mature organization does not necessarily dictate successful software delivery. The framework is mainly focused on controlled and repeatable processes that are adhered to in a project.

The Zachman Framework

Myles Standish is introduced to an organization that has adopted the Zachman Framework (ZF) as an approach to structured technology development. This group is composed of mostly senior IT technologists and their adoption of the Zachman Framework has been successful in managing many enterprise-scale technology initiatives at Canaxia. The group has successfully applied many of the company's required processes for technology delivery and has also created a series of additional process definitions to satisfy all the dimensions of the ZF perspectives. Myles notices though that the culture of this group is centered around its framework and that, regardless of project size or intention, the entire framework is required to be applied, thus inducing an impressive initial overhead just to support the framework.

The Zachman Framework, originally authored by John Zachman in the 1980s at IBM, has since become widely adapted by IT organizations as a framework for identifying and disciplining the various perspectives involved in an enterprise architecture. In practice, the ZF summarizes a collection of perspectives based upon an architecture. Those perspectives are described in a two-dimensional matrix that has axes defined by type of stakeholders and aspects of the architecture. The rows in Table 5–2 represent the views of different types of stakeholders. The columns, respectively, represent different aspects or views of your architecture as shown in Table 5–3.

There are three important concepts to understand about the ZF:

- Within a column, the models are evolved/translated to reflect the views of the stakeholders for each row.
- The models within a single row should be consistent with one another, with the caveat that agile models are just barely good enough, so the models may not be perfectly consistent with an agile instantiation of the ZF.
- The ZF does not define a process for architecture. Rather, it defines the various perspectives that architecture should encompass. The ZF is a template that must be filled in by the processes specifically required by the organization. If the processes do not exist already, the ZF will help identify these gaps in the architecture.

Figure 5–2 is an example instance of the Zachman Framework. For each perspective defined by the two axes, a process is defined that is required for each perspective of the framework.

Tables 5–2 and 5–3 describe the details for each item in the two axes described in Figure 5–2.

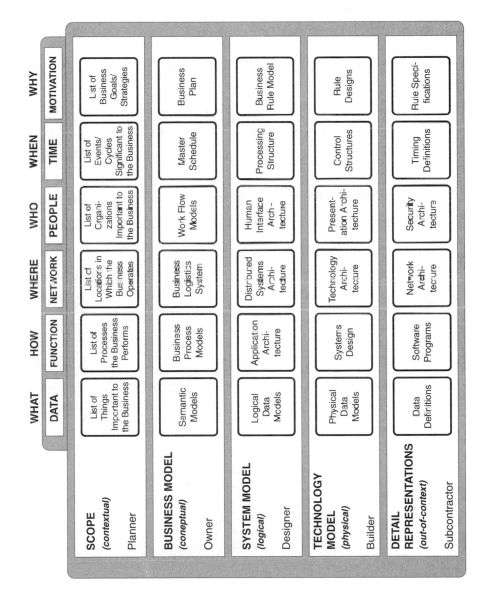

Figure 5–2
Zachman Framework.

Table 5–2

The rows of the Zachman Framework.

Row	Description
1. Scope (Planner's view)	Defines your organization's direction and purpose, defining the boundaries of your architecture efforts.
2. Enterprise Model (Business owner's view)	Defines in business terms the nature of your organization, including its structure, processes, and organization.
3. System Model (Architect's view)	Defines the enterprise in more rigorous terms than row 2, basically taking the model to a greater level of detail. In the original version of the ZF, this row was originally called *information system designer's view.*
4. Technology Model (Designer's view)	Defines how technology will be applied to address the needs defined by the previous rows.
5. Detailed Representation (Builder's view)	Defines the detailed design, taking implementation language, database storage, and middleware considerations into account.

Table 5–3

The columns of the Zachman Framework.

Column	Description
1. Structure (What)	Focus is on the entities/objects/components of significance, and the relationships among them, within your organization. This column was called *data* in the original version of the framework.
2. Activities (How)	Focus is on what your organization does to support itself and its customers. This column was called *function* in the original version of the framework.
3. Locations (Where)	Focus is on the geographical distribution of you're organization's activities. This column was called *network* in the original version of the framework.
4. People (Who)	Focus is on who is involved in the business of your organization.
5. Time (When)	Focus is on the effects that time, such as planning and events, has on an organization.
6. Motivation (Why)	Focus is on the translation of business goals, strategies, and constraints into specific implementations.

Benefits and Shortcomings of the Zachman Framework

The primary strength of the Zachman Framework is that it explicitly shows that many views need to be addressed by architecture. An immediate benefit of the views shown in Figure 5–2 is that they provide a reminder of the issues you need to consider in your architecture, whether or not you decide to adopt the ZF. Another implication is that one model does not fit all, as Agile Modeling (AM) multiple models principle implores. Furthermore, a single level of detail isn't sufficient either. Hay's data-driven approach in *Data Model Patterns*, requires several flavors of data model in the first column, whereas Moriarty's object-driven approach, in *Business Rules Forum* 2002 *Presentation on Model Driven Architecture*, requires several different flavors of class model. They do this because the audience for each row changes. A related strength is that the ZF explicitly communicates that architecture has several stakeholders in addition to the architects and developers. An implication is that you need to involve your stakeholders in the development of your architecture to ensure that it meets their needs, and ideally you want to follow the practice of active stakeholder participation. Unfortunately, ZF also has several potential problems:

- *The ZF can lead to a documentation-heavy approach.* There are thirty cells in Figure 5–2, each one of which needs to be supported by one or more artifacts. This is potentially a lot of documentation, so you have to really think about what information you actually need versus what information is nice to have; in other words, adopt AM's travel light principle. The value of creating and maintaining a document must be that it exceeds its cost.

- *The ZF can lead to a methodology-biased approach.* It is very easy to use the ZF to promote your preferred way of working, to use it to beat your methodological drum. That might work very well for you, but is it really the best option for your organization or your clients? It can be countereffective if you are not in a position to choose the right artifacts for your situation, artifacts that reflect your organizational culture, your business environment, your technical environment, and the skills of the people involved.

- *The ZF can lead to a process-heavy approach to development.* In Figure 5–2, you can see immediately the necessity of defining a collection of rigorous processes to support the ZF. To maintain traceability among the artifacts in those thirty cells, you need to develop and maintain a detailed traceability matrix or database of metadata. That sounds good in theory, but these activities quickly add overhead that grinds progress to a halt.

- *The ZF is not well accepted within the development community.* Although the ZF seems to be growing in popularity within the IT architecture community, it doesn't seem to have made it into the mainstream development culture.

- *The ZF promotes a top-down approach to development.* When people first read about the ZF, they tend to think that it implies a top-down approach in which you start with the models in row 1, work on row 2 models, and so on. This doesn't have to be the case. A top-down approach works in some situations, sometimes a bottom-up approach works, and other times a middle-out approach works. Start in whatever cell is most appropriate for your situation and iterate from there.

Model-Driven Architecture

A group in Canaxia is looking to adopt the model-driven architecture (MDA) for some new development efforts. The group is composed of some software architects and modelers who are excited about applying this implementation-independent approach to technology. Myles Standish talks with a few of the software modelers in this group and reviews their plans to bring this methodology into the enterprise. The modelers are fairly up to date with the semantics for MDA, but they have found many of the tools necessary to translate these models into their implementations to be either buggy or unavailable yet for specific platforms. Though it is an excellent academic approach to technology solutions, Myles is not convinced that this approach is ready for Canaxia.

A model-driven architecture defines an approach to modeling that separates the specification of system functionality from the specification of its implementation on a specific technology platform. In short, it defines guidelines for structuring specifications expressed as models. An MDA promotes an approach where the same model specifying system functionality can be realized on multiple platforms through auxiliary mapping standards or through point mappings to specific platforms. It also supports the concept of explicitly relating the models of different applications, enabling integration, interoperability, and supporting system evolution as platform technologies come and go.

The MDA is based on the idea that a system or component can be modeled via two categories of models: Platform Independent Models (PIMs) and Platform Specific Models (PSMs). PIMs are further divided into Computation Independent Business Models (CIBMs) and Platform Independent Component Models (PICMs). As the name implies, PIMs do not take technology-specific considerations into account, a concept that is equivalent to logical models in the structured methodologies and to essential models within usage-centered techniques. The CIBMs represent the business requirements and processes that the system or component supports, and the PICMs are used to model the logical business components, also called *domain components*. PSMs bring technology issues into account and are, effectively, transformations of PIMs to reflect platform-specific considerations, see Figure 5–3.

The MDA is part of a collection of modeling-oriented standards from the Object Management Group (OMG). These standards include the following:

- XML *Metadata Interchange* (XMI). XMI is a standard interchange mechanism used among various tools, repositories, and middleware. XMI also can be used to automatically produce XML (DTDs) and XML schemas from UML and MOF models, providing an XML serialization mechanism for these artifacts.

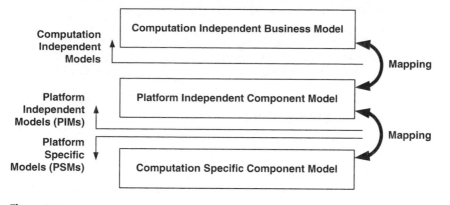

Figure 5-3

MDA overview.

- *Unified Modeling Language* (UML). UML defines the industry-standard notation and semantics for object-oriented and component-based systems.

- *Common Warehouse Metamodel* (CWM). CWM is the OMG data warehouse standard and is a good example of applying the MDA paradigm to an application area.

- *Meta Object Facility* (MOF). The MOF provides the standard modeling and interchange constructs that are used in the MDA. The common foundation of the MOF—the UML and CWM—are both MOF-based, enabling the potential model/metadata interchange and interoperability among tools. The MOF is the mechanism through which models are analyzed in XMI.

Other mappings among the various types of models describe a system/component: mappings that represent transformations. For example, there is a mapping between the CIBM and the PICM for a given system, and from the PICM to the PSM for a system. It is these mappings that provide the glue among the various representations of a system/component, mappings that a sophisticated development tool perhaps would be able to use to generate system code.

The relationships among models in different systems/components are also a critical aspect of the MDA. For example, there are relationships among the CIBMs of each system, their PICMs, and their PSMs. These relationships support integration among the systems, and thus promote large-scale reuse within an organization.

It's important to recognize that a CIBM, PICM, or PSM may be comprised of several artifacts. For example, a CIBM could include a collection of business rule definitions and a UML activity diagram used to describe the overall business process supported by the system/component. A PICM could be described via a UML component model and a collection of interface definitions. A PSM could be comprised of a UML class diagram, several UML sequence diagrams, several UML state chart diagrams, and a physical data model. Furthermore, you may decide to have several PSMs for any given system/component, one for each platform on which you intend to deploy it.

Benefits and Shortcomings of the MDA

The MDA has the following primary strengths:

- *The* MDA *defines a coarse separation of views.* When you are modeling, it is important to consider issues such as what the system should do and what processes the system should support, without having to worry about how it will support them because it enables you to consider a wide range of options. It can also be beneficial to consider the logical domain architecture separately from the physical implementation architecture because the logical architecture will change much more slowly than the underlying technologies, allowing you to reuse your logical model as the system evolves over time.
- *The* MDA *defines a viable strategy for system integration.* The MDA's explicit support for modeling relationships among systems and components can help to ease system integration, and hence can promote greater levels of reuse, within your organization. Legacy integration is a significant issue for most software development efforts.
- *The* MDA *may motivate a new breed of modeling tools.* The separation of views offers the potential for tools that automatically generate the next model down, in particular PSMs from PIMs, based on automated mappings.
- *The* MDA *may support tool integration.* Part of the overall vision of the OMG is to provide a set of standards for tool vendors to follow, and thereby to support integration of those tools.

Although the MDA is interesting, and in the near term will probably gain significant support from the OMG and its supporters, you should be aware of several potential challenges:

- *There are other competing, and arguably better, strategies for system integration.* The OMG isn't the only organization working on the issue of system integration. For example, there is the entire Web services strategy supported by technologies such as .Net and Sun ONE and various Internet standards bodies. Web services are something that developers understand and are eager to work with it, unlike the MDA. Common Object Request Broker Architecture (CORBA), another standard developed by the OMG, is also a viable option. Luckily for the MDA, developers will need tools and techniques to understand the interfaces to Web services and CORBA objects, something that the MDA may be well suited for.
- *The* wonder tools *will prove elusive.* The idea that you can (mostly) automate the creation of platform-specific models from your platform-independent models is theoretically sound. However, this will

probably only occur within niche technical environments. The underlying technology changes too quickly and by the time the automated mappings are in place for a given platform, it will have changed or will no longer be in demand. Furthermore, there is a plethora of platforms. Both of these factors will force tool vendors to choose a subset of platforms to support.

- *Tool integration will also prove elusive.* Each tool vendor is compelled to support the MDA in their own way, if they support it at all. This can be attributed to the fact that vendors will not be interested in opening up their technologies to potential competitors . . .

- *The* MDA *is complicated.* The underlying premise of the MDA is that developers will have significant modeling skills. Although this is an ideal vision, it isn't realistic. Most developers struggle to create UML State Charts or use case models, if they even know what these models are.

- *The* MDA *doesn't appeal to developers.* When was the last time you heard a programmer say "I'd really like to work on an MDA project"? When was the last time you bumped into a programmer who even knew what the MDA was? The MDA might appeal to academics and professional modelers who haven't written a line of code in years, but that's about it.

- *There is a bias toward object-and component-based technologies.* Because the MDA is based on the UML, and the UML is used to model object- and component-based systems, there is an underlying assumption that components will be your underlying building blocks.

In Canaxia there are organizations in the company that are utilizing Rational Unified Process (RUP) for software development projects with varying degrees of success. Myles Standish sees that because of the steep learning curve required to understand the UML syntax, some of the groups are struggling with creating consistent artifacts at each stage of a project's development. What Myles finds is that the groups that are more mature in the use of RUP are effectively creating reusable components and have solid specifications and documentation to support those components. The RUP-oriented development teams are directed more toward software framework than the other organizations and have defined components that can be used easily for new project developments. The business groups that work with these RUP-oriented development teams are having a hard time picking up all the syntaxes required to create the deliverables associated with this process. It seems that though the quality of the documentation associated with the design and implementation of the projects is exceptionally high, the quality of the requirements specification artifacts are inconsistent.

RUP is an evolution of the practices and process definitions created by Rational Software over the past 15 years. Identified as the Unified Process back in 1998, this process definition was the next generation of Rational's Objectory Process, which encompassed software development for object-oriented and component-based systems. Despite the changing of names, RUP continues to be a software engineering process framework for defining,

Rational Unified Process

implementing, and deploying software applications. At its core, RUP utilizes the Unified Modeling Language (UML) to clearly communicate requirements, architectures, and designs. The great benefit of basing the process framework around UML is that it is an industry-accepted language for modeling software systems. Though UML has a focus in describing object-oriented systems, the modeling syntax is a well defined and ubiquitously accepted standard across today's technology industry.

One of the characteristics of RUP is the well-defined grammar and terminology used throughout the process definition. At the highest level, RUP defines the following phases of a software project's delivery:

- *Inception*: The Inception phase is synonymous with the concept and specification phases described in the SDLC. This phase of a project is used to define the business case for any new software-development endeavor. It is also used to start describing the scope of a project's delivery, the primary actors that will interact with the software, and the criteria for evaluating the success of a project delivery.

- *Elaboration*: The elaboration phase is generally synonymous with the design phase described in the SDLC. Its purpose is to analyze the domain of the application design and establish a sound architectural foundation. The elaboration phase is many times the most important phase of a project's delivery, as many of the high-risk areas are dealt with during this phase and an overall "mile-high, inch-deep" description of the system is created during this phase.

- *Construction*: The construction phase of a RUP project encompasses the development and integration of each of the application components. The management mind-set undergoes a transition from the development of intellectual property during inception and elaboration to the development of deployable products during this phase of a project.

- *Transition*: The transition phase focuses on the activities required to place the software into the hands of the end-users. Typically, this phase includes several iterations that include beta releases and general availability releases, as well as bug-fix and enhancement releases. A large amount of effort is dedicated in this phase to develop user-oriented documentation, train users, support users in their initial product use, and react to user feedback.

- *Evolution*: The evolution of a software project is the ongoing activities associated with managing and deploying new releases of a product. Each evolution cycle encompasses another entire series of phases that include inception, elaboration, construction, and transition.

The Unified Modeling Language (UML)

It is important to understand the role and history of UML in the RUP. UML is a software modeling language used to describe the structure and processes encompassed by software systems. UML is the product of an evolution of various second-generation, object-oriented methods that were developed during the 1990s. Starting with Rational Software Corporation and three of the most prominent methodologists in object-oriented information systems, Grady Booch, James Rumbaugh, and Ivar Jacobson combined their respective approaches into a unified syntax for modeling software systems. Over the years, UML has pervaded the industry and was adopted as a standard for software modeling by the software consortium, the Object Management Group (OMG), in 1997.

Core Process Disciplines

Along with the four RUP phases of a software development release, nine core process disciplines are associated with a project in a RUP software delivery process. The nine core process disciplines are as follow:

1. *Business modeling discipline*: One of the key problem areas defined in software development projects is that the business users and the technical teams do not communicate properly because of differences in perspectives, knowledge, and semantics. Business modeling defines a common syntax to document business processes that can be translated into business use cases. These use cases can be readily analyzed by both the development and the business members.

2. *Requirements discipline*: The requirements work flow is used to define what the system will do. This process usually entails hashing out all the use cases that will be required to describe the behavior of the entire system. The use cases are then used as a unifying thread throughout the system's development cycle to analyze, design, and ultimately test the developed application.

3. *Analysis and design discipline*: This work flow deals specifically with defining how the system will realize all the requirements defined by the use cases in the context of the technology that will be used. Activities in this work flow include creation of the component design models, the definition of all the architectural details, and the analysis of how the components will interact in a software system.

4. *Implementation discipline*: The implementation work flow encompasses all the activities associated with defining the organization of the code, the implementation of classes and object, unit testing, and integration of the code across the software team.

5. *Test discipline*: The test work flow is used to verify the quality and behavior of the new software system. This work flow includes verifying the proper integration of all the implemented components, verification that all the use cases have been satisfied, and identification of any defects found in the software that can be used to provide feedback to the development team.

6. *Deployment discipline*: The deployment work flow defines the activities required to successfully manage software product release and to deliver the software to the end-user. Activities in this work flow include packaging software, installation of software in the

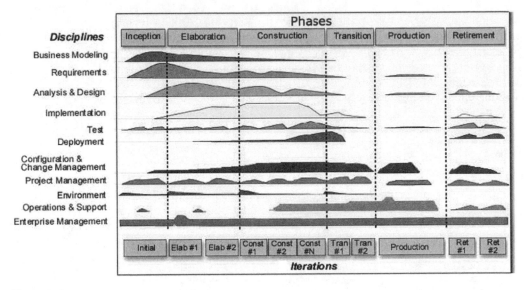

Figure 5–4
RUP life cycle by phase, task, and effort.

deployment environments, providing support to the end-users, and coordinating the formal acceptance of the new software system by the end-users.

7. *Project management discipline*: This work flow details the activities that are required to effectively balance competing objectives, project risks, project cost, and project schedule. This work flow identifies activities to manage the planning, staffing, budgeting, and tracking of a software development effort.

8. *Configuration and change management discipline*: All the deliverables associated with a RUP project are known as *project artifacts*. This work flow defines the activities associated with managing the versioning and update notification associated with developing and maintaining the software artifacts.

9. *Environment discipline*: The environment work flow is an ancillary set of activities that identify the processes and tools that are used to support the development team.

Figure 5–4 describes the relationship of the core process work flows in relation to where effort is applied during the various phases described by the RUP methodology.

The Rational Suite of Tools

Along with providing the thought leadership, process information, and training for deploying RUP in an organization, Rational also provides a suite of software tools designed to work effectively in facilitating a RUP process implementation. Rational Software, acquired by IBM in the spring of 2003, provides commercial tools to support the full development life cycle of software. The following list is a subset of tools that are recommended by Rational for the various parts of the core process work flows. These tools are not required to implement RUP in an organization, but they greatly facilitate the maintenance and adherence of RUP standards at all stages during a software delivery.

- *Rational Requisite® Pro.* This tool is used to capture and organize the requirements for a software project. This software is used to manage the activities associated with business modeling and requirements management.
- *Rational ClearQuest™.* This is a Web-based change-request management product that enables project teams to track and manage change activities that occur throughout the development life cycle.
- *Rational Rose®.* This tool is an industry-leading software product used to analyze and model software systems. The tool has all the UML concepts and syntaxes built in to facilitate the creation and maintenance of UML-based component and process designs.
- *Rational TeamTest.* This tool is used to create, maintain, and execute automated functional tests, allowing you to more manageably test code and determine that the software meets project requirements.
- *Rational ClearCase®.* This is a configuration management tool used for version control and tracking project progress.

The Benefits and Shortcomings of RUP

RUP is a software development process that has been developed and championed across the IT industry for almost a decade. The process definition is based upon a language (UML) that is in accord with industry standards and is widely accepted as the de facto modeling language for object-oriented and component-based systems. Throughout its evolution, RUP has matured into a variety of applications, and today one of the key characteristics that Rational is touting for this methodology is that the process can be tailored for the needs of an organization. Varieties of RUP have been defined that incorporate using RUP in a CMM organization or to attain CMM certification. Process-light versions of RUP have been developed to manage smaller, more agile projects. At the same time, this software development methodology is scalable to the full software delivery life cycle and includes details for managing software across organizations and the enterprise. Lastly, Rational provides the suites of tools, training, and process information that can be used to roll out RUP effectively across a company.

The first and most apparent shortcoming of RUP is, because it is based on UML, that it is biased to supporting OO and component-based software projects. For companies that support hybrid application environments where some systems may not fit directly into an object-oriented metaphor, UML is not as effective at incorporating these systems into its modeling language. The next shortcoming is that RUP can be very complex. The modeling syntax requires far more notation than what the average developer wants or needs.

Figure 5–5
The Enterprise-
Unified Process
diagram.

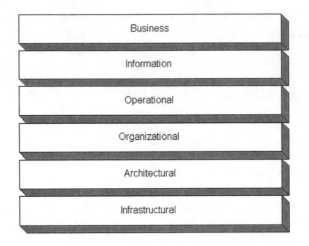

The third shortcoming is that purchasing the tools and training for RUP tends to be very expensive for an organization. Probably because RUP is proprietary to Rational and is its flagship product offering, implementing RUP in the enterprise can be costly in terms of software licensing and training support.

RUP is a software development methodology that has some limitations, specifically when dealing with the entire software life cycle. The Enterprise Unified Process (EUP), described in detail in Chapter 6, extends the RUP to make it a complete life cycle. As you can see in Figure 5–4, it adds two new phases, Production and Retirement, as well as two new disciplines, Enterprise Management and Operations & Support. Mid-to-large sized organizations find that they require these additions to have a life cycle that meets actual real-world needs, see Figure 5–5.

Using These Methodologies

After having toured all the development groups in Canaxia, Myles Standish has a sweeping perspective on the development capability of the entire enterprise. In his review of the groups, he has seen the strengths and weaknesses of the various groups and has been able to bring them into the context of the software development methodologies that are rolled out across the company. Myles knows that consistency in software development is a great benefit for improving the overall quality of development efforts. Project consistency enables easier tracking of projects by company management. It also allows for easier transition of development staff from organization to organization. At the same time, Myles has also seen that when software projects are inundated with software procedures, the processes actually hinder progress rather than facilitate it. Knowing the nature of all the different methodologies used throughout the enterprise, Myles put together a plan for managing software development at an enterprise scale.

The methodologies described in this chapter are not directly comparable. In fact, it is not uncommon to see RUP processes used in conjunction with a CMM framework, or RUP used in conjunction with an XP project, or Zachman's Framework used with CMM. The nature of these methodologies is to be as flexible as possible while still maintaining the integrity of the quality of a project's delivery. That said, each of the methodologies can be modified and combined with best practices from other methodologies to fulfill the needs of an organization or, as in Myles Standish's case, an entire corporation's enterprise. The first thing Myles needs is a consistent process framework for tracking the progress and risk of projects. He is not interested in, nor would he be capable of, keeping up with all the project initiatives at Canaxia. Yet Myles needs to be able to review project information and to identify and assist in software projects that may be experiencing risk.

Knowing that a number of organizations are already on track for CMM certification, Myles recommends that all software development efforts become compliant with the CMM initiative. Myles is not looking for all the development groups to standardize on all process definitions across all teams. This would be a nightmare to implement and enforce and would actually hinder development groups from delivering software solutions effectively to the user groups. Rather, each of the software development groups can continue using its existing software development processes but these processes must satisfy the process maturity requirements of the enterprise. Each of the methodologies described—RUP, XP, Zachman's Framework, and MDA—can be used in the context of a CMM-mature organization. Also, by complying with CMM's standards for process maturity, the entire enterprise can view project material from any type of project delivery and the structure of the information can be assumed consistent. CMM is the most recognized frameworks for capturing procedures related to evaluating process performance in an organization. CMM can adapt as the enterprise matures its capability to deliver software. With performance metrics available for describing the progress of the various software projects at Canaxia, Myles plans eventually to take a proactive role in identifying and assisting groups that are experiencing problems with software development. With CMM defined as an umbrella framework for software development projects, all the software development project teams can continue to deliver software solutions for their respective user groups as each deems most effective.

Myles Standish also created an enterprise services group that is responsible for evaluating, implementing, and maintaining reusable application components that can be shared throughout the enterprise. This application framework group uses both RUP and MDA as software methodology as the end-users for these developers are other development teams that can leverage existing components. Because RUP and MDA are based upon the widely accepted UML industry standard for software definition and design, it can be effectively used among development teams. Specifically, MDA approaches are designed to be implementation independent and, therefore, may be more appropriate for design-reusable software across the enterprise.

Leveraging CMM-mature processes across the enterprise, Myles Standish also knows that the company can benefit in the various development conditions. Offshore development has become a more popular and economical approach to software development, but inherent problems arise when developing this model. Because of disparate locations and time zones, it is difficult to maintain high levels of communication. Also, it is always a concern of companies to impose its own standards of quality and maintainability of software development done outsourced. In response to this, many outsourcing companies are committed to CMM process certification. For example, outsourcing companies at CMM level 3 have set procedures and process mechanisms to manage the consistency and quality of software projects. CMM-certified corporations that contract out development to other CMM-certified organizations will have the added benefit of sharing their documented procedures and consistent project artifacts.

Myles Standish knows that the practice of software development is continuing to mature, just as the processes at Canaxia will continue to develop. The methodologies he has put into place will provide for him exposure across all the development activities at Canaxia. With this exposure, Myles is confident that he can support areas where an enterprise architecture perspective can help with individual projects. Also with this exposure, Myles has the information available for him to steer the enterprise direction of software development at Canaxia.

Conclusion

This chapter is a tour of a variety of technology-delivery methodologies available across industries. To use them effectively, it is important to understand that project delivery requires a balance of flexibility and discipline. This balance is not a hard and fast rule either, but rather it is unique to the technology circumstance according to the business problems, the people, the organizations, the project type, and the technology used. No company exists whose enterprise can be managed by any one of the methodologies described. It is important for the enterprise architect to understand the scope and approach of each and to be able to utilize the strengths and identify the weaknesses in applying each to any delivery circumstance.

chapter 6

Enterprise Unified Process

The reasonable man adapts himself to the world; the unreasonable one persists in trying to adapt the world to himself. Therefore all progress depends on the unreasonable man.

George Bernard Shaw (1856–1950),
Man and Superman (1903)

The Rational Unified Process (Kruchten 2000) is swiftly becoming an industry standard for prescriptive software development. This makes sense, when you consider RUP's strengths:

- The RUP is based on sound software engineering principles, such as taking an iterative, requirements-driven, and architecture-based approach to development.

- The RUP provides opportunities for concrete management visibility. The most important opportunities include the creation of a working architectural prototype at the end of the elaboration phase, the creation of a working (partial) system at the end of each construction iteration, and the go/no-go decision point at the end of each phase.

- Rational Corporation (2003), now a division of IBM, has made, and continues to make, a significant investment in its RUP product, a collection of HTML pages and artifacts that your organization can tailor to meet its exact needs.

The Canaxia case study makes it very clear that the RUP unfortunately suffers from several weaknesses:

- The RUP is only a development process. Like most organizations, Canaxia is concerned not only with developing systems but also with operating and supporting them once in production. Furthermore, Canaxia has found that it eventually needs to retire systems as well. The RUP only includes phases for the development of systems, not the entire system life cycle.

141

- Multisystem development is missing. Canaxia is clearly interested in cross-system issues such as enterprise architecture, enterprise business modeling, and strategic reuse efforts, but the RUP does not explicitly include these activities.
- Multisystem management is missing. Canaxia has several IT projects underway at any given time and many more in the queue. Canaxia clearly needs to manage both its staff and its portfolio of projects, but once again the RUP doesn't include this.

Although the RUP may be adequate for the development of a single system, it is not adequate to meet the real-world needs of modern organizations. The RUP may become part of Canaxia's overall process solution, but it isn't the entire solution. Luckily you have a choice, the Enterprise Unified Process (EUP), which extends the RUP to address these critical issues.

The Enterprise Unified Process

So how do you enhance the RUP so that it meets the real-world needs of typical organizations? The place to start is to expand the scope of the RUP to include the entire software process, not just the development process. Your organization likely has several software projects that it's currently managing. You likely have some systems that you are currently operating and supporting in production. The actual focus of most organizations isn't on the development of a single project but on the development, operation, support, and maintenance of a collection of systems. This implies that processes for operations, support, and maintenance efforts need to be added to the RUP. Second, to be sufficient for today's organizations, the RUP also needs to add support for the management of a portfolio of projects, something other processes have called *program management*, *multi project management*, *infrastructure management*, or *enterprise management*. These first two steps result in an enhanced version of the RUP life cycle first described by Scott Ambler and Larry Constantine (2000a; 2000b; 2000c; 2002) and later evolved into what is depicted in Figure 6–1.

> To learn more about the Enterprise Unified Process (EUP) visit *www.enterpriseunifiedprocess.info*.

The EUP extends the RUP, as depicted in Figure 6–2. Each project team will follow a tailored version of the RUP called a *development case*, which is a deliverable that meets the unique needs of your environment discipline efforts. Alternatively, you could use another software development process in place of the RUP, such as eXtreme Programming (XP) (Beck 2000) or Feature-Driven Development (FDD) (Palmer and Felsing 2002). What is important is that the team has a software process to follow that reflects its situation. Figure 6–2 makes it clear that the EUP makes four major additions to the RUP life cycle:

- The production phase
- The retirement phase
- The operations and support discipline
- The enterprise management discipline

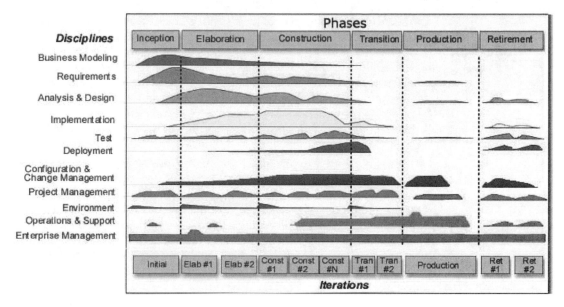

Figure 6–1
The life cycle of the Enterprise Unified Process (EUP).

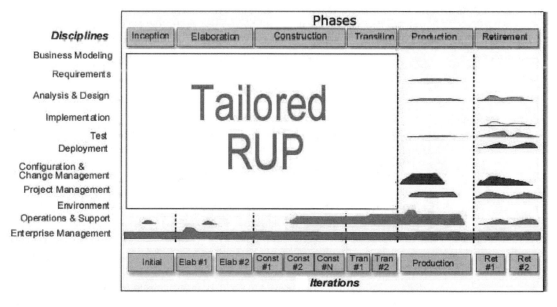

Figure 6–2
The EUP additions to the RUP life cycle.

The EUP's production phase represents the portion of the system life cycle in which the release of a system is in actual use. As the name implies, the goal of this phase is to keep your software in use until it is either replaced with a new version—from a minor release such as a bug fix to a major new release—or it is retired and removed from service. Note that there are no iterations during this phase, or there is one iteration, depending on how you look at it, because this phase applies to the lifetime of a single release of your system. To develop and deploy a new release of your software, you will need to run through the four development phases again, a concept depicted in Figure 6–3.

The EUP life cycle depicted in Figure 6–3 is interesting because it depicts critical concepts that aren't always clear to people new to the Unified Process. The large arrows across the top of the diagram show that once a system is released into production, you often continue working on a new release of it. Depending on your situation, work on the next release will begin either in the inception, elaboration, or construction phase. Along the bottom of the diagram, the phase milestones are indicated to make them more explicit (hence you are less likely to bow to pressure to move into the next phase even though you haven't achieved the appropriate milestone).

The focus of the retirement phase is the successful removal of a system from production. Systems are removed from production for two basic reasons:

1. *They are no longer needed.* An example of this is a system that was put into production to fulfill the legal requirements imposed by government legislation. Now that the legislation has been repealed, the system is no longer needed.

2. *The system is being replaced.* For example, it is common to see home-grown systems for human resource functions replaced by commercial off-the-shelf (COTS) systems.

Activities of the retirement phase include the following:

1. A comprehensive analysis of the existing system to identify its coupling to other systems.

2. A redesign and rework of other existing systems so that they no longer rely on the system being retired. These efforts will typically be treated as projects in their own right.

3. Transformation of existing legacy data, perhaps via database refactoring (Ambler 2003b), because they will no longer be required or manipulated by the system being retired.

4. Archival of data previously maintained by the system that is no longer needed by other systems.

5. Configuration management of the removed software so that it may be reinstalled if required at some point in the future (this is easier said than done).

6. System integration testing of the remaining systems to ensure that they have not been broken via the retirement of the system in question.

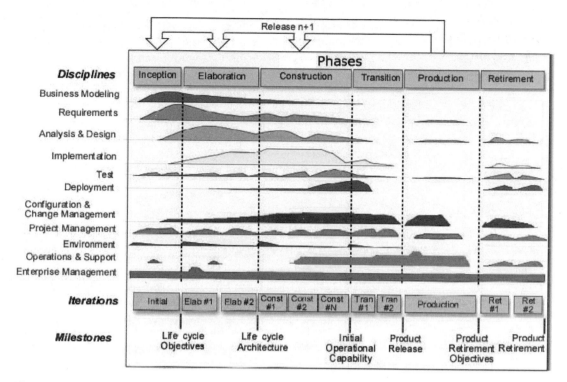

Figure 6-3
The augmented view of the EUP life cycle.

The retirement, or sunsetting, of a system is often a difficult task that should not be underestimated.

The goal of the operations and support discipline is exactly as the name implies, to operate and support your software. Operations and support can be very complex endeavors, that need processes defined for them. During the construction phase, and perhaps as early as the elaboration phase, you will need to develop operations and support plans, documents, and training manuals (some of this effort is currently included in the RUP's implementation discipline). During the transition phase, you will continue to develop these artifacts, reworking them based on the results of testing, and you will train your operations and support staff to effectively work with your software. During the production phase, your operations staff will keep your software running, performing necessary backups and batch jobs as needed, and your support staff will work with your user community in working with your software. This will also occur during the retirement phase as you turn down the legacy system.

The Operations and Support Discipline

Enterprise Unified Process

The enterprise management discipline focuses on the activities required to develop, evolve, and support your organization's cross-system artifacts, such as your organization-wide models, software processes, standards, guidelines, and reusable artifacts. Table 6–1 summarizes the major activities of the enterprise management discipline. As you can see, it is this discipline that effectively brings enterprise architecture into the unified process.

The activities of this discipline occur throughout the system life cycle. These efforts are often supported by enterprise groups. For example, in Chapter 7 you will learn that it is possible to define an agile enterprise architecture team that owns the enterprise architecture and works with project

Table 6–1
The major activities of enterprise management.

Activity	Description
Program/Portfolio Management	The identification, prioritization, initiation, and oversight of the system projects within your enterprise. This includes systems that are in development, as well as those in production or in the process of being retired.
Enterprise Modeling	The modeling of the business processes and high-level requirements of your organization.
Enterprise Architecture	The identification, modeling, and support for common, enterprisewide architectures within your organization.
Enterprise Asset Management	The management of the hardware and software assets of your organization. This extends configuration management efforts to the level of the enterprise, not just a single project.
People Management	Traditional human resource (HR) issues such as hiring, firing, promotions, transfers, and career management. Also includes training and education efforts outside the scope of a single project.
Strategic Reuse Management	The identification, development, harvesting, and support of reusable assets within your organization.
Standards and Guidelines Management and Support	The development and support of standards and guidelines, such as coding standards or logical data definitions, within your organization.
Software Process Management	The evolution and support of your organization's software processes and/or best practices.

teams to take advantage of it. Similarly, it is possible to take similar approaches with your enterprise modeling, strategic reuse, and standards and guidelines efforts, or you could choose to implement a more prescriptive approach: It's your choice.

If your organization has adopted, or is thinking of adopting, the RUP and it wants to also include effective enterprise architecture efforts, it needs to look at the entire system life cycle. The EUP does this, and the RUP clearly does not. In this situation, the primary advantage of the EUP is that it explicitly includes enterprise-scope efforts in the project life cycle, making it clear to developers that they need to think beyond the confines of their current project and to take enterprise issues into account.

Why Adopt the EUP?

This chapter summarized the Enterprise Unified Process (EUP), an extension to the Rational Unified Process (RUP). The EUP adds two phases and two disciplines to the RUP to make it truly ready for the real-world needs of midsize to large organizations. This includes an enterprise management discipline, which is where enterprise architecture efforts belong. If your enterprise architecture efforts are to succeed, they must be explicitly included in your software process.

Conclusion

chapter 7

Agile Architecture

Aim for success, not perfection. Never give up your right to be wrong, because then you will lose the ability to learn new things and move forward with your life.

Dr. David M. Burns

Enterprise architecture processes can range from something that is very formal and prescriptively defined to something that is simple yet still effective. Enterprise architectures can be described via models and documents that are several hundred pages in length or by a concise document that provides a simple overview. Architects can work in virtual seclusion from the rest of the organization, or they can work side by side with the people actively involved in software development. This chapter describes how to take an agile approach to enterprise architecture that is simple and effective, which produces concise documentation, and in which architects work side by side with their customers.

This chapter explores the following topics:

- Agility in a nutshell
- Potential problems with existing architecture efforts
- Existing architecture and architectural modeling techniques
- An agile approach to architecture
- What agile architecture efforts should produce
- Agile architecture at Canaxia
- Introducing agile architecture into your organization
- Potential problems with an agile approach

To address the challenges faced by software developers, an initial group of seventeen methodologists formed the Agile Software Development Alliance (www.agilealliance.org), often referred to simply as the Agile Alliance, in February 2001. An interesting aspect of this group is that all members came from different backgrounds yet were able to come to an agreement on issues that methodologists typically don't agree upon. This group of people defined a manifesto for encouraging better ways of developing software, and then based on that manifesto formulated a collection of principles that define the criteria for agile software development processes.

The manifesto is defined by four simple value statements. What is most important to understand about these statements is that while you should value the concepts on the right-hand side, you should value the concepts on the left-hand side (presented in italics) even more. A good way to think about the manifesto is that it defines preferences, not alternatives, encouraging a focus on certain areas but not eliminating others. The Agile Alliance manifesto values the following:

1. *Individuals and interactions* over processes and tools. Teams of people build software systems, and to do that they need to work together effectively, including but not limited to programmers, testers, project managers, modelers, and customers. Tools and processes are important; it's just that they're not as important as working together effectively. Remember this old adage: A fool with a tool is still a fool.

2. *Working software* over comprehensive documentation. When you ask users whether they would want a fifty-page document describing what you intend to build or the actual software itself, what do you think they'll pick? Ninety-nine times out of a hundred, they'll choose working software. If that is the case, doesn't it make more sense to work in such a manner that you produce software quickly and often, giving your users what they prefer? Documentation has its place, and when written properly it is a valuable guide for people's understanding of how and why a system is built and how to work with the system. However, never forget that the primary goal of software development is to create software, not documents—otherwise it would be called documentation development.

3. *Customer collaboration* over contract negotiation. Only your customers can tell you what they want. Yes, they likely do not have the skills to exactly specify the system. Yes, they likely won't get it right the first time. Yes, they'll likely change their minds. Working together with your customers is hard, but that's the reality of the job. Having a contract with your customers is important, but a contract isn't a substitute for communication. Successful developers work closely with their customers, they invest the effort to discover what their customers need, and they educate their customers along the way.

4. *Responding to change* over following a plan. People change their priorities for a variety of reasons. As work progresses on your system,

your project stakeholder's understanding of the problem domain and of what you are building changes. The business environment changes, and technology changes over time, although not always for the better. Change is a reality of software development, a reality that your software process must reflect. There is nothing wrong with having a project plan, but it must be malleable, allowing room to change it as your situation changes.

To help people gain a better understanding of what agile software development is all about, the members of the Agile Alliance refined the philosophies captured in their manifesto into a collection of the following twelve principles:

1. Our highest priority is to satisfy the customer through early and continuous delivery of valuable software.

2. Welcome changing requirements, even late in development. Agile processes harness change for the customer's competitive advantage.

3. Deliver working software frequently, from a couple of weeks to a couple of months, with a preference for the shorter time scale.

4. Businesspeople and developers must work together daily throughout the project.

5. Build projects around motivated individuals. Give them the environment and support they need, and trust them to get the job done.

6. The most efficient and effective method of conveying information to and within a development team is face-to-face conversation.

7. Working software is the primary measure of progress.

8. Agile processes promote sustainable development. The sponsors, developers, and users should be able to maintain a constant pace indefinitely.

9. Continuous attention to technical excellence and good design enhances agility.

10. Simplicity—the art of maximizing the amount of work not done—is essential.

11. The best architectures, requirements, and designs emerge from self-organizing teams.

12. At regular intervals, the team reflects on how to become more effective, then tunes and adjusts its behavior accordingly.

Stop for a moment and think about these principles. Is this the way your software projects actually work? Is this the way you think projects should work? Reread the principles again. Are they radical and impossible goals as some people would claim, are they meaningless motherhood-and-apple-pie statements, or are they simply common sense? They sound like common sense to us.

Over the years we have observed a common set of problems that organizations seem to experience when it comes to architecture. None of us has yet seen an organization that experiences all these problems, although some suffer from all but one or two. The potential problems with existing traditional approaches to architecture include the following:

1. *There isn't an architecture effort.* Every system has an architecture whether or not the project team chooses to manage it effectively. As you will see in this chapter, architecture efforts don't need to be a complicated endeavor.

2. *Skewed focus.* Architecture models act as bridges between the business and the technical sides of your project. A model that focuses primarily on business issues, or on technical issues, will not meet your real-world needs. When business stakeholders or IT professionals do not see concepts that they can understand, and mappings of those concepts to the ideas that they may not immediately comprehend, they will soon abandon the architecture efforts. You need to find the model that meets everyone's needs.

3. *Developers don't know that the architecture exists.* Many project teams suffer serious breakdowns in communication.

4. *Developers don't follow the architecture.* Developers don't take advantage of the architecture in many projects, and more commonly they only follow part of it and reinvent other portions, due to one or more of the following problems.

5. *Developers don't work with the architects.* Some developers will follow the architecture but will not work with the architects, stumbling a bit due to lack of guidance. The architects also suffer because they don't get the feedback they require, ensuring that their work reflects what developers actually need. Several common reasons explain this problem. First, the architects do not realize the importance of gaining concrete feedback regarding their work. Second, the architects think that coding is "beneath them" and therefore are unwilling to work closely with developers. Third, they are working in a bureaucratic environment that leads them to believe that the best way to communicate their work is through models and documentation. Unfortunately, practice shows that this is the least effective means of communication (Ambler 2002a; Cockburn 2002). Fourth, developers may have little respect for the architects, perceiving them as out of touch or overly academic.

6. *Outdated architecture.* Architecture must evolve over time to reflect new business needs and technological approaches. When architecture becomes outdated, or is perceived to be so, the chances of developers following the architecture decrease dramatically.

7. *Narrowly focused architecture models.* A system is a complex entity, and a single view isn't sufficient to model it. For example, a data model can be an important part of your architecture model if you use it effectively, but it's only one of several parts. What about

your network architecture? The business processes that your system supports? Your organization structure? Software architecture? Business rules? You need a robust architectural model comprised of many views that takes into account all the issues that developers face—one or two narrowly focused views are not good enough.

First and foremost, the values, principles, and practices of Agile Modeling (AM) (see Chapter 8) should help to guide your architecture modeling and documentation efforts. However, this is only a good start. To be successful at architecture, you need to rethink your overall approach and address seven fundamental issues. These issues are connected in a synergistic manner; you must address all them, otherwise you will put your effort at risk:

- Focus on people, not technology or techniques.
- Keep it simple.
- Work iteratively and incrementally.
- Roll up your sleeves.
- Build it before you talk about it.
- Look at the whole picture.
- Make your architecture attractive to your customers.

Focus on People, Not Technology or Techniques

Architects span the boundaries between developers and the people within your organization who have the long-range vision—very often senior IT and senior business executives. The architects work closely with senior executives to understand and evolve their vision for the system. The architects will then reflect this vision in their work and will communicate the vision to the project. The feedback they receive from developers will be fed back into the visioning process; thus the architects act as a communication bridge between senior executives and developers.

Alistair Cockburn (2002) likes to say that software development is a communication game, that to succeed you must ensure that the people (developers and project stakeholders alike) are able to communicate with one another effectively. Figure 7–1 depicts a modified version (Ambler 2002a) of Cockburn's communication modes diagram, indicating that the options on the lower curve support documentation efforts, whereas the options on the upper curve support modeling activities. Several interesting points can be derived from this diagram. First, people can communicate in many ways with one another, and you should vary your approach depending on the situation. Second, some techniques are clearly better than others, so given a choice you should prefer to apply the most effective option available to you. Third, although permanent documentation is clearly important, it is the least effective way to communicate. The implication is that if your current strategy is to simply model and then document your architecture and hand it off to developers, you are very likely going to fail.

Figure 7–1
Communication
modes.

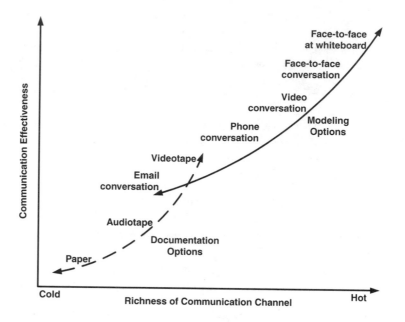

Agile architects will work with their customers, including developers, in the most effective manner possible. Sometimes this will be drawing sketches face to face with them at a whiteboard. Sometimes it will be working with project teams via video conferencing. Sometimes it will be posing questions and receiving answers via email. Sometimes it will involve publishing models and documents. We highly suggest following the AM practice of Display Models Publicly for your architectural models and documents—publish them online at an internal Web site and consider putting up paper versions of critical diagrams in the work spaces of your audience. It isn't enough for architects to put their diagrams on the walls within their work areas; these models must be available to everyone.

This concept isn't new. Fred Brooks (1995) wrote that "The quality of the people on a project, and their organization and management, are much more important factors in success than are the tools they use or the technical approaches they take." The reality is that architectures are developed, evolved, and followed by people. All the arguments over which model is right, which notation is right, and which paradigm is right are meaningless if you don't have a viable strategy for working together effectively. You could create a perfect architecture model, but it doesn't matter if developers can't or won't take advantage of it.

An interesting observation is that enterprises have two organizational structures—the formal one documented by your organization chart and the informal one that people use to get things done. Within IT departments there are always the "go-to guys" that developers work with to get things done, very often other developers who have critical skills or knowledge. Agile architects understand this and actively seek to become "go-to guys."

Keep It Simple

Another of AM's core principles is Assume Simplicity. This principle advises you to assume that the simplest solution is the best solution. You should not overbuild your software, and in the case of architecture, you should not depict additional features in your models that your audience doesn't really need. A supporting principle is Model with a Purpose, which advises you to know who the audience is for your work and to know their use for it. This knowledge enables you to create models and documents that actually meet their needs and permits you to streamline your efforts because you don't need to guess what it is that they actually want. In other words, work together effectively with your audience.

These principles lead to two core practices, Depict Models Simply and Create Simple Content. The first practice implores you to depict your models and documents as simply as possible, to use the simplest notation available to you, and to follow modeling style guidelines (Ambler 2003a) wherever possible. The second practice says that you should apply the simplest solution that gets the job done; avoiding unnecessary complexity that would require greater development, testing, and maintenance efforts and thus higher cost (another AM principle is Maximize Stakeholder Investment).

A critical concept is that your architecture models and documents only need to be good enough, they don't need to be perfect. It is naïve to assume that you can produce perfect artifacts—you're only human, and you will never get it perfectly right and nobody expects you to anyway. Furthermore, even if you did manage to create perfect artifacts, they'd be out of date the day after you published them because something within your business or technical environment would change (Embrace Change is also an AM principle). Why is this important? Our experience is that a hand-drawn sketch today can often be far more valuable than a fully documented and validated document several months from now. Timely guidance from an agile architect who understands the current environment and the future vision for the enterprise, even when this guidance is imperfect and based on incomplete information, is often far better than the uneducated guesses that developers will make on their own while they wait for the official architecture to be published.

By keeping your architecture artifacts simple, you increase the chances that your audience will understand them, that developers will actually read them, and that you will be able to keep them up to date over time. Overly detailed documents might look impressive sitting on a shelf, but a simple model that project teams actually use is far more impressive.

Work Iteratively and Incrementally

Agile architects work in an iterative and incremental manner, preferring an evolutionary approach as opposed to a "big design up front" (BDUF) approach. Agile architects will follow the practice Apply the Right Artifact(s) and use a wide variety of modeling techniques as required (more on this later). They will also follow the practice Iterate to Another Artifact when they realize either that the model they are working on isn't the appropriate one with which to depict a concept or that they are simply stuck and need to break out of their analysis paralysis. They will also follow the Agile Modeling practice Create Several Models in Parallel so that it is easy for them to iterate back and forth among artifacts. Instead of holding a use-case modeling session, an agile modeler will focus on requirements modeling, or even just modeling, and work on use cases, business rules, change cases, and whatever other artifact is required to get the job done. The advantage of these practices is that the right model is used for the task at hand.

Agile architects also follow the practice Model in Small Increments, modeling just enough to fulfill the purpose at hand and then moving on to the next task. They don't try to create complete models; instead they create models that are just good enough. When they find that their models are not sufficient, they work on them some more. The advantage of this approach is that they evolve their models incrementally over time, effectively taking a just-in-time (JIT) approach that enables them to get the models in the hands of their customers as quickly as possible.

On the preceding advice, some readers may say to themselves "All this sounds great, particularly for a programmer, but architecture is different. It's more complex. It's more important. It requires significant modeling up front to get it right." Aaarrrrggghhh! That's old-style thinking. Agile architects can work in an iterative and incremental manner if they so choose.

Roll up Your Sleeves

Fair or not, many application developers have little respect for IT professionals who do not write code. You may not agree with this, but that's the way it is and, frankly, this attitude is reasonable. Think back to all the "architects" you've met. We bet that the best ones always seemed to be willing and able to roll up their sleeves and get involved with hard-core software development when needed. However, this wasn't their only skill. They were also very good at abstraction, at thinking through both logical and physical architecture issues.

Although an important part of an architect's job is modeling and documentation, that should not be their primary focus. Supporting the architecture within your project team should be the primary focus, particularly coaching developers in the architecture and architecture skills. The best way to do this is to get actively involved in development, to work with developers to help them understand the architecture, and to try it out in practice. This approach has several benefits:

- You quickly discover whether or not your ideas work and, if so, how well they work.
- You improve the chance that project teams understand the architecture because you're working with them face to face. As Figure 7–1 shows, this is a far more effective way to communicate.
- You gain experience in the tools and technologies that the project team works with, as well as the business domain itself, improving your own understanding of what it is that you're architecting.

- You obtain concrete feedback that you can then act upon to improve the architecture, enabling it to evolve over time to meet the actual needs of your organization.
- You gain the respect of your primary customers, the developers, because they see that you're participating and not simply pontificating.
- You actively help to build software-based systems, which is the primary goal of IT professionals.
- You can mentor the developers on the project teams in modeling and architecture, improving their skill sets.
- You provide clear benefit to application teams because you're helping them to fulfill their immediate goals, forsaking the "Do all this extra work because it's good for the company" attitude for a more attractive "Let me help you achieve your goals, and by doing so together we'll do something good for the company" attitude.

Build It Before You Talk About It

Agile architects will ensure that their technical ideas actually work by writing a small version of them to validate the idea. This is called a *spike solution* in eXtreme Programming (XP) (Jeffries, Anderson, and Hendrickson 2001) and a technical prototype or skeleton in the Unified Process (Ambler 2001b; Kruchten 2000). The idea is that you write just enough code to verify that that what you think will work actually does so. This helps to reduce technical risk because you're making technology decisions based on known facts instead of good guesses.

Look at the Whole Picture

Agile architects believe in the principle Multiple Models and thus strive to look at the whole picture. They don't just focus on data models, or object/component models, or business models, or whatever type of model might tickle their fancy. Instead they strive to model from several points of view so that their understanding and description of the architecture are more robust.

Why several views? First, architecture has several audiences—the business community, application developers, database administrators (DBAs), network professionals, and so on—each of whom has different priorities. Second, each type of model has its strengths and weaknesses, and no single view is sufficient because architecture is such a complex issue.

The concept that you require multiple views to sufficiently model your architecture isn't new. Kruchten (1995) suggests a five-view approach for software architecture and the Zachman Framework (described in Chapter 5) suggests thirty views for architecture in its entirety. Looking at the whole picture is the norm, not the exception.

Make Your Architecture Attractive to Your Customers

Agile architects realize that they need to make their work, including their services, attractive to their customers (developers and business stakeholders). If your customers perceive that you have value to add and that your architecture efforts will aid them in their jobs, they are much more likely to work with you. If, on the other hand, they think you're wasting their time, they won't work with you. Rather, they'll find ways to avoid you, to cancel or postpone meetings with you, or to find ways around you.

What Should Agile Architecture Efforts Produce?

If you're hoping for an exact list of deliverables here, you need to go back and reread this chapter because you don't understand it yet. However, it is important to define a set of goals that should be achieved. In priority order, these goals are as follow:

1. *Support for the customers of the architecture.* We cannot stress this enough: Agile architects spend the majority of their time working with software developers to mentor them in the architecture, in modeling skills, and in architecture skills in general. They do this by being actively involved in projects, thus helping the project teams to achieve its short-term goals in a manner that reflects the long-term vision of the organization. They also work closely with senior business stakeholders to mentor them in the architecture, in modeling skills, and in developing that long-term vision.

2. A *vision and plan to achieve that vision.* Architects are often keepers of the vision whether they take an agile approach or not. Developers and project stakeholders will look to them for the vision, so agile architects need to be prepared to communicate that vision to developers.

3. A *collection of models and documentation describing the architecture.* Architecture models and documents are important, but alone they are not sufficient for success, as many organizations have found in practice. These artifacts should be just barely good enough and should reflect the values, principles, and practices of Agile Modeling.

Agile Architecture at Canaxia

Is it possible for Canaxia to take an agile approach to its enterprise architecture efforts? Canaxia's situation certainly isn't ideal:

- It is a large, multinational organization, which implies that the business rules, culture, and laws are likely to be very different in each country in which it conducts its business.

- It needs to support a wide range of business applications (finance, production, human resources, and so on), some of which have very little to do with others.

- There may not be a perceived need to change. Because the current architecture has remained relatively unchanged for two decades, chances are very good that many people within IT are perfectly happy with the status quo.

Although any one of these issues would provide Canaxia with a good excuse not to try to be agile, that doesn't mean it should take it. Too many IT professionals like to use the "Technique XYZ is fine for everyone else, but we're unique" excuse to not try new approaches. The reality is that every organization is unique, including Canaxia. Yes, they have some problems. The fact that they are a large multinational organization is likely the largest problem to overcome because it introduces several barriers to communication, but that's going to be an issue whether they take an agile approach or not.

Canaxia's first step should be to form a core architecture team (CAT) that is responsible for developing, supporting, and evolving the enterprise architecture. This CAT team should include people who represent the overall IT constituency. There should be one person, although two are better, from each regional office as well as headquarters. Furthermore, the team must represent the various types of applications within Canaxia, and the easiest way to do that is simply to have a representative from each major project on the team. At the same time, Canaxia should strive to keep the size of the team under ten people, ideally no more than five to seven people, because the larger the team gets the more unwieldy it will become.

The CAT is responsible for defining the initial architecture, getting it just good enough so that Canaxia's development teams have some guidance regarding the enterprise architecture. As depicted in Figure 7-2, the CAT would define the initial enterprise architectural vision and models, a process that would likely take several days or even a week or two. Any longer and the CAT will be at risk of developing architectural models that don't actually reflect something that will work in practice. Remember, your models need to be just good enough, not perfect. The key idea is that your enterprise architecture model(s) start out small and are fleshed out over time based on the feedback you receive from both the business community and from project teams.

The CAT would work with Canaxia business stakeholders while they are modeling the architecture—and this isn't simply an intellectual task for the team. An enterprise architecture must reflect the actual needs of the business. Therefore, part of your architecture efforts must be to identify architecture-level requirements. Without requirements you are effectively "hacking in the large," a recipe for disaster. Therefore, the CAT should follow the AM practice of Active Stakeholder Participation and work closely with business stakeholders, including Canaxia senior executives and other subject matter experts (SMEs). Agile enterprise architects will often find themselves in the position of leader, facilitating senior executives in the identification and evolution of the vision for the system.

The CAT must communicate its models to the larger business stakeholder community. Canaxia chose to enlist the stakeholders who were involved with the modeling efforts for this purpose. The stakeholders must communicate the models to the business community, give several interactive presentations, and publish summary information specifically targeted at business professionals. Their efforts are critical to the success of the enterprise architecture efforts within Canaxia. The business stakeholders will be actively involved in the development and use of business systems. Therefore, they need to understand the overall vision and direction of the organization. A side benefit of this effort is that they'll provide valuable feedback about

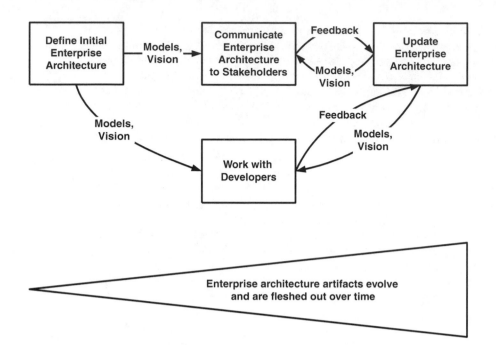

Figure 7–2

An incremental and iterative approach to architecture.

your architecture: Sometimes a simple question from someone in your presentation audience can identify a serious weakness in your approach.

Figure 7–2 depicts another important activity, which is for CAT members to actively work with developers on project teams to communicate the enterprise architecture. This will provide the technical feedback required to update and evolve the architecture models and documents over time. Agile enterprise architects spend their time modeling and documenting the architecture, communicating it to business stakeholders, and working with developers to both ensure that the enterprise architecture reflects the actual realities faced by the team and that it is implemented in practice. In this respect, the architects find themselves in the role of coach, helping to transition skills and knowledge to customers, business stakeholders, and developers.

When Canaxia organized the CAT, it decided to gather the team at Canaxia's world headquarters in the United States for a two-week, initial modeling effort. It also chose to fly in several business experts from each region to ensure adequate representation and to send out the message that Canaxia was serious about the effort.

Immediately following this initial meeting, the team kept in contact via email, a shared documentation repository, impromptu phone calls, and video conference sessions. At first, regular video conference sessions were held each week to discuss common architectural issues, but once the team got used to working together in an impromptu fashion, these meetings were held every second week and eventually once a month.

Once a quarter, the team got together physically for one week at one of the five regional headquarters. At least one person from each region was required to attend, and often they would bring one or two senior developers with them from project teams to help share information with the enterprise architecture team. During the week that the architecture meetings were held, the architects were made available to local development teams, as well as local business stakeholders, to provide advice to the teams as well as to learn from them. When CAT team members were at their home locations, they were co-located with project teams, working as active team members.

Canaxia decided to take a flexible approach with tools. The CAT decided that all documentation would be written as HTML files using simple picture formats (.jpg and .gif) but that members could use any tools that they liked. Most members chose to work with simple tools such as an HTML editor and whiteboard; they took digital snapshots of their diagrams and then cleaned them up using WhiteboardPhoto (www.pixid.com). A few members chose to create presentation-quality diagrams using Visio (www.microsoft.com), which was already a corporate standard. Although Canaxia owned several licenses for sophisticated enterprise modeling tools and was willing to purchase licenses for other tools as needed, the architects decided to wait until they needed the features of the tools before using them—and they never did.

Introducing an Agile Approach into Your Organization

Introducing the techniques and philosophies described in this chapter will prove difficult in many organizations, particularly those that have an established architecture group that follows a traditional approach. Adoption of agile techniques requires a change in mind-set—agile architects are service oriented, realizing that it is their job to help project teams to succeed and to work with senior stakeholders to define and evolve the corporate vision. Agile architects realize that they need to make it as easy as possible for other people to work with them and that they must provide perceived value to the teams they work on. They realize these matters and act accordingly because they know that the people they are supposed to serve will ignore them if they don't. In the end, it's all about people and the way that you interact with them.

Ideally, you'll need to build your architecture team, something that very well could start as a single-person effort, with people who have robust skill sets. If you don't have people like this, which is very often the case, at the very least you need people with open minds who are capable of gaining those skills. These people need the humility to realize that just because architecture is important to them, it doesn't mean that it's important to everyone else. They realize that it will take time to prove themselves and become accepted, and senior management within your organization must allow them that time.

Agile architects must have real-world experience on agile software development projects. They must understand the techniques and philosophies of agile software development, a learning process that could take several years. Simply labeling your existing traditional architects as agile architects isn't going to work—they need to live and breathe the agile paradigm before they can effectively support agile software development efforts.

The best way to introduce agile architecture techniques into an organization is to start small and grow your strategy over time. This approach allows you to gain some initial successes, to learn from your experiences (because everything won't go perfectly according to plan), and to evolve your strategy based on those learnings. You need to build a solid foundation from which to work, to build up the proof that the approach actually works.

It is important to have a growth strategy for your architecture team, and the best strategy is to keep an eye out for potential candidates among your development community and then to mentor potential candidates. This is likely the exact same approach you've taken in the past when building traditional architecture teams; the only change is that you have slightly different qualification criteria against which you're judging candidates.

Are Other Architecture Approaches Agile?

We described the Zachman Framework, the OMGs, Model-Driven Achitecture (MDA), and the Unified Modeling Language (UML) in Chapter 5. Are these approaches agile? This is actually a trick question because the answer depends on how you choose to implement them. Each of these techniques makes it really easy to overcomplicate your modeling efforts, to make them harder than they need to be, and to motivate you to write more documentation than you really need. For example, you can apply the artifacts of the UML in a very agile manner, something that agile modeling aptly demonstrates, or you can apply them in an incredibly dysfunctional manner. You could easily apply the principles and practices of AM to the Zachman Framework and make it very agile. Or you could use the Zachman Framework to justify a complex and documentation-heavy modeling process that requires a large architecture group to administer and control. It's your choice. Table 7–1 summarizes strategies for how each technique could be used in an agile manner.

Table 7–1
Strategies for applying each technique in an agile manner.

Technique	Strategies
Model-Driven Architecture (MDA)	Keep it simple.
	Adopt the concept of platform independent models (PIM) and platform specific models (PSM), with mappings in between, but keep them agile by ensuring that they are just barely good enough.
	Adopt good tools based on the MDA that add value to your efforts.
	Avoid documentation-heavy, bureaucratic processes centered around the MDA.
	Remember that your goal is to develop working software, not to create lots of fancy models and documentation.
Unified Modeling Language (UML)	Keep it simple.
	All developers should have a thorough grasp of UML modeling techniques, including knowing when to use them and when not to use them.
	Adopt the values, principles, and practices of Agile Modeling.
	Remember, UML is not complete but defines the core of your modeling techniques.

Technique	Strategies
Zachman Framework (ZF)	Keep it simple.
	Adopt the concept that your architecture efforts must reflect a wide range of perspectives.
	Adopt an augmented form of the ZF, renaming the "Data" column to "Structure," to avoid methodology bias.
	Avoid documentation-heavy, bureaucratic processes centered around the Zachman Framework.
	Remember, your goal is to develop working software, not to create lots of fancy models and documentation.

No approach to enterprise architecture is perfect, including this. We would be remiss if we didn't identify the following known issues:

Potential Problems with an Agile Approach

1. It *does not include an explicit way to ensure compliancy.* There is something to be said about the philosophy "If you build it, they will come," as long as you build something people actually want. We highly suggest that you do not force anyone to work with your architects and that instead you make it an option. For example, the CAT members at Canaxia should make themselves and their work available to project teams and should wait for the teams to find ways to best take advantage of their offer. This forces agile architects to provide services in such a way that they are attractive to development teams, that they actually provide immediate value to developers. The risk with this approach is that an application team will still decide to opt out and do things on its own, potentially producing a system that does not conform to the existing environment or to the overall corporate vision. The implication is that you need to either accept this risk or to put a mechanism in place to mitigate it. A good place to start would be to identify why the project team has chosen to opt out and then to address the actual root cause.

2. It *depends on people being responsible.* People need to be willing to work together. People need open minds and to be willing to learn new techniques. People need to accept that they make mistakes, and that they don't know everything.

3. It *requires you to actively strive to keep things simple.* Process entropy, the tendency of processes to become more complex and slower over time, is a serious danger to agility. Each new process step, such as the addition of a checklist or a review, always sounds like a good idea at the time—and they almost always are. Unfortunately, a price must be paid, which is often forgotten. Follow AM's Maximize Stakeholder Investment principle when you're improving your software process, and ensure that all process improvements truly are improvements. Canaxia kept things as simple as possible.

4. *It requires you to accept an agile approach to modeling and documentation.* Many architects wait until they've got it "just right" before they publish. Sometimes they try to wait out fluctuations in technology or deficits in skill sets before they publish anything. The end result is that they may never publish anything or may publish too late. Everyone, including the architects, needs to accept that architecture models don't need to be perfect; they just need to be good enough. This can be very difficult for some people to accept.

Conclusion

The approach described in this chapter works incredibly well if you let it. Your most important take-away point is that it's all about people. Sophisticated tools based on theoretically sound frameworks, metamodels, or modeling languages are great to have, but they won't do anything for you if developers don't use them. It's all about people. Complex models and documents are interesting to create, but they offer little value if nobody reads them. It's all about people.

chapter 8

Agile Modeling

*Sometimes people carry to such perfection the mask they have
assumed that in due course they actually become the person
they seem.*

W. Somerset Maugham (1874–1965),
The Moon and Sixpence

Modeling often proves to be one of several dogmatic issues within the
software industry. Traditional software developers will either insist on
developing sophisticated models before coding, or they will think that modeling is a paper-intensive, overly bureaucratic waste of time. Traditionally,
architects often fall into the pro-modeling camp, whereas many programmers
seem to fall into the anti-modeling camp. Unfortunately, both groups could
improve their approaches by finding the appropriate balance between over-
modeling and not modeling at all. Architects must realize they don't need to
get everything right, that they need only to think through the larger issues
and to leave the details to the developers, that they are much better off taking an evolutionary approach to their work. Similarly, programmers must recognize that sometimes it is significantly more productive to a sketch to think
through an idea, or to compare several different approaches to solving a
problem, and thereby avoid unnecessary churn when coding.

The AM methodology (Ambler 2002a) is a chaordic collection of practices
that are guided by principles and values. AM is not a prescriptive process, and
it does not define detailed procedures for how to create a given type of
model. Rather, it provides advice for how to be effective as a modeler. AM is
more an art than a science.

An agile modeler is anyone who models following the AM methodology,
applying AM's practices in accordance with its principles and values. An agile
developer is someone who follows an agile approach to software development. An agile modeler is an agile developer. Not all agile developers are
agile modelers.

165

AM has three goals:

- To define and show how to put into practice a collection of values, principles, and practices for effective, lightweight modeling.
- To address the issue of how to apply modeling techniques to software projects taking an agile approach, such as eXtreme Programming (XP) (Beck 2000) or Feature-Driven Development (FDD) (Palmer and Felsing 2002).
- To address how you can improve your modeling activities following a "near-agile" approach to software development, and in particular project teams that have adopted an instantiation of the Unified Process (UP), such as the Rational Unified Process (RUP) (Kruchten 2000) or the Enterprise Unified Process (EUP) (see Chapter 6).

It is critical to recognize that AM is independent of other processes, such as XP and the UP, that it is used only to enhance those processes. This is because AM is not a complete software process. AM's focus is on effective modeling and documentation; AM doesn't address programming, testing, project management, system deployment, system operations, system support, or a myriad of other issues. As Figure 8–1 depicts, you need to use AM with another, full-fledged process such as XP, Dynamic System Development Methodology (DSDM) (Stapleton 2003), FDD, or the UP. You start out with a base process and then tailor it with AM and other techniques to define a process that reflects your unique needs.

Let's explore the values, principles, and practices of AM in detail.

Values

In the book *Extreme Programming Explained* (Beck 2000), one of the most poignant aspects of XP was how Beck first defined a foundation for his methodology. He did this by describing four values: communication, simplicity, feedback, and courage. He had found a way to describe some of the fundamental factors that lead to success in the software development game, and he managed to do it in such a way as to personalize it for individual developers. Agile Modeling adopts all four of XP's values and adds a fifth: humility. Agile software developers are humble enough to recognize that they can't do it alone but instead must work with others, including business stakeholders. Furthermore, they realize that they don't know everything, that they will never know everything, and as a result that they always must be looking for opportunities to learn. Table 8–1 discusses each AM value in detail.

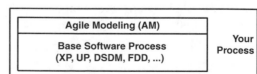

Figure 8–1
AM enhances other software processes.

Table 8–1

The values of agile modeling.

Value	Description
Communication	Communication is a two-way street: You both provide and gain information as the result of communication. Good communication—among everyone involved in your project, including developers and project stakeholders—is a requisite for software development success. Modeling helps you to communicate your ideas, to understand the ideas of others, to mutually explore those ideas, and to eventually reach a common understanding.
Courage	Agile methodologies ask you to do much that requires great courage, particularly much that you've never attempted before. You need to work closely with other people, to trust them and to trust yourself. You should do the simplest thing that you can, to trust that you can solve tomorrow's problem tomorrow. You should create documentation only when you absolutely need it and when stakeholders are willing to invest in it, not just when it feels comfortable to do so. You must let businesspeople make business decisions, such as prioritization of requirements, and technical people make technical decisions, such as how the software will fulfill individual requirements. You must trust your coworkers, to trust that programmers can make design decisions and, therefore, that you do not need to provide them with as much detail.
Feedback	The only way you can determine whether your work is correct is to obtain feedback, and that includes feedback regarding your models. You can obtain feedback by developing the model as a team instead of by yourself, by reviewing models with the target audience (better yet, get them involved early on with modeling), by implementing the model, and through acceptance testing of the actual system.
Humility	The best developers have the humility to recognize that they don't know everything. Agile modelers understand that their fellow developers and their project stakeholders have their own areas of expertise and, therefore, have value to add to a project. Agile modelers have the humility to respect the people they are working with, realizing that others likely have different priorities and experiences than they do and will, therefore, have different viewpoints.
Simplicity	Keep your models as simple as possible. Model today to meet today's needs, and worry tomorrow about tomorrow's modeling needs. Follow the KISS (Keep It Simple, Stupid) rule and not the KICK (Keep It Complex, Kamikaze) rule. In other words, don't overmodel.

The Principles of Agile Modeling

Agile Modeling's values, in combination with the values and principles of the Agile Alliance (2001a, 2001b), are used as the foundation of AM's principles. When applied to a software development project, these principles set the stage for a collection of modeling practices. Some of the principles have been adopted from XP, which in turn adopted them from common software engineering techniques. For the most part, the principles are presented with a focus on their implications to modeling efforts. As a result, material adopted from XP may be presented in a different light.

Table 8–1 describes AM's core principles, which you must adopt in full to be truly able to claim that you are agile modeling. Table 8–2 describes AM's supplementary principles, which you may optionally tailor into your software process to increase its effectiveness. Why distinguish between core and supplementary principles? AM strives to avoid a problem that XP suffers from: people who claim to do XP, but who really don't, who then blame XP for their failure. Like XP, the principles and practices of AM are synergistic, and if you remove some, the synergy is lost. By failing to adopt one of the core principles or practices of AM, you reduce the method's effectiveness. You should feel free to adopt whatever aspects of AM you see fit to use, just don't claim that you're doing AM when you've only adopted it partially.

Table 8–2

The core principles of agile modeling.

Principle	Description
Assume Simplicity	As you develop you should assume that the simplest solution is the best solution.
Embrace Change	Agile modelers accept the fact that change happens. Your requirements change, as does your understanding of them. The technology you are working with changes over time, as does your strategy for using it.
Enabling the Next Effort Is Your Secondary Goal	Your project can be considered a failure even when your team delivers a working system to your users. Part of fulfilling the needs of your project stakeholders is ensuring that your system is robust enough to be extended over time. As Alistair Cockburn (2002) likes to say, when you are playing the software development game your secondary goal is to set up to play the next game.
Incremental Change	To embrace change, you need to take an incremental approach to your own development efforts, to change your system a small portion at a time instead of trying to get everything accomplished in one big release. You can make a big change as a series of small, incremental changes.

Principle	Description
Maximize Stakeholder Investment	Your project stakeholders are investing resources—time, money, facilities, and so on—to have software developed that meets their needs. Stakeholders deserve to invest their resources the best way possible and to not have them frittered away by your team. Furthermore, stakeholders deserve to have the final say in how those resources are invested or not invested. If it were your money, would you want it any other way?
Model with a Purpose	If you cannot identify why and for whom you are creating a model, why are you bothering to work on it at all?
Multiple Models	You have a wide range of modeling artifacts available to you. These artifacts include but are not limited to the diagrams of the Unified Modeling Language (UML), structured development artifacts such as the physical data model which depicts a portion of Canaxia's database schema in Figure 8–2, and low-tech artifacts such as essential user interface models (Ambler 2001a; Constantine and Lockwood 1999) Visit www.agilemodeling.com/essays/modelingTechniques.htm for a list of potential modeling artifacts (It's interesting to note how many non-UML artifacts there are) and www.agiledata.org/essays/umlDataModelingProfile.html for a description of the notation used in Figure 8–2).
Quality Work	Agile developers understand that they should invest the effort to make permanent artifacts, such as source code, user documentation, and technical system documentation, of sufficient quality.
Rapid Feedback	Feedback is one of the five values of AM, and because the time between an action and the feedback on that action is critical, agile modelers prefer rapid feedback over delayed feedback whenever possible.
Software Is Your Primary Goal	The primary goal of software development is to produce high-quality software that meets the needs of your project stakeholders in an effective manner.
Travel Light	Traveling light means that you create just enough models and documentation to get by. No more, no less.

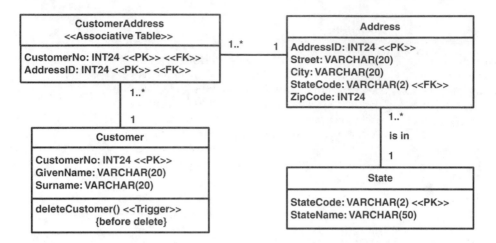

Figure 8–2
A physical data model.

Table 8–3
The supplementary principles of agile modeling.

Principle	Description
Content Is More Important Than Representation	Any given model could have several ways to represent it. For example, a UI specification could be created using Post-It™ notes on a large sheet of paper (an essential or low-fidelity prototype), as a sketch on paper or whiteboard, as a traditional prototype built using a prototyping tool or programming language, or as a formal document including both a visual representation and a textual description of the user interface. For example, Figure 8–3 depicts a high-level business model for customer contact at Canaxia. Although it uses some UML notation, in particular the stick figure representing an actor, the rest of the diagram is clearly free-form. Although it doesn't conform to an official notation, this diagram still provides values to its users.
Everyone Can Learn from Everyone Else	Agile modelers have the humility to recognize that they can never truly master something and that there is always opportunity to learn more and to extend their knowledge. They take the opportunity to work with and learn from others, to try new ways of doing things, to reflect on what seems to work and what doesn't.
Know Your Models	You need to know the strengths and weaknesses of each type of model, know when to create each one, and how to create each one effectively.

Principle	Description
Know Your Tools	Software, such as diagramming tools or modeling tools, has a variety of features. If you are going to use a modeling tool, you should understand its features, knowing when and when not to use it.
Local Adaptation	AM is designed so you can tailor it to reflect your environment, including the nature of your organization, your coworkers, your project stakeholders, and your project itself.
Open and Honest Communication	People need to be free to offer suggestions. Open and honest communication enables people to make better decisions because the quality of the information they are basing them on is more accurate.
Work with People's Instincts	As you gain experience at developing software, your instincts become sharper, and what your instincts are telling you subconsciously can often be an important input into your modeling efforts.

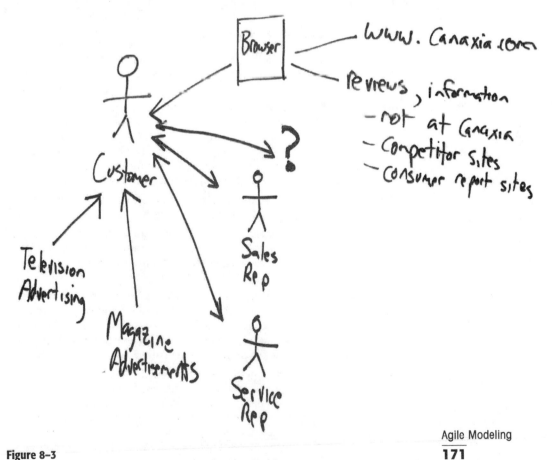

Figure 8–3
A high-level business model for customer contact at Canaxia.

The Practices of Agile Modeling

The heart of AM is its practices. It is those practices that you apply to your projects, those practices that are guided by AM's values and principles. They are organized into core practices (Table 8–4) that you must adopt and optional supplementary practices (Table 8–5) that you may adopt. You must adopt all AM's core practices to be able to claim that you are "doing AM." However, you may still benefit if you only adopt some of the practices, perhaps because that is all that your organization's culture will allow.

Table 8–4

The core practices of agile modeling.

Practice	Description
Active Stakeholder Participation	Project success often requires a significant level of involvement by project stakeholders. Senior management needs to publicly and privately support your project, operations and support staff must actively work with your project team toward making your production environment ready to accept your system, other system teams must work with yours to support integration efforts, and maintenance developers must work to become adept at the technologies and techniques used by your system.
Apply the Right Artifact(s)	This is AM's equivalent of the adage "Use the right tool for the job." In this case, you want to create the right model(s) to get the job done. Each artifact—such as a UML state chart, an essential use case, source code, or data flow diagram (DFD)—has its own specific strengths and weaknesses, and therefore is appropriate for some situations but not others.
Collective Ownership	Everyone can work on any model, and ideally any artifact on the project, if they so need.
Consider Testability	When you are modeling, you should be asking yourself constantly "How are we going to test this?" If you can't test the software you are building, you shouldn't be building it.
Create Several Models in Parallel	Because each type of model has its strengths and weaknesses, no single model is sufficient for your modeling needs. By working on several at once, you can easily iterate back and forth between them and use each model for what it suits best.
Create Simple Content	You should keep the actual content of your models—your requirements, your analysis, your architecture, your design—as simple as you possibly can while still fulfilling the needs of your project stakeholders. The implication is that you should not add additional aspects to your models unless they are justifiable.

Practice	Description
Depict Models Simply	Use a subset of the modeling notation available to you. A simple model that shows the key features you are trying to understand—perhaps a class model depicting the primary responsibilities of classes and the relationships among them—often proves to be sufficient. For example, the models depicted in Figure 8–3 and Figure 8–4 are both fairly simple and use minimal notation, yet they depict important information.
Display Models Publicly	This supports the principle of Open and Honest Communication on your team, because all the current models are quickly accessible to it. It also satisfies your project stakeholders because you aren't hiding anything from them.
Iterate to Another Artifact	Whenever you are having difficulties working on one artifact—perhaps you are working on a use case and find that you are struggling to describe the business logic—that's a sign that you should iterate to another artifact. By iterating to another artifact, you are freed immediately because you are making progress working on that other artifact. For example, as you're developing a use case, you may discover that your stakeholders are having trouble describing the usage logic, so you decide to change tack and work on sketching a few supporting screens. A few minutes later, your stakeholders suddenly realize what needs to occur in the use case as the result of approaching the problem from another direction (in this case UI design).
Model in Small Increments	With incremental development you model a little, code a little, test a little, then deliver a little. No more big design up front (BDUF) where you invest weeks or even months creating models and documents.
Model with Others	Software development is a lot like swimming: It's very dangerous to do it alone.
Prove IT with Code	A model is an abstraction, one that should accurately reflect an aspect of whatever you are building. To determine if it will actually work, you should validate that your model works by writing the corresponding code.
Use the Simplest Tools	The vast majority of models can be drawn on a whiteboard, such as the diagram in Figure 8–3, on paper, and even on the back of a napkin. Note that AM has nothing against computer-aided software engineering (CASE) tools—if investing in a CASE tool is the most effective use of your resources, by all means use it to its maximum benefit.

Table 8–5

The supplementary practices of agile modeling.

Practice	Description
Apply Modeling Standards	Developers should agree to and follow a common set of modeling standards on a software project. Good sources of modeling standards and guidelines are *The Elements of UML Style* (Ambler 2003a) and www.modelingstyle.info.
Apply Patterns Gently	Effective modelers learn and then appropriately apply common architectural, design, and analysis patterns in their models. However, both Martin Fowler (2001a) and Joshua Kerievsky (2001) believe that developers should consider easing into the application of a pattern, that they should apply it gently.
Discard Temporary Models	The vast majority of the models you create are temporary/working models—design sketches, low-fidelity prototypes, index cards, potential architecture/design alternatives, and so on—models that have fulfilled their purpose but no longer add value now that they have done so. For example, Figure 8–4 depicts a whiteboard sketch of a potential technical architecture for Canaxia applications. The architects drew this diagram as they discussed the issue but eventually erased it in favor of another approach. The fate of most models is to be discarded like this.
Formalize Contract Models	Contract models are often required when an external group controls an information resource that your system requires, such as a database, legacy application, or information service. A contract model is formalized when both parties mutually agree to it and are prepared to mutually change it over time as required.
Model to Communicate	One reason why you model is to communicate with people who are external to your team or to create a contract model.
Model to Understand	You often create models to explore the problem space, to understand the requirements for the system. Similarly, you will compare and contrast potential design alternatives to understand the solution space.
Reuse Existing Resources	Agile modelers can take advantage of a wealth of resources by reusing them.
Update Only When It Hurts	You should update an artifact such as a model or document only when you absolutely need to, when not having it updated is more painful than the effort of updating it.

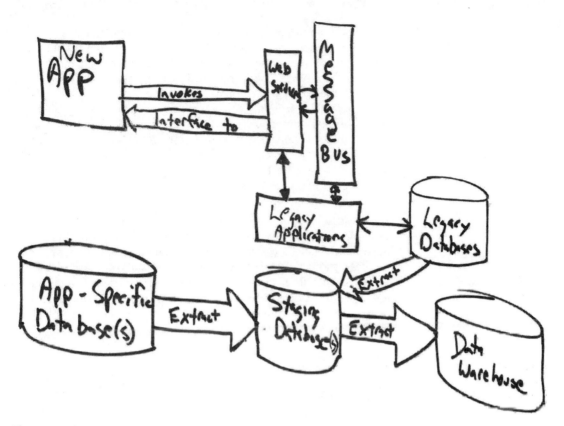

Figure 8–4
A free-form diagram depicting high level technical architecture.

A model is an abstraction that describes one or more aspects of a problem or a potential solution addressing a problem. Traditionally, models are thought of as zero or more diagrams plus any corresponding documentation. However, nonvisual artifacts such as collections of CRC cards, a textual description of one or more business rules, or the structured English description of a business process are also models. An agile model is a model that is just barely good enough. But how do you know when a model is good enough?

Agile Models

Agile models are just barely good enough when they exhibit the following traits:

- *Agile models fulfill their purpose.* If you don't know why you need to create something, don't create it. That wouldn't be agile.
- *Agile models are understandable.* A requirements model will be written in the language of the business that your users comprehend, whereas a technical architecture model will likely use technical terms with which developers are familiar. Style issues, such as avoiding crossing lines, will also affect understandability—messy diagrams are harder to read than clean ones (Ambler 2003a). The level of detail in your models and their simplicity also affect understandability.

- *Agile models are sufficiently accurate.* When a street map is missing a street, or it shows that a street is open but you discover it's closed for repairs, do you throw away your map and start driving mayhem through the city? Of course not. You can tolerate some inaccuracies. It's the same with models: The nature of the project, the nature of the individual team members, and the nature of the organization all determine how accurate your models need to be. For example, Figure 8–5, modified from *Agile Database Techniques* (Ambler 2003b) depicts the basic logic for optimistic locking although it isn't necessarily the exact way you would actually implement it (you don't need near that many database accesses). It isn't perfect, but it gets the job done.

- *Agile models are sufficiently consistent.* In an ideal world, all your artifacts would be perfectly consistent, but the world isn't ideal nor does it need to be. There is clearly an entropy issue to consider regarding accuracy and consistency. If you have an artifact that you wish to keep as official documentation, you will need to invest the resources to update it as time passes, otherwise it will quickly become out of date and useless. There is a fine line between spending too much time and not enough time updating documents.

Figure 8–5
A UML sequence diagram.

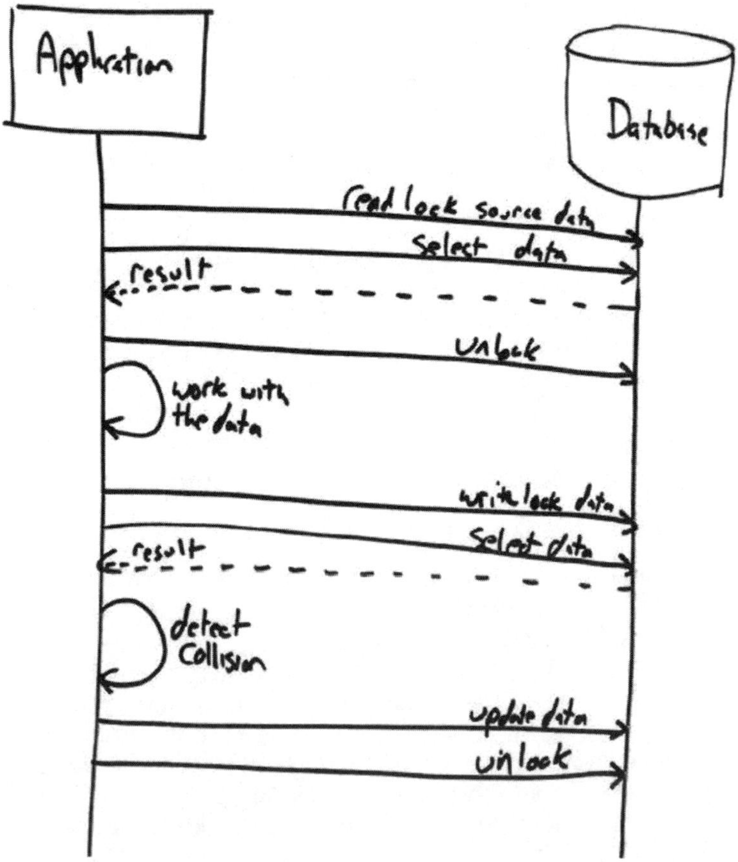

- *Agile models are sufficiently detailed.* A road map doesn't indicate each individual house on each street because that would be too much detail. However, when a street is being built, the builder requires a detailed map showing each building, the sewers, electrical boxes, and so on. Sufficient detail depends on the audience and the purpose for which it is using a model. For many projects, a couple of diagrams drawn on a whiteboard and updated as the project progresses are sufficient to describe the architecture. For example, Figure 8–2 doesn't depict the indices needed to support this data structure, yet you likely could create a working database schema from this diagram.

- *Agile models provide positive value.* A fundamental aspect of any project artifact is that it should add positive value. Does the benefit that an architecture model brings to your project outweigh the costs of developing and (optionally) maintaining it? If not, find more cost-effective ways to create it.

- *Agile models are as simple as possible.* Strive to keep your models as simple as possible while still getting the job done.

The supplementary AM practices of Discard Temporary Models, Update Only When It Hurts, and Formalize Contract Models support the concept of agile documentation. A document is agile when it meets the following criteria:

- It *maximizes stakeholder investment.* The benefit provided by an agile document is greater than the investment in its creation and maintenance. Ideally, the investment made in that documentation was the best option available for those resources. In other words, no better approach was available to you.

- It is *"lean and mean."* An agile document contains just enough information to fulfill its purpose. It is as simple as it can possibly be.

- It describes *"good things to know."* Agile documents capture critical information that is not readily obvious, such as design rationale, requirements, usage procedures, and operational procedures.

- It *has a specific customer and facilitates the work efforts of that customer.* You must work closely with customers, or potential customers, for your documentation if you want to create something that will actually meet their needs.

- It is *sufficiently accurate, consistent, and detailed.* Agile documents do not need to be perfect; they just need to be good enough.

Implications for Architects

Although Chapter 7 describes an agile approach to architecture in detail, it is worth noting several implications that AM has for architects:

- It's *about people, not models and documents.* An effective architect focuses on people. You must work closely with your stakeholders, including both business experts and developers, to ensure that the architecture reflects the actual needs of your organization.

- *Models do not equal documents.* A model isn't necessarily a document, and a document isn't necessarily a model. A sketch or stack of index cards might be a model, but it's doubtful you'd consider them to be documentation.

- *You can't think everything through from the start, and you don't need to anyway.* Requirements change. A person's understanding of the requirements change. Technologies change. Your strategy changes.

- *You must embrace multiple models.* There's more to architecture than data. There's more to architecture than process. There's more to architecture than objects. There's more to architecture than hardware. There's more to architecture than [Fill In Your Favorite View Here].

- *Be prepared to take an iterative and incremental approach.* Effective architects work in a way that reflects the software development followed by the project teams with which they work. Because modern software development processes, such as the RUP, FDD, and XP, take an iterative and incremental approach, so must architects. The BDUF approach to development simply isn't acceptable for the vast majority of projects.

- *Your work needs to be just barely good enough. It doesn't need to be perfect.*

- *The longer you go without feedback, the greater the risk that your architecture doesn't reflect the needs of your stakeholders.*

- *It's your stakeholder's money that is being spent, not yours, therefore they should determine what they choose to fund.* The implication is that the decision to invest in an architecture model, and in architectural documentation, belongs to the stakeholders, not to you. You should inform stakeholders of their options and the trade-offs among the options, and then let them decide how much they intend to invest in architectural efforts. Effective architects who can actually provide value on a project team should welcome this approach; less-than-effective architects are typically threatened by it.

The Agile Modeling methodology defines an important collection of values, principles, and practices for architects to have in their intellectual toolkits. Extensive models and documents are one extreme, no models and documents are another. Your goal is to identify when your models are just barely good enough for your situation. Anything beyond just barely good enough is a wasted effort, effort that could be better spent elsewhere.

Conclusion

Understanding and being able to apply the values, principles, and practices of Agile Modeling is an important skill that agile enterprise architects should have if they are to work effectively with agile software developers. In this chapter, you have seen that it is possible to gain the benefits of modeling and documentation without the disadvantages of having to endure bureaucratic processes—if you choose to work that way.

chapter 9

Presentation Tier Architecture

Computers are useless. They can only give you answers.
Pablo Picasso (1881–1973)

Presentation tier is where the users and the system meet each other. This tier is responsible for generating the user interface (UI) for the users of the system. Presentation tier architecture is the act of defining the blueprint or the underlying schematics used to map out or design a system. Since UI is the most visible part of the system, it ends up being the most frequently changed part. This is perhaps the main reason for separating the presentation tier from the other back-end code in multi-tiered software architecture.

The basic concept of a tiered architecture involves breaking up an application into logical chunks, or tiers, each of which is assigned general or specific roles. Tiers can be located on different machines or on the same machine where they are virtually or conceptually separate from one another. The more tiers used, the more specific each tier's role. Multi-tier architecture concepts are fast evolving, whereas in most architecture a clear separation exists between the front end that contains the code for generating the UI and the back end that contains the code for business logic and the databases.

In this chapter we will discuss some of the following:

- Business needs and presentation requirements
- Key presentation tier components
- General design considerations
- Key architectural considerations

Business Needs and Presentation Requirements

Kello James at Canaxia is reviewing his presentation needs. Kello is well aware of the pitfalls of a poorly designed presentation tier. The metrics from Canaxia's projects indicate a surprisingly high cost in the overall spending **179** related to the presentation tier. Some projects were actually spending nearly 30 to 40 percent of the overall development budget on addressing the needs related to the presentation tier. What has made this more painful is that a large portion of the spending has been due to cost overruns and spending in support and maintenance. Although a detailed cost analysis of the spending in the presentation tier area is beyond the scope of this book, several industry research groups are reporting a large increase in presentation tier spending. It is not uncommon to find companies today that have a larger presentation tier cross-functional team than other development teams.

The Standish Group reports that U.S. companies are wasting as much as $145 billion a year on failed IT projects. Only 9 percent of technology investments are completed on time and within budget.

The growing complexity in presentation needs is related to the transforming business paradigm. This is apparent to Kello as he looks at how Canaxia is continuing to transform the way it does business. A large part of the complexity was introduced some years ago when Canaxia decided not only to connect and consolidate its global IT systems but also to open them to channel partners and customers. Mattie Lee Mitchell, Canaxia's CIO, had outlined this in her company broadcast: "Our business needs to reach out to our partners and customers. We will reach out to them via channels that they are most comfortable using and with messages that they are most familiar with. Doing business with Canaxia should be exciting and mostly transparent to them. Although we need to work as one company, we need to adapt to the local ways in every country that we do business in. We need to prepare our IT systems for the future or we will be lost to the competition."

The complex IT needs become apparent immediately. With the core application and system needs remaining the same, the presentation tier architecture needs to support some of the following:

- Internationalization and localization
- Personalization and co-branding
- Support for multiple device and access points
- Support for local business processes and data presentation
- Support for multiple technologies
- Potential exposure of the applications to other systems as services

To better prepare Canaxia for the future, Kello James was considering adopting the multi-tiered architecture shown in Figure 9–1. This figure illustrates a three-tier architecture that has also become a model for many enterprise applications. One of the major benefits of this architecture is its potential for a high level of maintainability and code reuse. This architecture is composed of the user system interface (the presentation tier), the process management (the business logic tier), and the database management (the data tier). In this architecture, the presentation tier has been separated into a primary tier and a secondary tier, corresponding to the activities related to the client and the server processes. The processes on the business and data tiers have not been elaborated.

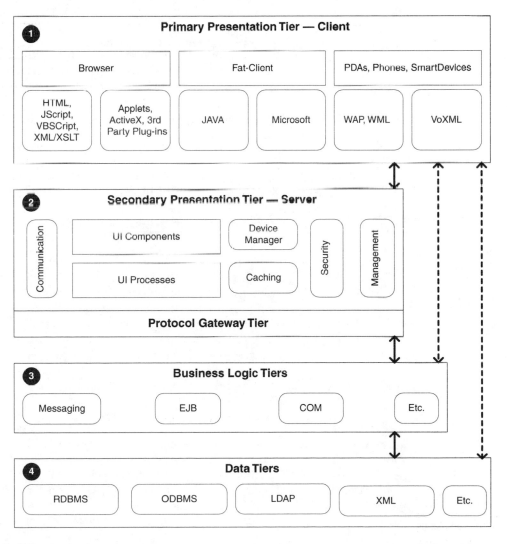

Figure 9–1
Multi-tiered software architecture.

An examination of most business solutions based on a layered component model reveals several common component types (in this case *components* refers to a piece or part of the overall structure). Figure 9–1 shows these component types in one comprehensive illustration. Although the list of component types shown in Figure 9–1 is not exhaustive, it represents the common types of software components found in most distributed solutions. These component types are described in depth in the following sections and throughout the remainder of this chapter.

Primary Presentation Tier Components

Most solutions today require users to interact with the system via a user interface. The primary presentation tier, called the *client*, consists of software that renders the user interface for the users to interact with the system. For smaller and less complex systems, users may be provided with only one client type. In recent years, many different types of client software, devices, and technologies have become increasingly popular. Users now expect systems to offer user interface in the client of their choice.

Discussion of all the client options is beyond the scope of this book. Some very important and popular client options have not been included in this chapter in the interest of maintaining the larger focus, including but not limited to character-based interface, terminal emulation, and voice response systems.

Among the many client options that are available today, the choices can broadly be grouped together in the following popular graphical user interface (GUI) categories.

Internet Browser

This client software is based upon the World Wide Web Consortium (W3C) specifications and is used for rendering Web-based applications. The Internet browser is based upon a request–response paradigm that requires accessing the Web server and downloading the client code to render the user interface. In most cases, the UI is updated only after a user makes an explicit request of the system. For the UI to be quickly available to the users, the code that is downloaded needs to be small in size, and therefore, it allows for little client-side processing. The browser is also called the *thin-client*. Internet Explorer from Microsoft and Netscape from AOL-Time Warner are the main Internet browsers available today.

Fat-client

When the software is preinstalled on the physical computer of users for access to the system, it is called a *fat-client*. Since the code actually resides on the users' computer, the size of the code can be potentially larger than that used for creating the UI via a thin-client. This makes it possible for the UI to be richer in both the user experience and processing. The fat-client also makes it possible for the users to do a large amount of (and sometimes all of) the work offline without requiring to send or receive information from a remote server. A key difference in paradigm between the Internet browser and a fat-client is that the fat-client can maintain a persistent connection with the back-end systems. This makes it possible for the server to send and update information on the client without an explicit request from the user. JAVA, an open-source technology from Sun Microsystems, and several proprietary technologies from various companies, including the popular Visual Basic and VC++ from Microsoft, are used for creating the fat-client.

Mobile Devices

Mobile access technology has gained a lot of attention recently. Interest in mobile access is strong among a wide range of people and organizations involved in mobile access technology, such as hardware manufacturers, software providers, communication service providers, content providers, and end-user organizations. W3C is working toward making information on the World Wide Web accessible to mobile devices. The key challenge is in the device that is characterized by small screens, limited keyboard, low bandwidth connection, small memory, and so on. These devices are highly portable and connect to the server using a wireless network. On one end of the spectrum are devices that are primarily phones, and on the other are smart devices that are primarily miniaturized computers. As the devices continue to grow in their telephony and computational power, their adoption is increasing manyfold. Several critical applications are offered now to users on their mobile devices. These applications include content serving, such as news; actual transaction processing, such as banking; and several others.

Secondary Presentation Tier Components

The secondary presentation tier consists of components that run on the server and prepare the presentation of the UI that is sent to the client for display to the users. Here is where most application developers tend to dilute the true modularity of the multi-tiered architecture. In a truly tiered architecture, the presentation tier has the following design requirements:

- Should use a well-defined interface to access the application's other tiers. Using APIs that the other tiers publish achieves this.
- Without requiring a change in the APIs, the presentation tier should not only be able to add newer ways of presenting an interface but also to allow the users to manipulate the data based upon their needs.
- Newer access mechanism can be introduced without requiring a change in the APIs.
- The system should be able to be deployed in any distributed configuration.

A popular architectural pattern used for generating the user interface and keeping it separate from the back-end API and data are the Model–View–Controller (MVC) pattern. The MVC pattern is surprisingly simple, yet incredi-

Figure 9–2
Model–View–
Controller pattern.

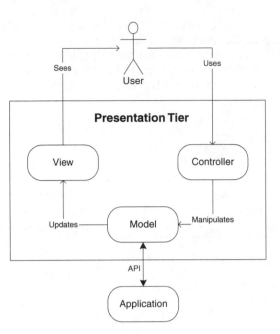

bly useful. Essentially, the pattern (Figure 9–2) forces one to think of the application in terms of the following three modules:

- *Model*: This is the information that the presentation tier receives from the APIs from the business logic tier (and other tiers). The model knows about all the data that need to be displayed. It also knows about all the operations that can be applied to transform the model. However, it knows nothing whatsoever about the user interface, the manner in which the data are to be displayed, or the UI actions that are used to manipulate the data.
- *Controller*: The user interface presented to the user to manipulate the application (model).
- *View*: The user interface that displays information about the model to the user.

While the model is the core responsibility of the other tiers (usually the business logic tier), the view (referred to as the user interface component in Figure 9–1) and the controller (referred to as the user process component in Figure 9–1) comprise the core responsibility of the presentation tier.

User Interface Components

Most solutions need to provide a way for users to interact with the application. In Canaxia's retail application, a Web site lets customers view automobile accessories and submit orders, and an application lets sales representatives enter order data for customers who have telephoned the company. User interfaces are implemented using various building blocks. Some building blocks include forms, Web pages, controls, or any other technology to render and format data for presentation on the UI. The controls may be related to the formatting UI or with presenting and manipulating data on the UI. The user interface components can be characterized as follows:

- *Generic native controls*: These are screen elements that the operating or the execution environment of the client makes available to the UI. Some controls are available across most client environments, although they may differ in their internal name, some attributes, and display characteristics. Label, text box, list box, radio button, check box, push button, and table are a few examples of such controls.

- *Proprietary native controls*: These controls are available for use from the operating or the execution environment but may not be available on all platforms. Spinners, sliders, and SWING extensions in VisualCafe are a couple of examples of such controls.

- *Widgets or custom controls*: These are either a complex collection of existing native controls or new controls. These often address specific presentation needs and may have prepackaged functionality. Grid, tree, and data table are examples of such controls.

- *Native screens*: These are screens that most operating or execution environments make available for the application to use. File Open and File Save are examples of such components.

- *Custom screens*: These are screens or a collection of screens created with prepackaged functionality. Wizards, shopping carts, and catalogues are some examples of such components.

The choice of the appropriate control or component and its presentation in a layout on the UI are critical to the overall usability and success of the solution. The software industry has struggled for several decades to address this issue and create a model and patterns that can define and describe this. Since the appropriate choice of the control depends upon the context, it becomes difficult to capture this information in one single manner. User Interface Markup Language (UIML) is one among a few initiatives that attempt to capture the display or the UI generation attributes in a UML-like meta language.

> For more information on User Interface Markup Language (UIML), see *www.uiml.org*.

User Interface Process Components

The user process component typically captures the controller-related information in the MVC paradigm. The responsibility of the controller includes, but is not limited to, housekeeping and session tracking: logging the request, managing session and local variables, tracking the user, keeping session data, and managing the connection. The controller knows what can be done to the model and what user gestures are required to get those things done. Controllers may be generalized to work at three levels:

- *Controllers that work on widgets or portions of the screen.* For example, one such controller would understand the dragging of the slider to increase or decrease the volume in a media player application. The position of the slider translates to the commands to the model to reflect the new volume level. Another controller might accept keyboard commands. Another might allow the user to change the volume by speaking to a speech-enabled application. Many controllers can manipulate the same model, as there are many views that display the model.

- *Controllers that work on screens or a group of screens.* For example, in Canaxia's retail application, customers could view the automobile accessories by first selecting an appropriate category from a list of available product categories and then selecting an individual product in the chosen category to view its details.

- *Controllers that work on a predefined process.* In many cases, a user interaction with the system follows a predictable process. In the Canaxia retail application example, when the user makes a purchase, the interaction follows a predictable process of gathering data from the user, in which the user first supplies details of the products to be purchased, then provides payment details, and then enters delivery details.

In some of the previous examples, the controller is dynamically generated from the information contained in the model. To help synchronize and orchestrate these user interactions and the work flow, it can be useful to drive the process using separate user process components. By doing this, the process flow and state management logic are not hard-coded in the user interface elements themselves, and the same basic user interaction can be reused in multiple user interfaces.

Application Adaptor Components

When the presentation tier needs to communicate with the business and data component, functionality must be provided in some code to manage the semantics of communicating with that particular component. These components require interfaces that support the communication (message-based communication, formats, protocols, security, exceptions, and so on) required by the different consumers.

Resource Components

Security, operational management, communication, caching, and device manager are a few examples of resources that the presentation tier may create and share with other components. The application also will use components to perform exception management, to authorize users to perform certain tasks, to communicate with other components/applications, for data persistence, and to map UI components to a particular client/device platform.

Business Tier Components

After the required data are collected and the model updated, the data can be used to perform a business process. For example, Canaxia's retail system would calculate the total value of the order, validate the credit card details, process the credit card payment, and arrange delivery of the goods. In this application, you would need to implement the functionality that calculates the total price of the goods ordered and adds the appropriate delivery charge. Business components implement the business logic of the application.

Regardless of whether a business process consists of a single step or an orchestrated work flow, the application will probably require components that implement business rules and perform business tasks. Additionally, the business logic function may take an indeterminate amount of time to complete, so the required tasks and the data required to perform them will have to be managed.

Data Tier Components

In a multi-tier architecture, the presentation tier is not expected to interact directly with the data tiers; rather, it needs the data that mirror the real needs of the users. For example, in the Canaxia retail application, the presentation tier needs product data from a database to display product details to the user, and it needs to insert order details into the database when a user places an order. The data are used to represent real-world business entities, such as products or orders.

The logic necessary to access data is abstracted into a separate layer of data access logic components. Doing so centralizes data access functionality and makes it easier to configure and maintain. Most applications require data to be passed between components.

When designing the presentation tier in a multi-tier architecture, the following recommendations should be considered:

- Analyze the user needs and plan for supporting appropriate client access options for the application. For example, Canaxia's retail application for scheduling delivery that is used by the back-office personnel may not require access via a mobile device. On the other hand, it is useful to have an application for notification on a cell phone when the automobile is ready for delivery or one that provides customers with the ability to query using SMS (Short Message Service) in Asia and the WAP (Wireless Access Protocol) browser in Europe to find the state of readiness of the automobile from a Canaxia service station.

- Identify the kinds of user interface components you will need, keeping in mind the client access paradigms that need to be supported. For example, if both Web site and cell phone access need to be provided, a separate UI control or component needs to be mapped for each target platform based upon device capabilities.

General Design Recommendations

- Determine the scope of internationalization and co-branding early. The static text and the look and feel of the UI may need to change to support such features. In most cases, keeping the content and the display attributes separate in the individual UI components may be sufficient. Either as a part of the build process or at run-time, the content and display attributes can be packaged together in the UI to create the desired internationalized and co-branded applications.

- Appropriate controllers must be chosen as part of the target platform selection. In a Web-based application, a one-screen-long input form may be sufficient to capture the requisite information and one submit button may be necessary to post the information back to the application. However, in a smaller WAP-enabled device, it may be necessary to split the form into several screen-long forms, the submit trigger may post smaller chunks of data, and the final submit may post all the data to the application, making the device specificity transparent to the application.

- Keep code that enforces policies (such as security, operational management, and communication restrictions) abstracted as much as possible from the application business logic. Try to rely on attributes, APIs, or utility components that provide single-line-of-code access to functionality related to the policies, such as publishing exceptions, authorizing users, and so on.

- Determine at the outset what kind of layering (tiers) you want to enforce. In a strict layering system, components in the presentation tier cannot call components in the data tiers; they always call components in the business logic tiers. In some cases, it may be appropriate for the presentation tier to call the data tiers directly so that the change in the model can immediately reflect on the UI. This reduces the intermediate layer that only acts as a pass-through layer. Monitoring-type applications are typically good candidates when relaxed layering may be appropriate.

Designing the Presentation Tier

The presentation layer contains the components required to enable user interaction with the application. The most simple presentation layers contain user interface components, such as SWING for JAVA clients. For more complex user interactions, you can design user process components to control the different user interface elements and the user interaction. User process components are especially useful when the user interaction follows a predictable flow of steps, such as when a wizard is used to accomplish a task.

In the case of the Canaxia retail application, several user interfaces are required: one for the e-commerce Web site that the customers use, another for the fat-client–based applications that the sales representatives use, another that is document based (such as Microsoft Excel) that the retail clerk uses to update bulk orders, and yet that is cell-phone–based to buy the merchandise. Figure 9–3 illustrates the use of multiple client access to the same application.

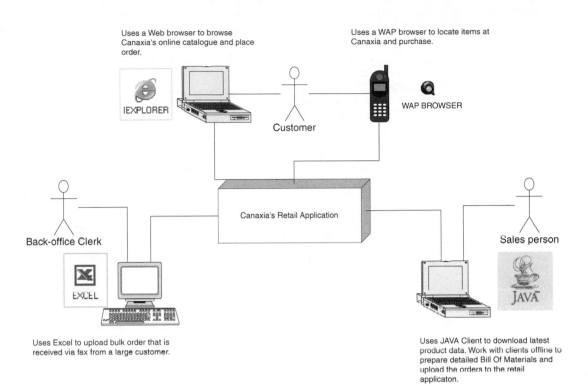

Uses a Web browser to browse Canaxia's online catalogue and place order.

Uses a WAP browser to locate items at Canaxia and purchase.

IEXPLORER

Customer

WAP BROWSER

Back-office Clerk

Canaxia's Retail Application

Sales person

EXCEL

JAVA

Uses Excel to upload bulk order that is received via fax from a large customer.

Uses JAVA Client to download latest product data. Work with clients offline to prepare detailed Bill Of Materials and upload the orders to the retail applicaton.

Figure 9–3
The Canaxia retail application.

All users may perform some common tasks through these user interfaces. For example, they may view the available product details, add products to an order, and specify payment details as part of the purchase process. This process can be abstracted in a separate user process component to make the application easier to maintain. In this section, we explore each of the client environments and understand the design considerations behind each. We also explore how the presentation tier needs to provide the architectural framework for providing access to different clients without affecting the underlying application.

Designing User Interface Components

You can implement user interfaces in many ways. As illustrated in Figure 9–3, the Canaxia retail application example requires a Web-based user interface, a fat-client–based user interface, a document-based interface, and a cell-phone–based interface. Other kinds of user interfaces, such as voice rendering, can possibly be included in the mix. User interface components manage interaction with the user. They display data to the user, acquire data from the user, and interpret events that the user raises to act on business data, to change the state of the user interface, or to help with progress in the desired task.

Presentation Tier
Architecture

189

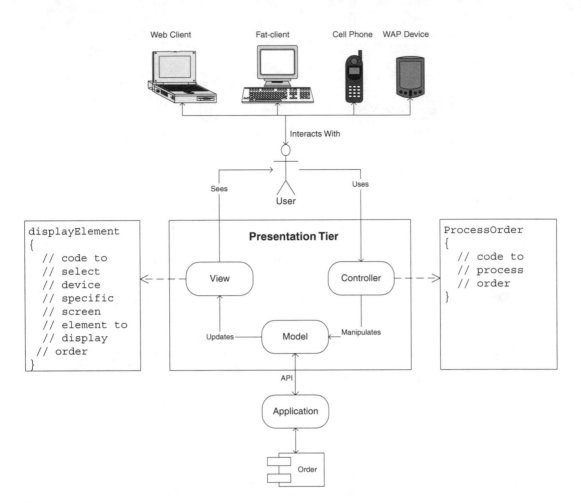

Figure 9–4
User interface design.

User interfaces usually consist of a number of screen elements or a form that displays data and accepts user input. For example, a fat-client–based application could contain a data-grid control displaying a list of product categories and a command button control to indicate that the user wants to view the products in the selected category. When a user interacts with a user interface element, an event is raised that calls code in a controller function. The controller function, in turn, calls business components, data access logic components, or user process components to implement the desired action and retrieve any necessary data to be displayed. The controller function then updates the user interface elements appropriately.

The user interface screen elements may map themselves to different and yet similar controls that are appropriate for different target platform or technologies. For example, the order list may be displayed in a data table in the Web application, as a data grid in the fat-client, as a spreadsheet in the document client, and as a bulleted list in the cell phone. Figure 9–4 shows the design of a user interface.

User interface components must contain all the information necessary to create and process the view and may also include methods for interacting with the controller and model functions. Definition of the following may be required to create a user interface component:

- Acquire and display data.
- Recognize and interpret events triggered by both users and the system.
- Filter actions based upon the context.
- Prevent triggering transactions outside the specified events.
- Validate user inputs.
- Maintain reference of the state with the controller.
- Maintain reference of the state with the model and update display when the model changes.
- Implement local caching.
- Implement features for pagination when dealing with long lists.
- Implement functions that create and interact with variables.
- Implement interaction with utility classes to provide functions such as undo, clipboard, and business functions (e.g., add total).
- Can encapsulate both the view and the controller functionality.

Since the users of the system interact and manipulate the interface components directly, it is critical that they support the necessary usability attributes. Following are some user-interaction and display-related design considerations:

- Interaction with the component is easy to understand.
- Visual assistance is available as necessary to the user.
- Erroneous inputs are prevented at an element level.
- Mandatory and valid data input are validated.
- Mapping among data elements is contained in the model with user-friendly terms appropriate for display.
- Values for display (such as date, currency, and other formatting) are formatted.
- Any localization work on the rendered data (for example, using resource strings to display column headers in a grid in the appropriate language for the user's locale) is performed.
- Users are provided with status information—by indicating, for example, when an application is working in "disconnected" or "connected" mode.
- Appearance of the application is customized according to user preferences or the kind of client device used.

Internet Browser User Interfaces

Canaxia's retail application requires a Web-based user interface so that customers can browse the catalogue and place orders via the Internet.

Web-based user interfaces allow for standards-based user interfaces across many devices (such as Internet browsers, WAP browsers on cell phones, and PDAs) and platforms (such as Microsoft Windows, Solaris, Linux, and Macintosh). This is very useful for extending the reach to the maximum within Canaxia's customer base.

Most user interfaces in Web-based applications require a dynamic page creation technology, such as ASP.NET, JSP, Cold Fusion, and so on. Even within the dynamic page creation, the applications can be grouped into two major categories:

- *Template-based pages*. The screen consists of a fixed layout of the user interface components. For example, the order screen has a fixed layout in which the order header presents the bill to, ship to, and sold to information, which is followed by the list of the products ordered, which is followed by pricing details. Individual orders may contain different information, but all follow the same structure or template.

- *Rule-based pages*. The screen is created based upon rules and previous user input. For example, a product locator feature solicits user input and then guides users through a series of screens, with each screen filtering the product choices progressively. Since the product attributes are large—especially when combined with user preferences and their relationships with other products—the choices quickly multiply and make it difficult to capture all possible combinations in any template-based pages. In such cases, the complete user interface definition is maintained in a rules set that is applied as users interact with the system to create the dynamic rule-based pages.

When you need to implement an application for a browser, you need to use several rich features offered by the technology of choice. The reason to move intelligence to the browser in a Web-based application is to reduce the to-and fro-traffic between the browser and the Web server. This is usually done by moving some processing to the browser—be it validation or parsing of the dynamic page (as in XML/XSLT, Extensible Markup Language/Extensible Stylesheet Language Transformation, in some recent browsers) or using DHTML (Dynamic Hyper Text Markup Language) to increase object manipulation in the browser's DOM (Domain Object Model). Following are some design considerations while architecting the browser application:

- Implementation of a validation framework is generally done using JavaScript and DHTML at the browser. In general, two types of validation are used for entered information. Field validation is the domain of the UI layer. It ensures that you entered a valid date, spelled the group message correctly, selected an employee only from the combo box, and so on. Data validation, on the other hand, is the domain of the business layer. It ensures that you didn't try to assign someone to a category for which they are unqualified or to ship a thousand widgets to a company that only uses sprockets (Burrows 2000). For performance and other reasons, you may wish at times to move some data validation to the client, but you must remember that the primary responsibility of this function still remains in the business logic tiers. Sometimes a JavaScript object is dynamically created and sent to the browser when the business logic object is accessed in the business tiers. This allows you to maintain the business logic in one place and to move intelligence to the client.

- With the increase in adoption of DHTML, browser-based applications are witnessing richer GUI. The basic HTML-form objects are not sufficient to create the necessary experience. Web application authors are creating custom controls. If you are creating Web user controls, expose only the public properties and methods that you actually need. This improves maintainability. Implement your controller functions as separate functions that will be deployed with your Web pages.

- Use a component to view state, to store page-specific state, and keep session and application state for data with a wider scope. This approach makes it easier to maintain and improves scalability. Your controller functions should invoke the actions on a user process component to guide the user through the current task, rather than redirecting the user directly to the page.

- Implement a custom error page and a global exception handler. This provides you with a catchall exception function that prevents the user from seeing unfriendly pages in case of a problem.

Mobile Device User Interfaces

With the increasing popularity of handheld PCs, Wireless Application Protocol (WAP) phones, and iMode devices, Canaxia recently opened access to the retail application to such devices. In concept, Canaxia adopted a popular WAP network architecture with the intention to reuse as much of the existing browser-based solution as possible.

In general, a user interface for a mobile device needs to be able to display information on a much smaller screen than can other common applications, and it must offer acceptable usability for the devices being targeted. Because user interaction can be awkward on many mobile devices, particularly mobile phones, you should design your mobile user interfaces with minimal data input requirements.

A common strategy is to combine the use of mobile devices with a fat-client or a browser-based application. The user can preregister data through the fat-client or the browser-based application and then select that data when using the mobile client. For example, in Canaxia's retail application, users register credit card details through the Web site, so that a preregistered credit card can be selected from a list when orders are placed from a mobile device.

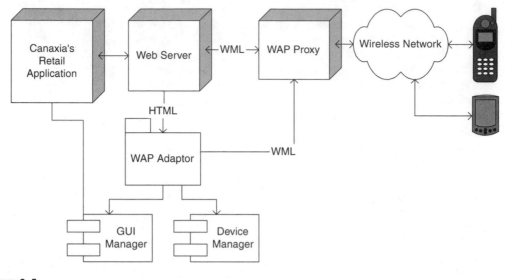

Figure 9–5
Mobile access architecture.

Figure 9–5 illustrates the mobile access architecture. This architecture uses the current browser-based GUI definition to extend it to the mobile devices. In the architecture, the GUI manager and the device manager are the two key presentation tier components responsible for creating the user interface for the mobile devices. The former component has the responsibility for mapping the screen-specific entities and information from the browser-based GUI to the display possibilities of the mobile device and the latter informing it about the device capabilities so that it can appropriately package the GUI code.

Given the limitations of the mobile devices, the mobile presentation tier strategy offers two basic choices:

- Create a new GUI manager component for mobile devices. This approach has the maintenance overhead of changing the GUI manager code when the basic application GUI needs to change and when a new device type is introduced.

- Adopt model-driven architecture for creating a platform-independent model for the complete presentation tier code. User Interface Markup Language (UIML) is an emerging language that captures the complete user interface definition, using a UML-derived notation. The GUI code is generated (potentially dynamically) and deployed from the model based upon the device profile and the technology choices.

Fat-client User Interfaces

There are three main reasons for adopting a fat-client user interface. You may wish to provide a persistent connection with the back-end system, to provide users with options of doing a large chunk of work in the offline mode (locally on their computers), or to provide a rich user interaction. With fat-client user interfaces, the user interface components are typically installed on the user's local computer. This leads to maintenance overheads, as the application needs to be reinstalled with every change to the client. The following deployment strategies have become popular recently:

- Download the application from a central server and check for newer versions when the users log on. Install patches and version upgrades in this manner. This may follow a pull paradigm in which the software is downloaded on explicit user request or a push paradigm where the software is downloaded automatically when the user is online.

- Provide architecture for the client, in two parts, in which the part that needs to change infrequently is installed on the user's local computer and the part that can change frequently is downloaded when the user connects to the central server.

- In download on demand, another option, the software is down-loaded and installed only for users who need that functionality and when they need it.

The technology choice for authoring the fat-client is based upon the requirement for deploying the software. Some technologies, such as JAVA, make it possible to create the application user interfaces that can run on any operating system. Others, such as Microsoft Windows, XMotif, and SystemX user interfaces can only run in a certain environment. They can, however, take advantage of a wide range of state management and persistence options and can access local processing power of the native operating system and the computer. Following are the four main types of fat-client user interfaces:

- In a *full-blown fat-client user interface*, all the client-side code is con-tained and installed on the user's local computer. This makes it possible to use the processing power of the user's computer to cre-ate the display. A richer interface and a highly interactive user inter-face can be offered in this paradigm. This may tie you to a client platform, and the application needs to be deployed to the users (even if the application is deployed by downloading it over an HTTP connection).

- You can use *additional embedded* HTML in your fat-client applications. Embedded HTML allows for greater run-time flexibility (because the HTML may be loaded from external resources or even a data-base in connected scenarios) and user customization.

- Embed *a fat-client within an* HTML *page*. This is done frequently using applets in the Java paradigm, ActiveX in the Microsoft paradigm, or third-party plug-ins, such as Macromedia Flash. Such plug-ins can provide an interface as rich as the full-blown fat-client, but they require a browser and some locally and successfully installed run-time environment on the user's local computer.

- Extend an existing application's features by *using your application as a plug-in*. This allows you to use all the existing framework of the native application.

Key design considerations for a fat-client include the following:

- *Maintain state information across several concurrent displays.* Changing the state in one instance can automatically change the display in another window. This is particularly useful if one is working with multiple views of the same data source and it is accomplished by data binding to keep the views synchronized.

- *Design the user interface components to promote reuse.* The reuse can happen at the individual screen or screen element level, at a set of screens that may include the dependent relationships of one parent screen with the child screens level, and at the set of screens that orchestrate a user-interface process level.

- *Implement frameworks for client-side validation and for creating user-friendly nomenclature for display to the users.*

- If you are creating custom user controls, *expose only the public properties and methods that you actually need.* This improves maintainability. Implement your controller functions as separate functions that will be deployed with your client.

- *Use a component to view state, to store screen-specific state, and to keep session and application state for data with a wider scope.* This approach makes it easier to maintain and improves scalability. Your controller functions should invoke the actions on a user process component to guide the user through the current task rather than redirecting the user to the page directly.

- *Implement a custom error page and a global exception handler.* This provides you with a catchall exception function that prevents the user from seeing unfriendly pages in case of a problem.

Document-Based User Interfaces

As Canaxia demonstrates, some users not only are familiar with document-based tools but also find them easy to use. In the retail example, the back-office clerk works with a wide variety of Excel documents, and it is convenient for them to prepare orders and then upload them to the retail application for further processing. Users often are more comfortable working with documents that reflect their real lives than they are with the form-based user interface provided by an application. For example, the accounting world relies extensively on spreadsheet-based applications such as Microsoft Excel, and most interaction among people is via word-processed documents, such as those produced in Microsoft Word. You may also need solutions that require interaction with documents that are created and often maintained outside your application. Consider the following document-based solutions:

- *Reporting data.* Your application (Windows- or Web-based) may provide users with a feature that lets them see data in a document of the appropriate type—for example, showing invoice data as a Word document or a price list as an Excel spreadsheet. Additionally, these documents may require displaying information collected from various others—for example, address for ship-to information that is maintained in your customer relationship management (CRM) system.

- *Gathering data.* You could let sales representatives enter purchase information for telephone customers in Excel spreadsheets to create a customer order document and then submit the document to your business process. Now the Excel spreadsheet may contain macros that perform several application functions, such as validations, calculations, and formatting that could potentially reduce processing overheads from your applications.

- *Synchronized data.* Sometimes these documents have direct connectivity with your back-end systems and provide a two-way interaction and manipulation of the model from the context of the document.

Designing User Interface Process Components

As presented previously in this chapter, user interface process components are the other key presentation tier piece that is responsible for providing the interaction to your application. Whether you are providing users the ability to interact with screen elements or widgets, with a complete screen, or with a collection of screens that are connected in some logical way, this piece of functionality is referred to as the controller (in the MVC paradigm, also discussed previously in this chapter). The user interface process component is typically implemented as a separate JAVA, .NET, or similar class. Sometimes this component may be bundled with the user interface components, but it is usually a good practice to keep it separate.

Sometimes the process component is dynamically generated from the model. This is useful when this component is providing a business process–like functionality, spans several user interfaces—such as those needed by different devices, or needs to generate a dynamic application interaction paradigm. For example, in the Canaxia retail application, users are required to enter product details, view the total price, enter payment details, and enter delivery address information. This process involves displaying and accepting input from a number of user interface elements, and the state for the process (which products have been ordered, the credit card details, and so on) must be maintained between each transition from one step in the process to another. To help coordinate the user process and handle the state management required when displaying multiple user interface pages or forms, you can create user process components. (*Note:* Implementing a user interaction with user process components is not a trivial task.)

The user interface component typically provides an interface to trigger the process component. For example, the Show Order button can trigger the controller component to interact with the model to create a view for displaying the list of products within the order. To increase the reusability of the component, it is advisable not to index a screen directly but to use the metadata to reference the display. Doing this will, as in the preceding example, allow reuse of the same component for displaying the list of products from

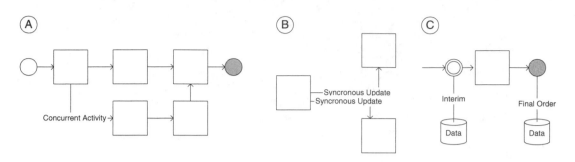

Figure 9–6
User interface process components.

the invoice screen. Designing user process components from multiple user interfaces will result in a more complex implementation and will isolate device-specific issues.

Separating the user interaction functionality into user interface and user interface process components allows the long-running user interaction state to be more easily persisted, thus allowing a user interaction to be abandoned and resumed, possibly even using a different user interface. For example, a customer could add some items to a shopping cart using the Web-based user interface and later call a sales representative to complete the order using the fat-client interface.

An unstructured approach to designing user interface logic may result in undesirable situations as the size of the application grows or new requirements are introduced. If you need to add a specific user interface for a given device, you may need to redesign the data flow and control logic. Partitioning the user interaction flow from the activities of rendering data and gathering data from the user can increase your application's maintainability and provide a clean design to which you can easily add seemingly complex features, such as support for offline work.

Let us use the Canaxia retail application example to illustrate the three key user interface design issues that are resolved by the process component. Figure 9–6 illustrates the three interaction issues:

- *Handling concurrent user activities.* Some applications may allow users to perform multiple tasks simultaneously by making more than one user interface element available. For example, a Windows-based application may display multiple forms, or a Web application may open a second browser window. User process components simplify the state management of multiple ongoing processes by encapsulating all the state needed for the process in a single component. You can map each user interface element to a particular instance of the user process by incorporating a custom process identifier into your design.

- *Using multiple panes for one activity.* If multiple windows or panes are used in a particular user activity, it is important to keep them synchronized. In a Web application, a user interface usually displays a set of elements on the same page (which may include frames) for a given user activity. However, in rich client applications, you may actually have many nonmodal windows affecting just one particular process. For example, you may have a product category selector window floating in your application that lets you specify a particular category, in which the products will be displayed in another window. User process components help you to implement this kind of user interface by centralizing the state for all windows in a single location. You can further simplify synchronization across multiple user interface elements by using data bindable formats for state data.

- *Isolating long-running user activities from business-related state.* Some user processes can be paused and resumed later. The intermediate state of the user process should generally be stored separately from the application's business data. For example, a user could specify some of the information required to place an order and then resume the checkout process at a later time. The pending order data should be persisted separately from the data relating to completed orders, allowing you to perform business operations on completed order data (for example, counting the number of orders placed in the current month) without having to implement complex filtering rules to avoid operating on incomplete orders.

User activities, just like business processes, may have a time-out specified, when the activity has to be cancelled and the right compensatory actions should be taken on the business process. You can design your user process components to be serializable or to store states separately from the application's business data.

Separating User Process from User Interface

To separate a user process from the user interface, use the following steps:

1. Identify the business process or processes that the user interface process will help to accomplish. Identify how the user sees this as a task (you can usually do this by consulting the sequence diagrams you created as part of your requirements analysis).

2. Identify the data needed by the business processes. The user process must submit this data when necessary.

3. Identify any additional state you will need to maintain throughout the user activity to assist rendering and data capture in the user interface.

4. Design the visual flow of the user process and the way each user interface element receives or gives control flow. You must also implement code to map a particular user interface session to the related user process:

   o A Web UI will have to obtain the information about the current user process by getting a reference from the session object or another storage medium, such as a database. You will need this reference in event handlers for the controls on your Web page.

○ Your windows or controls must refer to the current user process component. You can keep this reference in a member variable. However, you should not keep it in a global variable because, if you do, composing user interfaces will become very complicated as your application user interface grows.

User Process Component Functionality

User process components include the following:

- Provide a simple way to combine user interface elements into user interaction flows without requiring you to redevelop data flow and control logic.
- Separate the conceptual user interaction flow from the implementation or device where it occurs.
- Encapsulate how exceptions may affect the user process flow.
- Track the current state of the user interaction.
- Do not start or participate in transactions. They keep internal data related to application business logic and their internal state, persisting the data as required.
- Maintain an internal business-related state, usually holding on to one or more business entities that are affected by the user interaction. You may keep multiple entities in private variables or in an internal array or appropriate collection type.
- May provide a "save and continue later" feature by which a particular user interaction may be restarted in another session. You may implement this functionality by saving the internal state of the user process component in some persistent form and providing the user with a way to continue a particular activity later. You can create a custom task manager utility component to control the current activation state of the process.

The user process state may be stored in one of the following places:

- If the user process can be continued from other devices or computers, you must store it centrally, such as in a database.
- If you are running in a disconnected environment, you must store the user process state locally on the user device.
- If your user interface process is running in a Web farm, you must store any required state on a central server so that it can be continued from any server in the farm.
- The internal state may be initialized by calling a business process component or data access logic components.
- Typically, the user process state will not be stored as enterprise services components. The only reason to do so would be to use the enterprise services role-based authorization capabilities.
- The user process may be started by a custom utility component that manages the menus in your application.

General Recommendations for User Process Components

When designing user process components, consider the following recommendations:

- Decide whether you need to manage user processes as components that are separate from your user interface implementation. Separate user processes are most needed in applications with a high number of user interface dialog boxes or in applications in which the user processes may be subject to customization and may benefit from a plug-in approach.

- Choose where to store the state of the user process. If the process is running in a connected fashion, store interim state for long-running processes in a central database; in disconnected scenarios, store it in local XML files, isolated storage, or local databases. If the process is not long running and does not need to be recovered if a problem occurs, you should persist the state in memory. For user interfaces built for rich clients, you may want to keep the state in memory. For Web applications, you may choose to store the user process state in the session object.

- Design your user process components so that they may be serialized. This will help you implement any persistence scheme.

- Include exception handling in user process components and propagate exceptions to the user interface. Exceptions that are thrown by the user process components should be caught by user interface components and published.

Accessing Data Access Logic Components from the UI

Some applications' user interfaces need to render data that are readily available as queries exposed by data access logic components. Regardless of whether or not your user interface components invoke data access logic components directly, you should not mix data access logic with business processing logic.

Accessing data access logic components directly from your UI may seem to contradict the layering concept. However, it is useful in this case to adopt the perspective of your application as one homogenous service—you call it, and it's up to it to decide what internal components are best suited to respond to a request.

You should allow direct data access logic component access to user interface components in the following instances:

- You are willing to tightly couple data access methods and schemas with user interface semantics. This coupling requires joint maintenance of user interface changes and schema changes.

- Your physical deployment places data access logic components and user interface components together, allowing you to get data in streaming formats from data access logic components that can be bound directly to the output of the user interfaces for performance. If you deploy data access and business process logic on different servers, you cannot take advantage of this capability. From an operational perspective, allowing direct access to the data access logic components to take advantage of streaming capabilities means that you must provide access to the database from where the data access logic components are deployed—possibly including access through firewall ports.

Network Connectivity and Offline Applications

In many cases, your application will require support for offline operations when network connectivity is unavailable. For example, many mobile applications, including rich clients for pocket PC or table PC devices, must be functional when the user is disconnected from the corporate network. Offline applications must rely on local data and user process state to perform their work. When designing offline applications, adhere to the following general guidelines. The online and offline status should be displayed to the user. This is usually done in status bars or title bars or with visual cues around user interface elements that require a connection to the server. The development of most of the application user interface should be reusable, with little or no modification needed to support offline scenarios. While offline, your application will not have the following:

- Access to online data returned by data access logic components.
- The ability to invoke business processes synchronously. As a result, the application will not know whether the call succeeded or will not be able to use any returned data.

If your application does not implement a fully message-based interface to your servers but relies on synchronously acquiring data and knowing the results of business processes (as most of today's applications do), you should do the following to provide the illusion of connectivity:

- Implement a local cache for read-only reference data that relates to the user's activities. You can then implement an offline data access logic component that implements exactly the same queries as your server-side data access logic components but accesses local storage.
- Implement an offline business component that has the same interface as your business components but takes the submitted data and places them in a store-and-forward, reliable messaging system such as message queuing. This offline component may then return nothing or a preset value to its caller.
- Implement UI functionality that provides a way to inspect the business action outbox and possibly to delete messages in it. If message queuing is used to queue offline messages, you must set the correct permissions on the queue to do this from your application.
- Design your application's transactions to accommodate message-based UI interactions. You will have to take extra care to manage

optimistic locking and the results of transactions based on stale data. A common technique for performing updates is to submit both the old and new data and to let the related business process or data access logic component eventually resolve any conflicts. For business processes, the submission may include critical reference data that the business logic uses to decide whether or not to let the data through. For example, you can include product prices alongside product IDs and quantities when submitting an order.

Conclusion

The presentation tier, being the most visible part of any system, is often considered the system by the users. It is a key tier in multi-tiered software architecture and distributed computing. This tier is responsible for packaging the data for display to users and for providing users with options for interacting with the system. This tier is becoming increasingly complex and is the cause for most project overruns and user adoption issues.

The presentation tier contains the client code (primary presentation tier) that executes on the user's local computer and the code that executes on the server (secondary presentation tier). Model–View–Controller (MVC) is an important design pattern for the presentation tier. The view (UI display component) and the controller (user interface process component) functions are the primary presentation tier responsibility.

The presentation tier is the key tier for supporting some of the following requirements:

- Internationalization and localization
- Personalization and co-branding
- Support for multiple device and access points
- Support for local business processes and data presentation
- Support for multiple technologies
- Potentially exposure of the applications to other systems as services

chapter 10

Usability and
User Experience

Computers make it easier to do a lot of things, but most of the things they make it easier to do don't need to be done.

Andy Rooney (1919–)

Architecture with the attribute of usability has become very popular in recent years, as well as accepted—particularly since the advent of the Internet. Still, it has been difficult to implement its practice within organizations. Perspectives on usability are often oppositional. Some people consider usability from a product-oriented, bottom-up perspective that identifies usability with ease of use. Others favor a broader top-down approach in which usability is interpreted as the ability to use a system for its intended purpose (Bevan 1995). The main problem with equating usability with ease of use is that one may come up with a product that is usable but is not useful. This contradiction is absent in the latter approach.

Usability has been interpreted by many and in differing ways. Some try to quantify it as a precise science, and others think of it as subjective art form. Although developers of code need to know specific attributes and are willing to incorporate them if that will increase the product's usability, presence or absence of predefined attributes cannot ensure usability, as it is usually impossible to know how users will react to a system unless they actually use it.

While industry and thought leaders across the globe are struggling to define usability, Canaxia—like many organizations—is going through its own usability transition. Nigel Longfellow, Canaxia's chief usability architect, has been leading the crusade within the organization for several months. Usability is now a much talked-about term within the organization. When Nigel first joined Canaxia's architecture team, he had very quickly realized the following:

- Unless usability was mentioned as an objective criterion in the requirement specification, little incentive would exist for putting resources into usability design.

- Measuring against usability objectives provides a means for judging how much additional work on usability is required to reach the objectives.

Early on, Nigel had adopted the ISO 9241–11 definition of usability that states, "Usability is the extent to which a product can be used by specified users to achieve specified goals with effectiveness, efficiency, and satisfaction in a specified context of use." Using this definition, Nigel had successfully set up a usability program within Canaxia. Different project teams that consulted on a wide variety of issues now frequently called upon Nigel. Nigel has had to fight many battles, though, including the following barriers:

- Usability was not defined in actionable terms. Very often, people mentioned that the GUI should be easy to use, but little else was defined.
- The project plans did not reflect usability activities or dependencies with other project activities.
- Customers, client managers, and even Canaxia's product management and marketing staff used to speak for users in their absence. At the extreme, some managers felt that it would raise product expectations if users were involved in application development activities.
- Feature lists drove application development, with more emphasis on making the feature work than on making it usable. Very often the team was more excited about the new technology to be used than about realizing the project goal.

Although a complete discussion of organizational barriers, and strategies for countering them, is beyond the scope of this book, this chapter offers some perspective on the five-point program that Nigel put in place, which helped him gain the acceptance for usability within Canaxia. This discussion will help you implement usability within your organization. Implementing usability within the organization still presents several challenges, including the following:

- *Spend development budget on each feature based upon its value to users.* A phase in the requirements cycle will help you evaluate the usefulness and scope of each new feature to be implemented. Very often this helps prioritize features to be developed and prevents overdesigning of less frequently used features.
- *Ensure participation from all development members.* This helps gain a common understanding context of use. Developer-level decisions will help attain the overall project goals.
- *Conduct usability tests often and report cost-benefit in financial terms.* This provides management with insight into the real value of the usability activities. (Cost-benefit is discussed elsewhere in this chapter in more detail.)
- *Make the project lead responsible for achieving usability objectives.* This helps create ownership within the project team rather than reliance upon an external person coming in to promote usability.

- *Share knowledge within the development teams.* Nigel created several training programs, monthly reports on usability accomplishments, and a discussion database for identifying and discussing usability and user interface issues. Nigel was also instrumental in creating a library of reusable UI components that extended the efforts of the reusability teams. He also published UI design standards and guidelines. In addition to these, Nigel facilitated a usability roundtable where development teams and management sat together to discuss successes and barriers to usability adoption within the organization.

Everything that Nigel did is not applicable to all organizations. An ongoing managed program is important for maintaining the organization's focus on usability. Any program you may create will benefit from recording usability issues and measuring and reporting usability attributes.

Let us further examine the keywords used in the following meaning-packed definition of usability, as well as the essence of those words: "Usability is the extent to which a product can be used by specified users to achieve specified goals with effectiveness, efficiency, and satisfaction in a specified context of use."

Understanding Usability

- *Specified users.* No product can be designed to suit everybody. At the outset of design, it is critical that the key user groups be identified. A software system can be optimized for one or two user groups, but any attempt to design it for more groups is a guarantee of failure.
- *Specified goals:* The key goals of each user group must be documented. Note that the user goal is different from the business or technical goals. For example, a data-entry application's business goal is to eliminate paper records and reduce maintenance cost. A potential technical goal could be to use the latest technology. The users' goal is to be able to enter an acceptable number of records with as few errors as possible.
- *Effectiveness:* Effectiveness is a measure of the use of a system in relation to the accuracy and completeness achieved by meeting the users' goals and subgoals. For example, the measure of the task effectiveness of the data-entry operator is calculated as the percentage of two attributes: the number of records entered and the quality (mistakes, formatting, and so on) of records entered.
- *Efficiency:* Efficiency is the measure of effectiveness at the rate of resource utilization. This is a valuable economic indicator. Continuing our example, when time is unlimited all the records can be entered with 100 percent effectiveness, but resources are always a constraint. Regardless, records need to be entered in a finite amount of time. In our example, the efficiency is calculated as the ratio of the effectiveness and the time taken to enter the records.
- *Satisfaction:* Satisfaction includes comfort and acceptability of use. Comfort refers to users' overall psychological and emotional responses to system use (whether users feel good, warm, and pleased or tense and uncomfortable). Acceptability of use may

measure either overall attitude toward the system or the user's perception of specific aspects, such as whether or not users feel the system supports the way they carry out their tasks, whether or not they feel in command of the system, and whether or not the system is helpful and easy to learn. If satisfaction is low while efficiency is high, it is likely that the users' goals do not match the goals selected for the measurement of efficiency.

- *Specified context of use*: Specified context of use is the technical, physical, social, and organizational environments in which users interact with the system.

The ISO 9241–11 definition of usability: "Usability is the extent to which a product can be used by specified users to achieve specified goals with effectiveness, efficiency, and satisfaction in a specified context of use."

Usability is the key quality objective of any system. Like other quality attributes of the system, it cannot be easily retrofitted as an afterthought. Usability is a systemic attribute and begins with project goal setting and system requirements gatherings. Clearly, if usability requirements are not adequately captured up front, the cost of introducing them, either by choice or by user demands, may be severe and at times prohibitive.

The terms that have been used to define usability are many and include usability design engineering, user-centered design, human-centered design, usage-centered design, human–computer interaction, user experience, and customer experience. Most of these terms strive to create their own niches, thereby hoping to increase their acceptance in organizational practice. Though it is beyond the scope of this book to provide a detailed view of the different practices, in this chapter we present key concepts from the different practices to create an overall view of usability practices.

User Experience Components

Although users of some systems may have preconceived impressions of perceived usability based upon marketing and other stimuli, users performing real-life tasks base the usability of systems upon the real-life use. Nevertheless, the impact on the system adoption stimuli may be significant. However, we will not consider them as they are only external factors and do not directly affect the usability.

To achieve the overall usability of the system, we must understand the physical user interfaces of the system that users may interact with while doing their tasks. Focusing on a few of the interfaces may lead to poor usability overall. Following are some of the user interfaces. Although the complete list of all types of user interfaces is huge, the types can be categorized broadly into the following areas:

- *Web-Based User Interface* (WUI): An Internet Web browser is used for displaying the user interface of the system. The browser is used to connect to the server to get the (latest) user interface and display to the user by accessing a Web site address (URL). The initial Web-based systems were largely hypertext documents; the focus of the user interface was on presentation. "If you don't grab the users' interest, you will loose them to other Web sites." This philosophy governed the majority of the initial Web systems. Later the Web-based applications inherited the same user expectation on presentation that "grabbed interest".

- *Thick-Client Graphical User Interface* (GUI): Unlike the browser-based Web user interfaces, thick-client interfaces must be installed on a computer for users to access the system. The application may contain all the business logic, and it may or may not require connecting to a server. Since most of the processing to display the UI happens on the user's computer, the sophistication and level of interaction of the GUI potentially can be much richer than the WUI or other types of interfaces.

- *Text- or Character-Based User Interface* (TUI *or* CUI): These are the earliest user interfaces, and they are still very popular. ASCII characters are used to create the user interface. Though much debate involves the usability of a GUI versus a TUI/CUI, several sophisticated users find the TUI/CUI easier and less cumbersome to use. To run, this interface requires very little use of input devices other than a keyboard and frequently requires very little in the way of computer resources. Most early systems that have limited processing capabilities use TUI/CUI to display the UI. Most mobile communication devices, such as PDAs, fall into this category. As these devices increase their processing capabilities, they attempt to incorporate richer UI.

- *Voice Response User Interface* (VRUI): Very often users think VRUI systems are different. Phones (the most popular VRUI input/output device) are not like computers. Pressing buttons on a phone keypad or speaking are very different and frequently less intimidating activities than is using a computer. Voice response systems are becoming increasingly popular. Banking, e-commerce, and several other industries have adopted such systems widely.

The grammar and physical nature of the different interfaces are diverse, but the underlying principles that result in the overall usability of a system are common. While selecting an appropriate user interface and engaging in an elaborate exercise of development, one needs to adhere to and plan for some of the human–computer interaction components that directly affect the usability of a system.

Human–Computer Interaction Principles

To understand some of the underlying human–computer interaction (HCI) principles that require careful planning by system architects, let us return to Canaxia and read some pages from Nigel's notebook. These are records that Nigel had written following his interactions with his colleagues at Canaxia. Although Nigel's notes are useful in illustrating the underlying HCI principles, you may need to apply the principles in your application context differently, as is true with any generalized example or derived principle.

October 5. Observed the Infrastructure IT Administrator, Lucy, while she was modifying security permissions for the department members following a reorganization at Canaxia. She was working from permissions forms sent to her by the various department heads. These forms defined the necessary security permissions for the department members. Setting the necessary permissions separately for each member is a very tedious undertaking. Lucy actually wrote scripts to aggregate similar users from across departments to apply the necessary security settings. This was very time-consuming, and it took Lucy several attempts to get it right. Lucy needs to repeat the process for setting up email access for these members and setting preferences such as mailbox size and other features. Since this is a different system, her earlier scripts are not useful. Lucy is frustrated. I will continue my observation later.

Usability Principle 1: Systems must provide a way to aggregate data and commands. Users frequently require performing one or more actions on more than one set of data objects.

October 6. I was standing next to the network printer that was printing a large document. When the document finished printing, the owner picked it up and threw it in the recycle bin. "I fired a print command only to realize that it needed additional edits. There is no way to cancel this thing. What a waste!"

I saw Lucy again later in the day. She was trying to install software only to realize that she did not have time to complete it. There was no way to cancel the operation. Lucy will miss the bus today.

Usability Principle 2: Systems should allow users to cancel commands. Users frequently make mistakes or change their minds about operations they do not wish to perform anymore.

October 7. I was observing Dan at the help desk expertly switching between his email and the call log application. He was reading the problem reports, replying to them on email, and entering everything in the call log. Just then a call came in and Dan needed to pick it up on the computer. I was very curious when he first put the call on hold and closed the email application before picking up the call. He said, "When I get a call I cannot seem to use the mouse in the call log application if my email application is running. It was spooky, and then Lucy told me that the voice application for the call conflicts with the email application. This is very irritating."

Usability Principle 3: Systems should allow concurrent use of applications. A user may want to work with arbitrary combinations of applications concurrently.

October 9. I ran into Robert, the technical writer. He was excited with the latest version of Microsoft Word. "You know," he said, "when I typed 'hte' instead of 'the', Word automatically corrected it. Wow! I don't need to watch common words closely." This made me think that depending on context, error correction can be enforced directly (e.g., automatic text replacement, fields that only accept numbers), or suggested through-system prompts.

"Hmm. . . . I really had to type "hte" twice as Word kept correcting it automatically!"

Usability Principle 4: Systems should check for correctness. A user may make an error that he or she does not notice.

October 9. I ran into Dan again. He was like a child, still excited about the toy: Microsoft Word. "I was writing this document and had not saved it when I accidentally pulled the power cord. The computer switched off, and I thought I had lost my work. But guess what? When I launched Word again, the document was automatically saved. I only lost the last five minutes of work."

Usability Principle 5: Systems should allow recovery from systemic failure. A system may suddenly stop functioning while a user is working. Such failures might include a loss of network connectivity or hard drive failure in a user's PC. In these or other cases, valuable data or effort may be lost. Users should be provided with the means to reduce the amount of work lost from system failures.

October 10. I found Lucy in a bad mood again. "This is the fourth change-password request today. When we were implementing the password policy, we thought of it as a great security idea. Now either people have them written on Post-it® notes stuck on their monitors or they call me every other day to reset them. If I get another call today, I will not be able to finish my other work. I really need to catch the bus today."

Usability Principle 6: Systems should allow retrieval of forgotten information: A user may forget information, such as passwords.

October 10. It was dark as I entered my rental car. I was pleasantly surprised to find the ignition lock glowing, and I had no problem putting my key inside and starting the car. What a simple and clever design had made my experience with the car so much better. It gave me assistance when I needed it. Now why couldn't software be so sensitive? The Paperclip in Microsoft Office is too obtrusive, the Tool Tip feature sometimes is nice, and context-sensitive help is good, too. Maybe software is not always bad.

Usability Principle 7: Systems should provide good help. The need of good usable help cannot be understated. Providing contextual, easily navigable, searchable help, written in an easy-to-understand language, with simple examples and cross-links, is a task that should not be underestimated and should be estimated for early in the life cycle.

October 11. I was working with Bob today, our back-office sales assistant. He had received more than ten email messages with orders for twenty products in every message. Bob needed to provide all this information electronically using our order management system. Bob had done this many times over. He started by copying and pasting the product SKUs and quantities into Excel. He then uploaded the Excel spreadsheet into the order management system. "I had to search for the SKUs, then add them to a list, then search for the next SKU, and so on. It used to take a full day. In the new system, I can prepare the list in Excel and upload it. If there is a bad SKU, it tells me. I can do the same work in a couple of hours now."

Usability Principle 8: Systems should allow reuse of existing information: A user may wish to move data from one part of a system to another. Users should be provided with automatic (e.g., data propagation) or manual (e.g., cut and paste) data transports between different parts of a system.

October 14. Robert's initial enthusiasm with Microsoft Office had diminished. "I just installed Visio and have been struggling with this diagram. I need to move this shape a little, and whenever I select the object and use the arrow keys, the page moves instead of the object."

Usability Principle 9: Systems should leverage users' existing knowledge. People use what they already know when approaching new situations. Such situations may include using new applications on a familiar platform, using a new version of a familiar application, or using a new product in an established product line.

October 14. I was looking through my notes of the previous usability test and realized that some of the critical changes had not been incorporated into the upcoming release. "Although the change looks to be simple, it has far-reaching implications. It will take me several days to do. It's impossible to fit it into this release cycle," the lead developer had told me during the release planning session. Upon probing further, I realized he was working with legacy code that was not modular in its structure and was, therefore, not easily maintainable.

Usability Principle 10: Systems should allow easy modificiation of interfaces. Iterative design is the lifeblood of the current software development practice.

October 14. Robert published a set of training slides on the Web server and asked me excitedly to look at the human factors section starting at slide 32. The browser contains no straightforward way to navigate to a different slide.

Usability Principle 11: Systems should allow navigation from within a single view. A user may want to navigate from data visible on-screen to data not currently displayed.

October 16. I was trying to change my password on the enterprise intranet and realized that the password field had a hidden input mechanism. On my third attempt I realized I had changed my password to the same value three times. Apart from increasing some server traffic, no harm has been done.

Usability Principle 12: Systems should display the system state. A user may not be presented with the system state data necessary to operate the system (e.g., uninformative error messages, no file size given for folders). Alternatively, the system state may be presented in a way that violates human tolerances (e.g., it is presented too quickly for people to read). The system state may also be presented in an unclear fashion, thereby confusing the user.

October 16. I saw Robert was quite rushed; he had a document deadline to meet. He was working feverishly on the document on his newly upgraded computer. The computer was a very fast machine, and whenever Robert tried scrolling by moving the cursor, the pages flew past and landed several pages ahead. He then had to scroll back painfully by using the Page Up button to reach the desired section.

Usability Principle 13: Systems should allow working at the user's pace. A system might not accommodate a user's pace in performing an operation. This may make the user feel hurried or frustrated. Systems should account for human needs and capabilities when pacing the stages in an interaction. Systems should also allow users to adjust this pace as needed.

October 17. Ran into Ravi, the lead developer, in the break room. He was waiting for the code to compile. I ran into him again a couple of hours later, and he was still waiting for the code to compile. When I asked him how long it would take and if he wanted to join me for lunch, he replied, "Five minutes or another hour—I don't know."

Usability Principle 14: Systems should predict task duration. A user may want to work on another task while a system completes a long-running operation.

October 18. To make matters worse, Robert spilled coffee on the manuscript. "I wish that I could do a CTRL-Z and undo this!" Though we take this feature for granted today, though there was a time, not too long ago, when applications, such as PageMaker and others, could revert back only to a previously saved state. Now applications such as PhotoShop allow the user multiple Undo and Redo actions, and they offer other advanced functions. On the other hand, almost all of today's Web applications do not support Undo. Experts studying user behavior in a given context are usually required to appropriately design and support Undo functionality.

Usability Principle 15: Systems should support Undo, whereby a user may use the Undo command to revert to the state prior to an action.

October 18. I saw Bob struggling with the new order management system. None of his previous 2 years of working with one order management system seemed to apply to the new system. The nomenclature of terms was different, as was the basic metaphor.

Usability Principle 16: Systems should help users working in an unfamiliar context. Discrepancies between this new context and the one the user is accustomed to may interfere with the ability to work. Systems should provide a novice (verbose) interface to offer guidance to users operating in unfamiliar contexts.

October 19. I was trying to copy a file to another location. After endless churning of the hard drive, I got an error message that the disk did not have enough available space. Darn, why couldn't it have told me this up front? Surely file size comparison is not a complex operation. Had I known the file was so big, I could have compressed it before copying it.

Usability Principle 17: Systems should verify resources before initiating an operation. This failure may cause errors to occur unexpectedly during execution. For example, some versions of Adobe PhotoShop may begin to save a file only to run out of disk space before completing the operation.

October 20. Met with Dan to hear his complaints about the new Help Desk tool. This was the latest state-of-the-art system. It allowed the customer support personnel to view the data that the users were working with as they were working with it. "If I could see the screen of the user on my Windows application, I can better guide them. The labels on my screen are different from those the user sees in the browser."

Usability Principle 18: Systems should operate consistently across views. A user may become confused by functional deviations among different views of the same data. Commands that have been available in one view may become unavailable in another or may require different access methods.

October 20. I was watching Robert work with a 200-page document. He was working with the outline view in Word and had most sections collapsed, except the section he was editing. This gave him a good view of where he was in the overall document, as well as the details of the section he was editing. With a click of a button, he could change the view to a print layout mode and see how it was going to look in print.

Usability Principle 19: Systems should support appropriate visualization. Systems should provide a reasonable set of task-related views to enhance users' ability to gain additional insight while solving problems.

Usability Principle 20: Systems should support comprehensive searching. A user wants to search some files or some aspects of those files for various types of content. For example, a user may wish to search text for a specific string or for all movies for a particular frame. Search capabilities may be inconsistent across different systems and media, thereby limiting the user's opportunity to work. Systems should allow users to search data in a comprehensive and consistent manner by relevant criteria.

Usability Principle 21: Systems should provide ways to evaluate the system. A system designer or administrator may be unable to test a system for robustness, correctness, or usability in a systematic fashion. For example, the usability expert on a development team might want to log test users' keystrokes but may not have the facilities to do so. Systems should include test points and data gathering capabilities to facilitate evaluation.

- *Usability Principle 1: Systems must provide a way to aggregate data and commands.*
- *Usability Principle 2: Systems should allow users to cancel commands.*
- *Usability Principle 3: Systems should allow concurrent use of applications.*
- *Usability Principle 4: Systems should check for correctness.*
- *Usability Principle 5: Systems should allow recovery from systemic failure.*
- *Usability Principle 6: Systems should allow retrieval of forgotten information.*
- *Usability Principle 7: Systems should provide good help.*
- *Usability Principle 8: Systems should allow reuse of existing information.*
- *Usability Principle 9: Systems should leverage users' existing knowledge.*
- *Usability Principle 10: Systems should allow easy modification of interfaces.*
- *Usability Principle 11: Systems should allow navigation from within a single view.*
- *Usability Principle 12: Systems should display the system state.*

- *Usability Principle 13: Systems should allow working at the user's pace.*
- *Usability Principle 14: Systems should predict task duration.*
- *Usability Principle 15: Systems should support Undo, whereby a user may use the Undo command to revert to the state prior to an action.*
- *Usability Principle 16: Systems should help users working in an unfamiliar context.*
- *Usability Principle 17: Systems should verify resources before initiating an operation.*
- *Usability Principle 18: Systems should operate consistently across views.*
- *Usability Principle 19: Systems should support appropriate visualization.*
- *Usability Principle 20: Systems should support comprehensive searching.*
- *Usability Principle 21: Systems should provide ways to evaluate the system.*

Note: The usability requirements have been updated and modified from the original works of Lenn Bass, Bonnie E. John, and Jesse Kates (March 2001).

Usability and User Experience Design Process

Several software engineering processes have attempted to incorporate the user interface design activity while trying to align the usability aspects of the system. The heavyweight process—Rational Unified Process (RUP)—as well as lightweight processes, such as Agile, have tried to incorporate some core processes that attempt to account for a system's elusive usability. Most of these efforts have taken an inside-out view. Despite good intentions, these methodologies fall short of ensuring usability attributes. The main problem with these methodologies is their focus on design and building of software. They assume that the user interface and the usage requirements are clear to the designer of the software. However, this is frequently not the case. A large part of the usability effort is directed toward the early part of the system requirements and design activities.

The usability process, Figure 10–1, is largely iterative. It is difficult to design it correctly the first time. Yet if the process is not planned well, changing the user interface frequently after the software has been built is not very economical, regardless of whatever new information and feedback are received. Figure 10–1 illustrates this process.

Most steps in a usability-related process can be divided into stages for (1) mapping to the system requirements; (2) design, development, and testing; and (3) deployment and ongoing refinement. These three stages correspond to the system development stages. The requirements stage has the maximum usability-related processes and techniques. Typically, the output of the requirements stage is a functional specification. Together with the prototype UI, this provides a good reference for the development teams. Next, the traditional software design, development, and testing stages kick in. At this point, most of the usability processes are geared toward assisting development and providing alternate solutions if development trade-offs become necessary. Toward the end of this stage, when the application has been developed and is reasonably stable, the application goes through usability testing. Once the application is ready, it is rolled out to users in the field for actual

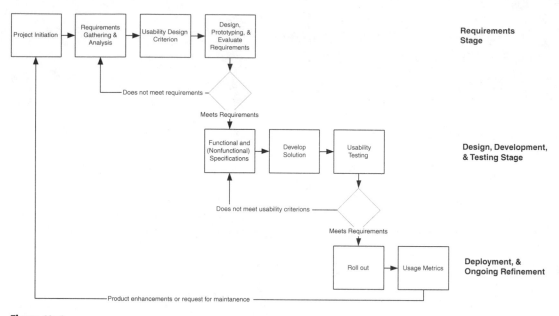

Figure 10-1
Usability process.

usage. At this stage, very little change to the application is possible or advisable. The focus shifts to gathering metrics for refining the applications.

Usability Techniques

This section describes standardized usability techniques. Using these repeatable techniques, high-quality system usability can be achieved. The techniques have been created based upon a model that can be tailored. The information in this section will help either the development project manager (in small projects) or the usability engineer in the selection of the appropriate methods and techniques from the resources suitable for the project.

Because they are standardized procedures, usability techniques provide results that can be compared. Results from a usability activity can be compared with existing results from previous projects, as well as with results from other organizations and companies if these parties agree to exchange such information. The following subsections contain brief summaries of key usability techniques separated into stages.

Requirements Stage

1. *Project Initiation*: In this stage, the project objectives have been defined. The key project leads are engaged in the various project-related planning activities. Since usability is still not tightly integrated into the overall system development processes, it may

need to be sold to the project sponsors. The key usability techniques used at this stage are the following:

- *Usability Planning*: Planning is essential for the success of any process. Usability planning requires identifying all the usability techniques to be applied during the project life cycle, identifying dependencies with other processes, and allocating the resources necessary for success.

- *Cost-benefit Analysis*: This technique involves working with the key stakeholders and analyzing the costs and benefits of the usability activities.

2. *Gathering and Analyzing Requirements*: In this stage, various usability techniques are applied to users, stakeholders, existing product versions, similar products, and competitor products to gather information that can be used for identifying the usability criterion and the functional requirements. Usability techniques may leverage marketing data, but they differ from marketing techniques in their unique focus on the user and stakeholder needs rather than marketing needs.

- *Group Discussion/Future Workshops*: Group discussions are based on stakeholders within the design process discussing new ideas, design options, costs and benefits, screen layouts, and so on, when relevant to the design process. The *future workshops* concept is designed specifically to allow participants to step forward though they are not used to having a voice in the discussion process.

- *Usability Context Analysis*: Usability context analysis (UCA) is a structured method for eliciting detailed information about a product and how it will be used, as well as for deriving a plan for a user-based evaluation of a product. For this method, stakeholders meet to detail the actual circumstances (or intended use) of a product. The objective of the method is to collect information—this should be done preferably through a well-prepared meeting, but it may also be done through a series of personal interviews (for example, if schedules in a busy company do not permit essential personnel to attend a general meeting).

- *Naturalistic Observation*: Observational methods involve an investigator viewing users as they work and taking notes on the activities taking place. Observation may be either direct, where the investigator is actually present during the task, or indirect, where the task is viewed by some other means, such as a video camera.

- *Surveys*: A survey involves administering standard questionnaires to a large sample population. Surveys can help determine customer preferences, work practices, and attitudes. The two types of surveys are (1) *closed*, in which respondents are asked to select from available responses and (2) *open*, in which respondents are free to answer as they wish.

○ *Ethnographic Approach/Contextual Inquiry*: The ethnographic approach emphasizes the understanding of behavior in context through the participation of the investigator in the situation being studied as an active member of the team of users involved in the situation. The ethnographic approach is essentially the traditional systems analysis approach enriched by contact with sociology and social anthropology. A close variant, *contextual inquiry*, has been adopted by Digital.

○ *Diary Methods*: Diary methods require the informants to record activities they are engaged in throughout a normal day. The structure of diaries varies from unstructured or open-ended, in which the informant writes in his or her own words, to highly structured tick-box questionnaires.

○ *Focus Groups*: A focus group brings together a cross section of stakeholders in an informal discussion group format. Views on relevant topics are elicited by a facilitator. Meetings can be audio or video taped for later analysis.

○ *Interviews*: Interviewing is a common technique in which domain experts are asked questions by an interviewer for the purpose of obtaining domain knowledge. Interviewing is not as simple as it may appear. The three types of interviews are *unstructured*, *semi-structured*, and *structured*. The type, detail, and validity of data gathered vary with the type of interview and the experience of the interviewer.

3. *Usability Design Criterion*: In this stage, the actual benchmarks and the usability criterions that become the design objectives are formulated. These criterions also serve as the usability test objectives. Each criterion is measured on the three attributes of *efficiency*, *effectiveness*, and *satisfaction*. Some criteria include, but are not limited to, learnability, helpfulness, meeting needs of trained users, meeting needs to walk up and use, meeting needs for infrequent or intermittent use, minimization of support requirements, error tolerance, legibility, and more.

4. *Design, Prototype, and Evaluate Requirements*: In this stage, the requirements and user needs are synthesized into multiple design options. Each design option focuses on emphasizing a different user need. Different usability techniques are then applied to synthesize the requirements. Some usability techniques help with the design and prototyping of the solution and some that assist in soliciting meaningful user feedback during the usability testing and evaluation sessions.

○ *Functionality Matrix*: This is a way of specifying which functions each user type needs. Identifying which tasks are critical allows more time for essential functions during design and usability testing. This technique is applicable to situations with tasks that are well defined.

○ *Task Allocation Charts*: A range of task allocation options is established between users and the computer system to identify the optimal division of labor needed to provide satisfying jobs and efficient operation of the entire work process. Task allocation charts are most useful for systems that affect whole work processes rather than single users or single-task products.

o *Task Analysis*: Task analysis can be defined as the study of what a user is required to do, in terms of actions and/or cognitive processes, to achieve a system goal. Task analysis is, therefore, a methodology that is supported by a number of techniques to help the analyst collect information, organize it, and use it to make various judgments or design decisions.

o *Wizard of Oz Prototyping*: This approach involves a user interacting with a computer system that is actually operated by a hidden developer, referred to as the *wizard*. The wizard processes input from a user and simulates system output. During this process, the users are led to believe they are interacting directly with the system. This form of prototyping is popular for testing voice response systems and artificial intelligence systems.

o *Paper Prototyping*: This method features the use of simple materials and equipment to create a paper-based simulation of an interface or system. Paper prototypes provide a valuable and cost-effective means of evaluating and iterating design options before a team gets committed to one implementation. Interface elements, such as menus, windows, dialogues, and icons, may be sketched on paper or created in advance using cards, acetate, pens, and so on. The result is sometimes referred to as a *low-fidelity prototype*. When the paper prototype has been prepared, a member of the design team sits before a user and moves interface elements around in response to the user's actions. A facilitator facilitates the session by providing task instructions and encouraging users to express their thoughts and impressions.

o *Scenario Building*: Scenarios are characterizations of users and their tasks in a specified context. They offer concrete representations of users working with a computer system to achieve a particular goal. The primary objective of scenario building is to generate usability requirements or targets. Scenarios also offer the opportunity to explore the implications of design options and to communicate interface issues to colleagues for comment and critical feedback. A variation of this technique has been adopted by the agile framework as user stories.

o *Storyboarding/Presentation Scenarios*: Storyboards are sequences of images that demonstrate the relationships among individual screens and actions within a system. A typical storyboard will contain a number of images depicting features such as menus, dialogue boxes, and windows. The sequencing of these screen representations conveys further information regarding the structure, functionality, and navigation options available within an intended system.

○ *Empathic Modeling*: This method has so far been mainly developed for use with disabled users. With empathic modeling, designers/developers strive to put themselves in the position of a disabled user. This is done by simulating the disability through various techniques. Similar methods are widely used in many application areas, but they are rarely referred to as empathic modeling. This is a general method that could be applied to a broad range of applications.

○ *Rapid Prototyping (software or hardware based)*: This method is concerned with developing different proposed concepts through software or hardware prototypes and evaluating them. In general, the process is termed *rapid prototyping*. The development of a simulation or prototype of the future system can be very helpful, allowing users to visualize the system and to provide feedback on it. Thus it can be used to clarify user requirements options.

Design, Development, and Testing Stage

1. *Creating the functional (and nonfunctional) specifications*: In this process stage, the prototype from the previous stage is used for documenting functionality with notes for the development team. This helps clarify for everyone engaged in the development and testing of the application what needs to be built and the intention for building it.

2. *Develop Solution*: This is a largely a development-intensive stage in which code is written. Usability parishioners are involved with the development team in deciding low-level design decisions and analyzing development trade-offs.

○ RAD (*Rapid Application Development*) *Workshops*: Workshops are set up in which eight to twenty individuals make decisions through the consensus-building leadership of a trained, unbiased facilitator who is not a stakeholder in the future system. A number of different formats for the method are offered. One variation produces formal outputs such as entity-relationship models, which can be input directly into the system specification.

○ JAD (*Joint Application Design*) *Workshops*: These workshops are specific variations developed within IBM. Here, users and information systems professionals are drawn together to design a system jointly in a facilitated group session. Six roles are defined, including session leader, user representative, specialist, analyst, information systems representative, and executive sponsor. A 20 percent to 60 percent increase in productivity over traditional design methods is claimed.

○ *Laboratory-Based Observation*: This approach to studying user behavior in the laboratory may be used at practically any stage in the development process with a representation of the software with which users may interact. *The Handbook on Usability Testing by Rubin*, 1994, is cited because of its clarity of exposition, but this approach is documented in many sources.

- *Co-operative Evaluation*: This is a cost-effective technique for identifying usability problems in prototype products and processes. The technique encourages design teams and users to collaborate on identification of usability issues and their solutions. Users work with a prototype as they carry out tasks set by the design team. During this procedure, users explain what they are doing by talking or thinking aloud. An observer records unexpected user behavior and the user's comments regarding the system. The observer also actively questions the user with respect to their intentions and expectations. This provides qualitative information concerning any difficulties that the users experience and the features or interface elements that give rise to these problems.

- *Parallel Design*: It is often helpful to develop possible system concepts with a parallel process in which several different designers work out possible designs. The aim is to develop and evaluate different system ideas before settling on a single approach as a basis for the system. In parallel design, it is important to have the designers working independently, since the goal is to generate as much diversity as possible. Therefore, the designers should not discuss their designs with each other until after they have produced their draft design concepts. When designers have completed their designs, it is likely they will have approached the problem in radically different ways that will give rise to different user systems. It is then possible to combine designs, taking the best features from each. It is important to employ parallel design for novel systems without established guidelines for how the system should operate best.

- *Walk-through*: A walk-through is a process of going step by step through a system design to obtain reactions from relevant staff, typically users or experts role-playing users' parts. Typically, one or two members of the design team will guide the walk-through, while one or more users will comment as the walk-through proceeds.

Deployment and Ongoing Refinements

1. *Rollout*: At this stage, the product has been tested and is ready for users to use. Very little usability is involved in this stage, other than using this opportunity for gathering requirements for future development activity. Most of the requirements stage techniques that involve observation of the users are applicable at this stage.

2. *Usage Metrics*: At this stage, both nonobtrusive and obtrusive methods are used to gather and analyze the actual usage of the system. Analyzing server log files, logging user clicks, and analyzing quality of data are some nonobtrusive techniques, while user surveys, interviews, and other subjective inquiries are obtrusive techniques.

Sharing the Usability Test Reports

Many factors affect a corporation's decisions about which software products to purchase. One key factor is any software's usability. In simple terms, usability reflects the following:

- How easy the software is to learn
- How easy the software is to use
- How productively users will work
- The amount of support users will need

Software developers employ a variety of techniques to ensure software usability. In general terms, these techniques involve studying users to develop an understanding of their needs and iteratively refining versions of the software based on usability testing results.

In making purchase decisions, companies and organizations have traditionally had little indication of how usable a product would be or how much training and support its users would need. The situation has made it difficult to compare products, to plan for support, or to estimate total cost of ownership. In October of 1997, the U.S. National Institute of Standards and Technology (NIST) initiated an effort, including the IUSER project, to increase the visibility of software usability. Cooperating in the IUSR project are prominent suppliers of software and representatives from large consumer organizations. The goals of the initiative are to:

- Encourage software suppliers and consumer organizations to work together to understand user needs and tasks.
- Develop a common usability-reporting format (CIF, ANSI/INCITS-354) for sharing usability data with consumer organizations.
- Create extensions/variations to the CIF for reporting in areas such as requirements, formative testing, and testing with hardware.

Usability testing can be valuable for a wide range of products, however the IUSR project is initially focused only on software. We recognize that the usability of hardware (printers, copiers, fax machines, and so on) is important and often tightly integrated with software. The initial focus on software was intended to narrow the focus of the initial project so that a pilot study could be conducted. Extending the scope of the reporting standard to include hardware and other products should be addressed later in the project.

Out-of-the-Box Experience

For some packaged software, the out-of-the-box (OOBE) is important. OOBE has been popularized by IBM's ease-of-use initiatives. (For more details about OOBE, please visit the IBM Web site mentioned in the bibliography at the end of the book.) A favorable experience goes a long way toward determining the perception of usability of the system. The following elements contribute to the overall OOBE:

- *Packaging* is the users' first encounter with products they have acquired. Their perceptions of product quality will reflect product packaging design, which addresses such aspects as number of boxes, size and weight, carrying and transportation, grouping and organization of items, identification and verification of contents, and conveying product/brand attributes.

- *Unpacking* should be an easy and efficient task. This requires attention to aspects such as unpacking instructions, opening outer boxes, order and organization of interior items, removing and unwrapping interior items, completeness and inventory checks, disposal of wrapping and packing materials, ease of repacking, and "In case of difficulty" instructions.

- *Hardware setup design* addresses aspects such as instructions and aids, physical arrangement of components, connectors, levels of setup, assembly, setup options, and "In case of difficulty" instructions.

- *Power-on* is the first plateau of achievement for the user. The design of the power-on experience addresses immediate feedback that setup was successful, rewards, thank-you notes, welcome messages and mementos, and "In case of difficulty" instructions.

- *Configuration of the system* addresses aspects such as installing and configuring post-setup options, such as passwords, device and network parameters, and system level defaults; removing unwanted software and features; agreeing to product license terms; submitting product registration information; subscribing to product information and updates; satisfying any warranty requirements; and getting assistance.

- *Introduction to use* considers design aspects such as product features and capabilities, sources of assistance, and "In case of difficulty" instructions.

- *Getting to work* addresses design aspects such as helping users achieve what they want to, providing active assistance as the default, teaching how to use supplied applications in everyday tasks, and providing easy and quick support in case of difficulty.

- *Further assistance* must be provided in multiple ways so that it is available at every step, including written instructions, tips, and troubleshooting guides, some period of free telephone support, Web sites for support and frequently asked questions, technical support via email, and user groups.

Conclusion

Usability is defined as the extent to which a product can be used by specified users to achieve specified goals with effectiveness, efficiency, and satisfaction in a specified context of use.

Usability practice requires complete enterprise buy-in to be successful. While the lack of usability in projects may lead to poor solutions, usability requires specialized knowledge of appropriate techniques if it is to be successful. Implementation of usability must be a planned activity with appropriate resources allocated for the successful execution of the project.

For the system to deliver on its usability promises, some known usability principles must be incorporated into the overall system architecture.

chapter 11

Data Architecture

*Real teams don't emerge unless individuals on them take risks
involving conflict, trust, interdependence and hard work.*

Katzenbach and Smith

It is rare for all but a few privileged organizations to have complete data
architectures. Data architecture is made up of the structure of all corporate
data and its relationships to itself and external systems. In far too many situations, the business community has to enlist the assistance of IT to retrieve
information due to the community's inconsistency, lack of intuitiveness, or
other factors. The goal of any architecture should illustrate how the components of the architecture will fit together and how the system will adapt and
evolve over time.

Taking an agile approach to data architecture will allow for the integration of existing corporate data and applications, allowing for new business
requirements and systems to be easily integrated into the organization's
technology nervous system. Enterprises everywhere find it increasingly necessary to incrementally change applications and their data in a rapid manner.
Sometimes this may result in building bridges, using a Service-Oriented
Architecture to overcome integration challenges or even rewriting legacy
applications to accommodate new data requirements.

---

*The practice of architecture is a long and rapid succession of sub-optimal decisions, mostly
made in partial light. Phillippe Kruchten, 1999*

An agile approach to data architecture will ensure that all mission-
critical information is well managed, accounted for, and appropriately
shared. It will also have the benefit of creating a common terminology for
corporate data elements and will add immense value to future software
development initiatives. This chapter will help you reach this goal.

Kello James, the CTO of Canaxia, has enlisted us to form a data architecture strategy that is closely aligned with his company's business objectives. Kello has asked the team to look at the following:

- Use of current databases for data mining of customer and competitor information
- Protocols used for EDI and XML-based Web services for integration with Canaxia's business partners
- Providing a unified view of customer information to all points within the organization
- Ensuring that the organization's data maintains integrity and is not exposed to misuse by hackers, business partners, or other parties

The organizational context (Figure 11–1) provides input into the data architecture and is the primary tool for the management and sharing of enterprise data. It enables architects, data modelers, and stakeholders to identify, classify, and analyze information requirements across the enterprise, allowing the right priorities for data sharing initiatives. Data architecture states how data are persisted, managed, and utilized within an organization (as shown in Figure 11–1). Data architecture also describes the following:

- How data are stored in both a transient and permanent manner
- How components, services, and other processes utilize and manipulate the data

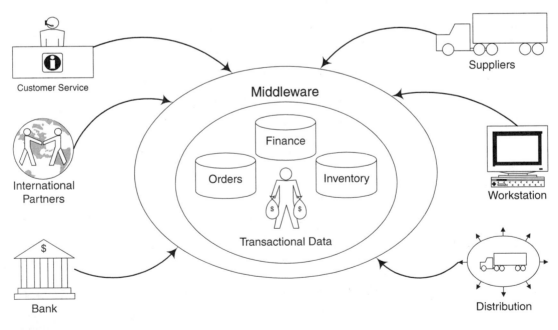

Figure 11–1
Organizational context.

- How legacy systems and external business partners access the data
- How common data operations (create, read, update, delete) should occur in a consistent manner

Now, let's see how we can help make Kello successful.

Baseline data architecture defines the business information needed to support the business functions that are encompassed in the baseline business model. It essentially contains information on high-level data areas and their classes. Additionally, it identifies the need for data warehouses and data marts. Data architecture is not a data model (entities, relationships, classes, elements, etc.). Data models are best created as part of a departmental project where business requirements are best understood. The data architecture cannot always anticipate all implementation details. In many situations, the data architecture can be compromised in places as long as the rationale behind it is understood and documented. In these situations, it is still the responsibility of the enterprise architect to ensure that the compromise does not affect the performance, integrity, or scalability of the overall system.

Canaxia has employed a well-respected consultancy to identify candidates for business objects. A business object is a person, place, thing, or event that Canaxia needs to keep data about in order to to conduct business. The consultancy created business definitions that reflect an understanding of each business object. Table 11–1 lists partial definitions for the creation of its data repository.

Table 11–1
Business objects.

Name	Definition	Identifiers	Characteristics	Notes
Agency	Department or administrative unit of a government entity	Title, type, ID number	Description, role, address, contact information (telephone, fax, Web address)	Legislative branches (Department of Transportation, Department of Motor Vehicles)
Agreement	An arrangement between two or more parties as to a course of action that identifies the roles and responsibilities of each	ID, title, dates, parties	Subject, scope, period of performance, funding, terms and conditions	Contracts, permits, collective bargaining, certifications and labor management agreements

continued

Table 11-1
Business Objects (continued)

Name	Definition	Identifiers	Characteristics	Notes
Authority	Specific rights and permissions assigned to an employee, person, and job	Type, data, name	Source, duration, level, scope	Rights, warrants, delegation orders, access rights to information, clearances, digital signatures, authentication, credit card information
Benefit	Pack of services and programs provided to employees	Date, name, type, grade	Description, duration, terms and conditions	Health insurance, counseling, massages, and free Krispy Kreme donuts
Budget	Estimated funds required for goods and services	Year, type, organization	Amount	Planning estimates, budget recommendations
Compliance	Conformance with legal, HR, and regulatory requirements	Date, type, mandate, department, name	Methodology, result	Audit reports, certifications, accident reports
Cost	Value of goods and services	Data, name, type	Amount, fiscal year, period covered, currency	Salary, benefits, products
Departments	Organizational units	Names, codes, acronyms	Mission, vision, function, head	Locations in each country
Dispute	Controversy among parties	Type, date, number, title	Description, resolution, status	Security clearances, HR policies, whistle blowers, union cutbacks, etc.
Document	Data that are contained within a physical or electronic media	Name, number, type, date	Content, description, format, media, sensitivity	Media can be hard copy, analog, digital, and can come in many forms
Employee	A person who works for Canaxia	SSN, employee ID	Education, name, type, grade, job title, skill, location	Does not include contractors or consultants
Goal	Desired outcome	Title, type, date	Content, event, source	Settled, closed, cancelled, etc.
Incident	Significant event where disclosure is required	Date, location, type	Sensitivity, severity, duration, department	Accident, injury, chemical release, security breach

Name	Definition	Identifiers	Characteristics	Notes
Intellectual property	Rights owned by Canaxia	Name, date, type	Concept, description, formulae, value	Copyrights, patents, trademarks, secrets
Job	Responsibilities of an employee	Title, position, job ID, date of creation, job grade	Description, job family, type, role, status	Enterprise Architect, Technology Director, Thought Leader
Mandate	Specific instruction	Identifier, date, topic	Authorization reference, context, type, approval	Law, regulation, policy, requirements (e.g., Healthcare Portability Act)
Measure	Standard of evaluation	Type, organization, date	Unit, scale, dimension, period, description	HR performance standards, miles per gallon
Product	Items that are created, manufactured, or distributed by Canaxia	Name, date	Description	Wheels, metal detectors for finding unicorns, etc.
Program	Grouping of related projects that have common attributes	Name, acronym	Scope, subject, context	NAFTA, financial management, customer relationship management
Project	Set of activities that are managed and funded together	Name, cost center, acronym, type	Scope, description, schedule	World domination, human genome
Proposal	Offer to provide product or services	Title, date, type	Value, approach, key personnel, deviations from norm	May result in agreement
Resource	Physical property used to accomplish a goal	Identifier, type	Description, location, age, quantity, availability, value	Equipment, space, supplies, buildings, inventory
Risk	Possibility of loss, failure, or other undesirable outcome	Name, type	Probability, impact, description, outcome, scenarios	Market, financial, litigation, security, safety, environmental, etc.
Task	A discrete unit of work	Title, number, date	Description, schedule, milestones	The lowest level of work, such as evaluate software for ERP

Frameworks

Kello received a call from Kathy Budhooram, director of the Data Center, who wanted his buy, in for a new database infrastructure and systems management framework and wanted to write a check for $55 million. Kello asked about the approach Kathy used to reach her decision on product selection. Kello also asked whether anyone from Kathy's staff performed trade-off analysis on alternative approaches and how it compared with other solutions in the industry.

Kathy admitted that she did not compare the recommended solution to anything else but highly admired the vendor's presentation and marketing materials. Kello then asked whether she talked with any of the database and/or network administrators who would have ultimate responsibility for the solution. Sadly this had not occurred.

While multiple objectives are behind building a data architecture (Figure 11–2), the main reason is to maintain an infrastructure that allows for the support of new business processes at the enterprise level in an easy manner. The organization should follow a framework for building a data architecture. Kello realizes that good data architecture will allow his organization to maintain the appropriate balance between business innovation and IT, and thus realize cost savings.

Let's look at the main components of a data architecture framework.

Figure 11–2
Layered data architecture.

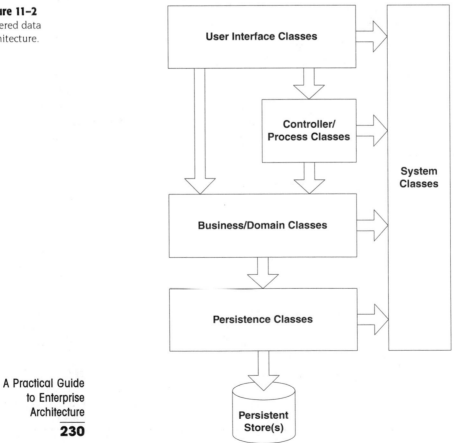

Business Architecture

Business architecture (conceptual architecture) identifies processes at the enterprise level and outlines the desired outcome the business seeks, as well as the steps necessary to accomplish it. In a vast majority of organizations, it will be relatively easy to find documentation on the solutions that have been implemented to date.

One may find at this step that many of the business processes are out-of-date and/or no longer provide any business value and were done solely for historic reasons. It is best to eliminate any business processes that do not provide business value at this step, as they should not occupy resources.

Use cases define goal-oriented interactions between external actors and the system under consideration. A complete set of use cases specifies the ways a system can be used and, therefore, the required behavior of the system. Use cases are common for RUP/EUP-based projects but not for others. For example, XP is based on user stories and FDD on features.

Business Object Modeling

Identifying business objects and the data that need to be associated, classifying business objects and their relationships to each other allows the architect to develop classification schemes that are necessary for creating metadata. In this step, it is a good idea to assign a unique identifier to each object, as well as to capture a description of the business processes the business object fulfills.

One should also consider attaching a representative sample of the data, as well as attaching a statement for the original motivation behind collecting this piece of data.

At this stage, one should make sure that processes and their associated data are consistently named throughout the enterprise. In all but the smallest organizations, it will be difficult to find the same process referred to with two different names. Usually this occurs across different business units. Inconsistencies in processes and their associated data may include assigning different labels to refer to the same type of process/data, associate the same label with different types of process/data, representing the same process/data using different formats, and so on. Eliminating these types of inconsistencies will remove hurdles now and in the future when integrating disparate business systems. It is important that one not get hung up on getting it perfect at this step.

Identifying the major business units within the enterprise and the relationships among them should be considered thoroughly at this stage. One will find that the identified business processes within each business unit should ideally map to the identified business objects.

Business Data

By capturing business data used in a business process, an organization can assess the effectiveness of a given business process. Additionally, identifying the data that are needed to achieve the desired outcome helps an organization know what data to keep as well as what data to discard.

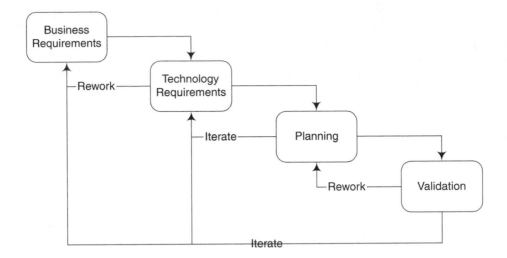

Figure 11–3
Architectural process.

It is important to identify how data are handled within various business processes. The data that are used by the process and used by other common processes, as well as those that are communicated externally, should be documented. By classifying data in this manner, it will become evident that certain transactions exist and must be supported by any new business processes (See Figure 11–3).

At this stage, an architect should be on the lookout for data integrity and for potential breaks in data integrity. Enough information has been collected to find spots where decision support systems have holes in the data they truly require to be complete. Sometimes, this may be due to vocabulary not caught at the previous stage. For example, within Canaxia's business process, the company uses the word *name* as both a noun and verb, where name can refer to a person (e.g., Fong Sai Yuk) or a promotion initiative (e.g., finding the next CTO).

One may also discover that the formats vary for the same data used by different business units. For example, date of manufacture is displayed by U.S. subsidiaries as 09/10/2001, when sold to the U.S. military as 09-OCT-2001, and by Caribbean subsidiaries as 10/09/2001. Other business units, such as manufacturing, may also append the time the unit rolled off the assembly line and could display local time or Greenwich Mean Time. This type of information is usually discovered only in discussion with participants from all parts of the organization, not from just a selected area.

The solution to this conundrum is the ability to have multiple views into the data. This is discussed in detail in Chapter 7, Agile Architecture.

"Discussion: A method of confirming others in their errors."—The Devil's Dictionary

---

Alternatively, for those who eschew waterfall approaches, you may prefer to see the diagram drawn as in Figure 11–4.

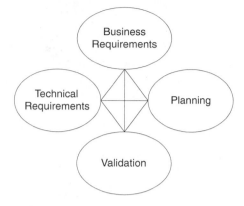

Figure 11–4
Architectural
process—the
agile view.

Architecture

At this stage, we have gathered all required information needed to construct a model for our data architecture. This model will reflect how Canaxia conducts business. Our framework suggests that we incorporate existing relationships and model them so that new systems and significant upgrades will support any proposed system's new processes and standards.

Validation/Final Review

Before any architecture is declared ready for production, it is important to consider what may have been forgotten. At this stage, it is important that the architecture support all the requirements the business needs to process information. This can be done by conducting a data gap analysis. Any concerns expressed by key stakeholders should be completely addressed here. Following are other gaps that should be identified:

- Data is not located where it is used.
- Required data is not available.
- Data is not available when needed.
- Data is not consumed.
- There are gaps in the data relationship.

The review should also consider qualitative criteria (e.g., security, performance availability, accuracy, costs, volumes, and so on) and provide criteria that are as measurable as possible. Following are some common items to measure:

- Privacy and confidentiality concerns met
- Maximum data volumes at peak times
- Minimum tolerable data losses

The goal at this step is to guide the data architecture efforts toward the qualities required in the processes that manage the data. This could also be extended to the applications that the organization builds or purchases, as well as the underlying technology infrastructure.

Many heavyweight frameworks for data architecture are available commercially and will be more impressive to the management team (at least those who are not aware of agile methods), cost an organization significantly more in the way of time and resources, and not produce the desired return on investment. We propose a lighter-weight approach that will result in better success. Using the framework we have suggested allows an enterprise to increase its data integrity through consistent implementation of business processes. This stage would be a good time to conduct a review with the goal of early detection of any mistakes made during the process.

> A good example of review framework approach is available at *www.cutter.com/itjournal/agile.html*.

Metadata

Canaxia's applications developed in-house were previously developed in a monolithic manner whereby each application performed every step in a process that was required to complete a business function. Additionally, different IT areas within Canaxia developed applications in a tactical manner with no thought on reuse or a shared enterprise view. This resulted in multiple sources for customers, accounts, billings, and manufacturing data, with no single database being the authoritative source. Each application had its own rendition of name, address, and contact information.

Kello James would like the data architecture to accommodate the establishment of an authoritative source for each data element. He has realized this will be difficult since each data element within each database is inconsistent in its usage and content. Canaxia has been good about using standard data modeling techniques and, in fact, incorporated this practice early in the application development life cycle. However, Canaxia now realizes that different modeling philosophies have emerged over time.

The various approaches to modeling have resulted in many anomalies within the Canaxia data architecture including, but not limited to, the following:

- Identification
- Semantic
- Synonym
- Homonym

Canaxia has no unified method for uniquely identifying an entity. In the sales lead database, each prospect is labeled with a sequentially assigned number, whereas in the customer database, customers are uniquely identified by their Social Security numbers. In the billing database, customers are assigned another unique identifier. No data source exists to identify how each record correlates across data sources.

Each database has semantically different ways of using different data values for the same data element. The Canaxia sales database refers to gender as *male* and *female*, whereas the billing database refers to gender as 0 or 1. Semantics are relevant when different values are associated with the same data element. Several of the databases have different field names for the same data element (*synonym*).

A data dictionary *stores data definitions.* A data repository *manages additional information, including data ownership, the systems that use the data, the organizations the data serve, and so on.*

Sometimes the same field name may exist for different data elements (*homonym*). For example, the term *race* could refer to a person and his or her genetic makeup, or it could refer to the action of a person, such as a *race for election.*

Homonyms occur where data exist within departmental applications. This will be the most difficult problem to solve. Usually the solution results in having distributed data sources with commonly defined definitions. This approach is sometimes referred to as *federated metadata.*

Metadata is information about data.

Federated Metadata

Federated metadata, when defined in a consistent manner, describes data the same way in each physical table in which the data are stored (Figure 11–5). The definition includes the name of the field, its length, format, and a list of valid values. When data have the same format, it is easier for exchanges of information to occur across systems.

A federated metadata approach can be implemented even when information is physically partitioned across disparate data sources. In the ideal world, all related data would exist within a single physical location, making application development easier. Reality dictates that information will be spread across multiple heterogeneous platforms and topologies. Defining this up front will simplify application integration. Data sharing can be further extended through reusable services using a service-oriented approach or by using a broker-based architecture. To access data, each application would send a request to the service. The service would execute the request and return the appropriate response to the application. This approach protects the integrity of data and guarantees that the data retrieved are both accurate and consistent.

To be successful in defining metadata, the first step is to define the appropriate owner of each data element. Usually data elements can be classified by who is the authoritative source. For example, Canaxia assigns each employee an employee number. The employee number is used by more than one department, including security, manufacturing, and legal, but the human resources department issues the employee number and is, therefore, the authoritative

Figure 11–5

Federated metadata.

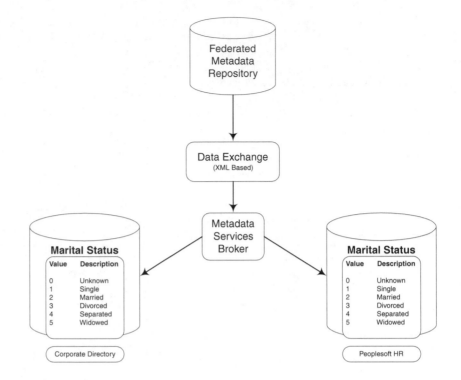

source. Sometimes, data elements are used by more than one department but are not identified as the authoritative source. For example, each employee of Canaxia within the United States has a Social Security number that is used in multiple applications, including payroll, employee benefits, and security. However, no department within Canaxia issues Social Security numbers.

Table 11–2 illustrates the use of the Social Security number within Canaxia's metadata repository.

Metadata also stores information about the location of databases and their aggregated content. Storing database information in the metadata repository allows information to be quickly located and shared. Additionally, Canaxia will benefit by using this approach to become compliant with the Healthcare Information Portability Act (HIPA), as well as to manage its data privacy concerns in a unified enterprise manner. A Big Five accounting firm that performs audits of Canaxia's business can additionally certify that data are being stored and used in an appropriate manner. At some future time, Canaxia can also extend this view to its customers and the public at large without grief or fear of wrongful disclosure.

The people at Canaxia realize that a metadata repository can help them overcome many of the business and technology problems they are experiencing, including the following:

- Building the enterprise data model
- Design reviews
- Use of XML DTDs and/or schemas for data exchange validation

Table 11-2

Canaxia's use of metadata.

Field	Values
Data Element Name	Social Security number
Element Definition	A 9-digit number assigned to an individual by the Social Security Administration
Business Format	999-99-9999
Business Length	11 positions
Business Type	Number
Exchange Format	9999999999
Exchange Length	9 bytes
Exchange Type	Character
Storage Format	999999999
Storage Length	9 bytes
Storage Type	Character or variable character
Scope	United States

Using the metadata repository to store data element definitions has the result of building the enterprise data model. In this usage, if the repository is kept up to date, the resulting enterprise data model is also up to date. By being able to start from either direction, the repository can serve as the tool that will empower an enterprise to determine how changes in data affect other processes. It will also help realize the goal of data reliability, reusability, and sharing across organizational boundaries.

Throughout the remainder of this text, the term schema *refers to tables, views, triggers, stored procedures, and other "objects" that are stored within a database.*

In small projects, design reviews are typically conducted by members of self-organizing teams. In larger projects, this model definitely breaks down. The ideal design review of data architecture would uncover any inconsistencies of data usage within and across applications and would reveal whether it is stored redundantly. The metadata repository will allow quick discovery of such scenarios. The other problem typically associated with a data architecture design review is the need to produce documentation that no one will look at once the review has been conducted. This step in the project life cycle will occur quickly because the repository will have the effect of uniformly stating which other applications receive data from this application and whether or not a requirement can be resolved by using an existing federated metadata element.

An industry trend is to use XML as a data transfer format for exchanging information between disparate applications. XML allows data to become self-describing. The metadata repository also will allow for instant creation of XML schemas since the repository is knowledgeable about each data element, its format, and the list of valid values. As the repository is updated, new schemas can be generated automatically, as appropriate.

XML schemas do not cover the semantics of the data. For additional information, visit *www.agiledata.org/essays/advancedXML.html*.

As part of its architecture, Canaxia has defined a metadata services broker (see Table 11–2) that adheres to the Open Applications Group Integration Specification (OAGIS). This specification defines a virtual, content-based business object model that allows an enterprise application to construct a virtual object wrapper around itself. Communication among software components occurs through the metadata services broker using a business object document to a virtual-object interface, as shown in Figure 11–6.

The business object document uses the metadata contained within the repository and is contained within an XML schema. By taking this approach, the business object document will contain not only data related to the business service request but also to the business data area. Each business service request (BSR) contains a unique verb/noun combination that drives the contents of the business data area (BDA). Examples could include post journal or sync password, which all systems can understand. The combination of the BSR and BDA in object-oriented terms, maps directly to the object name, method, and arguments in a method invocation.

For more information on OAGIS, visit *www.oag.org*.

Metadata has the ability to become dysfunctional easily. It is important to keep metadata streamlined, making it easy to work with so that it stays

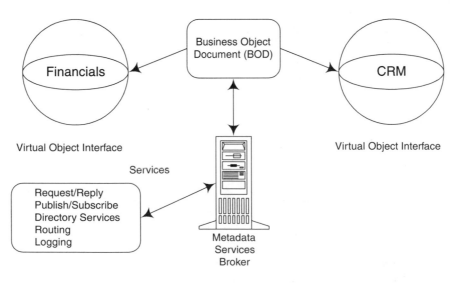

Figure 11–6
OAGIS virtual business object model.

current. Metadata access should never be held back unreasonably from developers or other interested parties.

The vast majority of metadata repositories are unidirectional. Modeling tools that extract, transform, and load information into the repositories are responsible for capturing both business (business metadata) and IT (technical metadata) meta information flow in only a single direction. A bidirectional metadata architecture allows information contained within the repository to be altered, and this information is then subsequently fed to its original source. For example, if a user could connect to the repository and alter the name of a property in an enterprise data warehouse, this change could be propagated back into the supporting data-modeling tool to update the physical model for the data warehouse.

This allows for metadata to become effective in that it allows for different vendor tools to share metadata information. This functionality provides a lot of benefit for decision support systems. The major problem with making this a reality is the simple fact that many enterprises have built their decision support systems using best-of-breed software rather than using integrated tool sets provided by a single software vendor. This approach has some merit but prevents integration at the tool level. Some tools do allow for integration but require jumping through complex hoops just to share this type of information and may require writing code to exchange meta information. A metadata approach that takes this into consideration would allow for enterprises to make global changes in their metadata repositories and have those changes propagated through all the tools within the organization.

> The Object Management Group (OMG) is working on a Common Warehouse Metamodel (CWM) standard. Additional information is available at *www.omg.org*.

Many enterprise tool vendors are trying to solve this particular problem, but several common organizational prerequisites must be considered before this can become reality. An organization would need to fully embrace the metadata repository approach for it to work and could not adopt it in bits and pieces. The repository will be required to store the latest version of the metadata source in which it will propagate changes. Concurrency issues will also arise in this situation. For example, if a user of the repository is updating information that needs to be propagated and another user is updating the schema at its source, collisions will occur. Finally, integration interfaces will have to be constructed to map and move metadata repository information back and forth to the metadata source.

> For more information on industry standard approaches to metadata, visit the Metadata Coalition and the Open Information Model (OIM) standard. *http://xml.coverpages.org/mdc-oim.html*.

Advanced Metadata Architecture

This type of approach can help solve many of the issues that enterprises are struggling with today. The most obvious business problem solved using this approach is with customer relationship management (CRM). The primary business driver for creating a customer relationship management system is the need for organizations to get single views of their customers. This statement is simple, but the work behind it is at best difficult as it requires integrating operational systems (orders, claims, customers, invoices, inventory, and so on) with business intelligence systems to provide a unified view. The ultimate goal is to enable customer-related information to be shared throughout the enterprise so as to provide higher levels of customer service (relations). Additionally, in industries such as banking, insurance, retail, and financial services, users want their systems to make certain business decisions for them without human interaction.

> Using a Service-Oriented Architecture is also a viable approach to solving the customer relationship management data integration challenge. This is discussed in Chapter 3, Service-Oriented Architecture.

Applying Metadata to Business Problems

Canaxia would like to expand its operations into selling aftermarket parts and accessories to owners of its automobiles. The company has expressed a desire for consumers to visit its Web site (www.canaxia.com) and to search for accessories that are appropriate for the vehicles they own. When an accessory is selected, the program interface will communicate with the customer relationship management system, will check for additional related accessories, will determine if any product recalls pertain to the vehicle, will locate auto dealers that could install parts, and will calculate applicable charges. Additionally, if the customer has never communicated using any channel (phone, fax, email) with Canaxia, it could offer the customer an online discount. Once the customer has completed the order, an additional request could be sent to the customer care center scheduling a follow-up call in 2 weeks to ensure that the customer was successful in installing the purchased accessories.

You may be wondering why you would not simply maintain this information in the operational system that is responsible for processing orders rather than separating it into distinct systems and services. The answer lies in whether your organizational philosophy allows for best-of-breed or single sourcing and whether a single system can support all your business requirements in an adaptable manner. Best-of-breed solutions would encourage a service-oriented approach, but this does not solve the decision support aspects. We have noted that a clear separation between operational and decision data is essential. By leveraging a metadata approach, you can access the best of all worlds.

By closing the loop, we can take metadata from the repository and feed it back into the enterprise operational systems. The use of a bidirectional approach allows for implementation of such business rules as when discounts apply to be fed to all systems in one global change.

The data that many organizations hold within the confines of their information technology systems is their most valuable asset. This holds especially true for financial services, banks, and insurance verticals. So far, this chapter has focused on the value of metadata repositories within the enterprise. To build upon this concept, we now focus on the data security architecture that should, ideally, extend the information contained with the repository.

Many large enterprises have groups of employees who are responsible for IT security. Some have even gone as far as creating a chief security officer position. Even with a large staff, organizations still experience breaches and lack any resources that allow them to quickly identify the impact of any attack. The existence of a metadata repository will also allow security personnel to identify and classify threats related to the following:

- Theft of information
- Malicious modification of data

Information theft can have a drastic impact on an enterprise violation of privacy and security regulations, on litigation, and—mostly—on damage to an organization's brand. Information theft at a minimum results in information being copied. In the wake of September 11, it is clear that this breach could also have an effect on national security. In many situations, it may also result in the destruction of data used to make critical decisions. This will result in a loss of productivity, as this information will need to be reproduced.

Malicious modification of data can sometimes be even more detrimental than either the theft and/or destruction of information since it could result in less-than-optimal decisions based on erroneous data. Unauthorized modification, especially if undetected, can compromise projects that depend on the integrity of information. Many organizations may expose this data to external systems or present this information on publicly viewable Web sites. Imagine if Canaxia's Web site were changed so that all its cars' names were altered to those of competitors' cars or if recall information were changed about defective tires on their sport utility vehicles. This threat category can also include nonmalicious, well-intentioned changes in data that can have the same effect. Nevertheless, the insecure actions of even trusted employees can compromise the security and integrity of valuable corporate information.

The metadata repository should also classify the various functional environments and create security policies to prevent unauthorized access to information. This information can then be used as a specification for upstream systems that leverage this data and can provide valuable input into an organization's compliance process. Canaxia has established data security policies and classified all data into five categories, as listed in Table 11–3.

Table 11-3

Classification

Category	Description
Unrestricted	Data that can be viewed by any party including the general public.
Research and Development	Data that is sensitive and contains preliminary research results that will be disclosed at a future date. Early disclosure could have detrimental consequences.
Operations	Data that is proprietary in nature and may contain information about Canaxia's customers, partners, and financials, as well as related information that is protected under privacy acts. Disclosure of this data could result in financial loss, damage to the brand, and legal recourse. This could also include data that are protected under the Freedom of Information Act (government entities).
Partner, Governmental Information	Data that is typically unclassified and protected in accordance with a sponsor's requirements and may contain trade secrets, competitive information, or other information deemed private. This could include information related to mergers and acquisitions, joint partnerships with governments in other countries, and information shared with financial auditors.
National Security	Information that requires special protection to support national interests and may include uses of special technologies. For example, Canaxia manufacturers the limousines for the presidents and prime ministers of many nations and specially equips them with antipersonnel devices, armor, and encrypted communication devices.

Agile Database Techniques

The goal of data architecture is to define the entities that are relevant to the enterprise and to avoid designing the logical and physical storage systems. At this point, you may be thinking about how to apply several of the topics discussed within this chapter for your database administrators. We feel that a slight deviation is warranted here. We will discuss techniques that database administrators (DBAs) may use to become more agile and to empower development teams.

> For additional reading, see *Agile Modeling: Effective Practices for Extreme Programming and the Unified Process* by Scott Ambler and Ron Jeffries.

The traditional database management approach has multiple problems, including but not limited to the following:

- Iterations of the data model or database are not allowed.
- Changes to the production environment are rare or not allowed.

- Migrating from one data model to another is a project in and of itself.
- There is usually only one development, QA, or other such database.
- The database administrator is a roadblock.

When considering how important databases are to the development of applications, one finds multiple opportunities for taking advantage of agile principles to save time and speed development. Now let's look at some agile principles we can apply to this discipline and then show how they can be realized.

Applying the Agile Approach

The agile approach to database management acknowledges that functionality in any undertaking should be done in increments. This is the first challenge to the previous bullet points. The agile approach is an advocate of automated testing. If one can have automated procedures for testing, one could potentially consider having more than one database for each release level (QA, development, etc.). If we could solve for this, both developers and QA could develop and test not only independently of each other but they could test different versions of future functionality. Also, the agile approach acknowledges the importance of team interaction. This challenges the notion that database administrators have to do everything related to databases, which sometimes causes developers to wait around while twiddling their thumbs.

Over time, both applications and databases grow more complex and undergo frequent rounds of refactoring. It becomes very important for architects to focus on the flexibility of the database. If an organization has an application in which business users can create complex scenarios within a half hour and run acceptance tests immediately, the importance of being agile is reduced. However, if the testing process requires intervention by multiple parties and running test scripts (even automated ones) for hours, if not days, then an enterprise can benefit by using agile approaches.

In an agile database approach, everyone gets his or her own copy of the database. A database should be thought of no differently than an application. In many Java shops, all developers are equipped with an application server on their desktops. The same should hold true for databases. This allows developers to work independently of other developers. Developers who understand how databases work (the vast majority) can have their own copies of the database so they can try out various changes to the database structure without involving the DBA. This allows developers to use the database as a scratch pad.

> To learn about sandbox diagrams, see *www.agiledata.org/essays/tools.html*.

If each person were to have an individual copy of the database, matters could get out of hand quickly—unless scripts (automation) allowed everyone to recreate a clean database at will. This illustrates a concept that can be manifested differently, depending upon the database in use (e.g., Oracle, MySQL, Pick, etc.).

Database administrators may ask "What's in it for me?" The answer is simple. In the agile approach, DBAs will receive fewer requests for work, allowing them to concentrate on what is truly important, which is maintaining the quality of the data and the structure of the production database. DBAs can maintain specialized data sets for each context (development, load testing, demos, etc.) that further empower the development team. By allowing each person to have a copy of their own database, developers can independently test incremental changes that allow for the migration of older data sets to newer versions of the application. For organizations that employ a release management process, the database can be thought of simply as just another component within the application and can be assigned a build number and context. In an agile approach, the DBA has more of a stewardship role toward databases instead of worker bee.

To make this work, several procedures must be put into place. First, modifications to the schema and setup data must be logged chronologically and the version controlled using the same manner as the application. By using version control practices, any member of the team can simply check out the appropriate scripts needed to support the version level they require and can execute them to get the proper version of the database. Since the schemas are within version control, this can happen on demand without DBA intervention. This same version control mechanism will allow old database instances to be rolled forward simply by applying the logged changes that were made to the schema and setup data.

In an agile database, everything starts with the notion of a database instance. Database instances are equivalent to application instances because they are a working copy of the system at a point in time. The vast majority of large projects use some form of source control (e.g., PVCS, Sourcesafe, Clearcase, etc.) that becomes the system of record for all project assets. For example, if the Canaxia development team were currently working on the sixth release of its enterprise customer relationship management system but expressed a desire to analyze the code base as of the fourth release, one would simply use the source control product and check out the code as of that release (Figure 11–7).

As we can see, the development team is working on the current release of software (version 6.0). When this build of software has been signed off on, exactly one version of the code base will be present at the end of the iteration. Part of this iteration includes an instance of the database that is comprised of the database schema and setup data. Since Canaxia uses scripts to create its database schemas and maintain setup data, the devel-

Figure 11–7
Development
timeline.

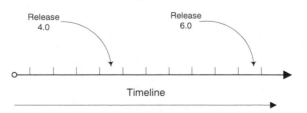

Table 11–4

Database iterations.

Version/Iteration	Function
4.0—Iteration 1	DBA makes a copy of certified schema from previous version and loads the database with programmatically generated data.
4.0—Iteration 2	DBA creates a new data set to allow for automated regression testing.
4.0—Iteration 3	DBA creates a new data set to allow for acceptance testing.
4.0—Iteration 4	Version has been certified. DBA creates production database.

opment team is able to recreate a functional database instance at any point in time and in the same manner as code.

The version control should also introduce the notion of context. Context represents the notion that multiple parties may require different sets of data loaded into the database for varying reasons, such as development, regression testing, acceptance testing, and production deployment. A development timeline is two-dimensional in that releases occur in order. Context establishes a third dimension that handles the usage of data within a development timeline. Table 11–4 presents a timeline to further explain this point.

Based on this scenario, you may have noted that each iteration had only one version of code data sets but multiple lineages (regression and acceptance testing). The schemas were the same throughout the iterations, yet the data sets could contain radically different data. For example, the development data set could contain only employees with the first name of Ernie. The acceptance data set could contain only data required to fulfill test cases that require preexisting data. Likewise, production databases created in the last iteration would be sizable and could require data conversion.

A lineage *is a preestablished context that is tracked across time and inherits its attributes from its ancestors.*

It is important to track the changes in database lineages in a manner different from what is done for typical code. Ideally, lineages should be maintained using scripts and storing them using version control. Sometimes, using lineages is not possible, so you may have to revert to snapshots. In any case, a lineage includes a master instance, a change log, an update list, and a collection of child instances that were derived from it. The first lineage of any application is the lineage that supports the application itself. Ideally, a new lineage is created every time an application branches or whenever the team requires a unique instance or specialized data set.

Data Architecture

Working with Scripts

Over time, the quantity of scripts required to create a database can become excessive. In such a situation, we recommend periodically creating new master scripts that essentially start a new lineage. This is referred to as the *master lineage*. The master should contain all changes to schemas and setup data from prior lineages.

Let's look at a database script and show the information that we will record within it.

```
/*
**      SUPPLIER.SQL
**      Creates table for supplier and signon.
**      Copyright 2003, Canaxia.      All rights
reserved.
**
**      Build: 2226
**      Release: 4.0
**      Date: September 10, 2001
**      Author: Little James
*/

use CRMDB
;

create table supplier (
        suppid int not null,
        name varchar(80) null,
        status char(2) not null,
        addr1 varchar(80) null,
        addr2 varchar(80) null,
        city varchar(80) null,
        state varchar(80) null,
        zip char(5) null,
        phone varchar(80) null,
        constraint pk_supplier primary key (suppid)
)
;

create table signon (
        username varchar(25) not null,
        password varchar(25) not null,
        constraint pk_signon primary key (username)
)
;
```

Scripts should be employed that handle the following tasks:

- Copy last certified release of database locally.
- Create a local copy of database specifying a version number.

- Create a new baseline and assign it a version number.
- Perform differential of local database versus last certified release.
- Perform differential of local database versus baseline.

Having the ability to use version control for databases will allow an organization to do the following:

- Conduct acceptance testing against a copy of current production data using a modified schema.
- Allow production databases to be migrated to a future state of development.
- Allow for changes to production databases to happen on a weekly or even daily basis since it is very easy to do so.

Normalization

Another important step toward having agile databases is not to be savage in the pursuit of normalization. In decision support applications, a star schema is typically used. Star schemas usually require fact tables to be third normal form and dimension tables to support second normal form. With most databases, 99 percent of the access occurs in a read-only fashion in which updates represent the other 1 percent. Using star schemas results in queries that are easy to write and run efficiently.

> Agile modeling techniques are presented in detail in Chapter 8.

Online transaction processing (OLTP) databases are typically used nowadays in conjunction with application servers for data access. For example, J2EE-based application servers support the notion of entity beans, which provide an object representation to a relational database. Since entity beans map one for one with a database's underlying table/view structure, it makes sense to consider, where appropriate, a less normalized view of databases. Many application servers can enforce the integrity rules that would otherwise be contained within the database, so following strict rules of normalization is no longer required. Traditionally, following rules of normalization resulted in an increase in performance. However, using this same mind-set with J2EE applications, and specifically with entity beans, could result not only in additional coding but also in lost performance since the application server has to manage relationships as well as create an object representation of each table/row run-time.

Star schemas are also easier to refactor because they are less normalized. They also map better to an object-oriented run-time model, especially when used in conjunction with adaptive object models that can build their representations using metadata obtained from a database.

When using star schemas, it is better to have a column containing precalculated values instead of performing calculations at run-time. This also has the effect of simplifying queries. For example, if your database supported a calendar table represented as a dimension in which each row at the day level has a "number of days since time began" column, your applications would be made simpler because would not have to calculate across month boundaries and so on. Dimension tables that are wide and contain pre-exploded values allow one to develop applications faster. Besides, columns are very easy to add to a database today.

One of the thoughts behind normalization was related to increasing the quality of data. Using normalization beyond Third Normal Form (3NF) does have the effect of potentially increasing data quality but comes at the expense of being agile. We believe a better approach is to build the quality information directly into the tables. The quality information could explain when, where, how good, etc., which is simply additional metadata.

Automating processes using metadata, creation of database scripts, and giving everyone the tools they need to become productive are the key outcomes of an agile process. DBAs should automate every process they perform on a repeated basis and, whenever possible, should ensure that these processes and the tools they use are accessible by team members. Process automation is the only activity that will allow DBAs to respond in a timelier manner.

We now present final best practices, which range across all the topics discussed previously in this chapter.

Establish an Infrastructure That Allows for Rapid Changes in Business Requirements and Database Technologies.

In most organizations, business requirements change frequently. The design of your data infrastructure must be agile and allow for easy and rapidly implemented changes to data models. Likewise, technology advances continue to outpace all but the most flexible organizations. Vendors are constantly adding new features to their engines that allow them to perform previously impossible tasks. The infrastructure must allow for replacing the database technology if necessary to gain advantage.

Data That Need to Be Shared and Current Should Be Centralized.

Transactional data that are high volume and shared across locations should be centralized. Additionally, if the data for all locations must be current, centralization becomes mandatory. Some organizations have tried to work around this by replicating updates to distributed databases in remote locations with limited success. Using a replication approach increases the complexity of an organization's data architecture and results in increased network traffic.

If any of the following criteria are present within your organization, a centralized database strategy is mandatory:

- *More than a handful of users requiring access to up-to-date data.* Usually this may include access to OLTP systems.
- *A handful of users and no distributed locations.* Sometimes an organization adopts the departmental mind-set, but this should be avoided.

- Multiple locations but a lack of appropriate skill sets and/or tools to manage distributed data.
- A *business requirement to provide consolidated data for federated metadata on an open platform.*

Avoid Monolithic Database Designs.

A good database design is aligned with the principles of a Service-Oriented Architecture whereby data are associated with a particular business service. When data for a particular process (service) needs to change, it is localized and does not have an effect on the entire application. Mapping your database design to a Service-Oriented Architecture allows an organization to realize quality attributes including the following:

- Scalability
- Performance
- Availability
- Flexibility
- Modularity

A modular database design allows databases to be backed up and recovered quicker than in a monolithic approach. Scalability and availability are also increased when data are partitioned along the lines of a service because that allows parallel tasks to be accomplished. A complex request can be divided into smaller chunks and processed by multiple databases simultaneously

To align the data architecture strategy with the principles of service-orientation, the following steps must occur:

- Clear definition of business processes.
- Clear definition of data requirements that the service will use.
- Accountability of business units for the integrity of data.
- Establishment of service levels to ensure consistency.

Use Access Rules to Protect Data.

Ideally, all data access should occur through a Service-Oriented Architecture that will have its own access rules. Data should not be directly accessible except through other processes that own the data. This practice will help prevent unauthorized access or its accidental destruction.

> For best practices on modeling, see Chapter 8, Agile Modeling.

Data Validation Should Occur at Multiple Tiers within an N-Tier Architecture.

Data can be represented in many forms, including EDI streams, XML documents, and SOAP messages. Validation in these scenarios should occur before data are sent across the network. This reduces errors within a distributed architecture and can increase performance in many situations. For example, if a GUI-based application captured user-entered data in a data entry screen, this can be corrected before data are written to the database. In a distributed environment, it may be more efficient to validate the data within the GUI instead of it having to travel through multiple and geographically dispersed systems, only for it to be rejected by a database constraint.

> For best practices on validation in the presentation layer, see Chapter 9, Presentation Tier Architecture.

Data Should Be Replicated Based on Business Requirements and Only When Necessary.

Our next best practice states that it is better to have a single version of a data source whenever possible. The only viable reasons for maintaining a replicated environment are either to increase performance or to create a decision support database that mirrors an online transaction processing (OLTP) database.

A data architecture that includes a replicated data source is much harder to design and maintain than a design that assumes a single stable location for data. Likewise, if data that is replicated are also updated frequently, the potential for latency and the potential for services to return inaccurate data are introduced.

A replication strategy is appropriate when users in different geographic locations need similar data that are not required to be current and a central data source is not possible. In such a situation, your business requirements should address nonfunctional quality attributes such as data availability, recoverability, freshness (near real-time versus 1 week old), and so on.

Replicated Data Should Be Read-only.

It is preferable that data architecture includes an authoritative source for data. This is where all updates should be directed. Allowing users to update replicated data unnecessarily complicates the replication environment and introduces potential data integrity problems. In a distributed environment, using a single source to guarantee data consistency is easier than managing updates in a multiple data source environment.

For example, if you have a replicated database that can be updated from multiple locations, you must consider the expected behavior when two people update the same record at the same time. Possible outcomes could include the following:

- Allowing the first update to succeed and undoing the last update (FIFO)
- Allowing the last update to overwrite the first update (LIFO)
- Canceling both updates
- Moving both updates to another table and allowing an administrator to determine the outcome

Obviously, multiple deviations on the above outcomes are possible. What is important to note is that they will make your data architecture a lot more complicated than it needs to be. By utilizing an authoritative source, other data sources can synchronize to the source of record, ensuring consistency.

The Replication Topology Implementation Should Meet Existing Business Needs.

Business requirements should define the following:

- Acceptable lag times
- Transformation
- Monitoring

By documenting the acceptable lag times in replication in a data architecture, service level agreements can be established along with the ability to determine appropriate replication schemes to be used along with scheduling. Data replication from an OLTP to a decision support system (DSS) usually results in data transformation. The business requirements should clearly articulate transformation requirements. This will allow an architect to determine any additional processing overhead on both the source and destination data sources and to make appropriate adjustments for performance and scalability.

Additionally, the business requirements should outline any monitoring requirements. Sound enterprise architecture will have a systems management component that will address configuration, monitoring, and administration.

Transparency of Location of Data by Accessing Applications Should Be Encouraged.

In an N-tier architecture, data access will usually occur through some form of middle tier (Figure 11–8). This allows applications not to know the location of their data sources. By introducing this principle into an architecture, one can restructure databases by changing schemas on the fly on backup sources using promotion/demotion schemes without the application knowing this occurred. For disaster recovery and high-availability situations, the underlying data source can be offline and restarted in another location, also without affecting the application. Furthermore, one can use this strategy for replatforming data sources, such as moving from Oracle on Solaris to Microsoft SQL Server on Windows 2000.

Figure 11–8

Separation of tiers.

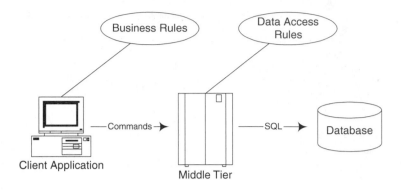

For example, a client should never send SQL requests directly to a database. It is preferable that a client send requests to services that handle processing. The service will receive the request from a client and send a message to the middle tier. The middle tier in turn will send an SQL call to the database. This approach means the client does not need to know data-specific language constructs, whether SQL, XML, or proprietary. The client is simply responsible for sending a request for work.

> The Command Pattern as outlined by the Gang of Four should be used. See *Design Patterns: Elements of Reusable Object-Oriented Software* by E. Gamma, R. Helm, R. Johnson, and J. Vlissides.

Implement Tools, Processes, and Policies to Ensure Data Integrity.

The responsibility for data integrity resides in the hands of both business and information technology personnel. Business users should determine functional security requirements, and IT should provide the mechanisms that guarantee that this requirement is met. It is the primary responsibility of IT to safeguard all data under its control.

The principles of systems management will ensure that all data are protected against corruption and loss by proving a mechanism to backup and restore data to an intact state after a system failure. Good backup and recovery strategies are mandatory so that data can be recovered in a timely manner regardless of the cause of loss. Systems management may also require reserving a portion of bandwidth between locations or even providing redundant connections to support replication in a disaster recovery environment. If the replicated/distributed data are mission-critical, it becomes important to make sure the data architecture considers performance and survivability under normal circumstances, as well as within degraded operations. In the latter situation, it may be necessary to record the flow of data across tiers (e.g., breadcrumbs).

When Designing a Database for Performance, It Should Include the Total Performance and Not Just Local Performance.

Performance should be viewed holistically. The performance of your data tier should be considered in conjunction with the capabilities of other tiers, such as network and application. Sometimes, performance of the data tier can be increased by employing caching strategies at other tiers, use of compression techniques at the network level, and so on.

However, when tuning the data tier for performance, consider the following whenever possible:

- Limit the number of indexes in a database.
- Limit ad hoc data access.
- Reduce the number of rows in a result set.
- Limit the number of joins.
- Avoid sorting.

For relational databases, an index is updated each time a record is updated. Logically, if a record has one corresponding index, the update will occur faster than if the record had ten corresponding indexes. By limiting ad hoc data access to a database, one can make data access patterns more deterministic and predictable. Ad hoc access can have an impact on the performance of a database.

By reducing the number of rows in a result set and/or at least potentially limiting the amount returning to the calling tier, performance can also be increased. In an OLTP system, users typically work with a single row displayed on the screen or with a couple of rows displayed within a grid or list box. Returning only the rows and columns that are needed at that instant will reduce the amount of network traffic, transformation, and other forms of processing associated with the request.

Limiting the number of joins in a result set also will have a profound effect on the performance of the data tier. By reducing the number of tables, the optimizer algorithms that many relational databases use can look at a smaller set of indexes and create a better data access plan. Sorts should be avoided on large amounts of data whenever possible. Additionally, sorting should occur only on indexed fields.

> For additional information on mapping, refer to *www.agiledata.org/essays/mappingObjects.html*.

Prefer Open Standards to Proprietary Extensions.

The temptation to use vendor-specific extensions to SQL should be avoided at all costs. Advocate for use of ANSI-standard SQL, and not proprietary extensions, in access to relational database stores. This concept is applicable to other forms of databases also. For example, an XML database should be exclusively accessed using XPath or XQuery.

> For additional information on XPath and XQuery, see *XQuery: Kick Start* by J. McGovern, C. Kagle, P. Bothner, J. Linn, and V. Nagarajan.

By utilizing a separate data access tier, data architecture can minimize the impact of calling applications since the APIs used by higher tiers do not change. The implementation of stored procedures is another form of proprietary access to a database that should be avoided. Stored procedures are specific to the database implementation in use and are difficult to migrate if a different implementation of a database is required.

> For more information on implementing a separate data access tier, see *www.agiledata.org/essays/implementationStrategies.html*.

Those familiar with Java and J2EE will see this principle represented by Enterprise Java Beans, and will notice the preference of the Java community to use container-managed persistence, which does not support the use of stored procedures. The Java community is slowly adopting APIs such as the Java Data Object (JDO) specification that allows for data store independence.

> For a great book on Java Data Objects, see *Core Java Data Objects* by Sameer Tyagi, Michael Vorburger, Keiron McCannon, and Heiko Bobzin.

Use of database triggers is also a proprietary extension of a database. It is a good practice to use database triggers for the sole purpose of supporting referential integrity and no more.

Protect Credit Card Information Using Encryption.

Credit card information is of special concern to enterprise architects as these data are usually the most vulnerable. Ideally, the protection of credit card information starts with the protection of the entry point into your organization. This may be in the form of a Web site that should be protected using a secure sockets layer (SSL). For one-time transactions, the credit card information should never be stored. Instead, it is preferable to pass this information to the payment gateway (provided by a bank) that the enterprise uses. Every transport used between systems should also support some form of encryption.

At times, it is preferable to allow applications to process recurring charges that mandate storing credit card information. In this situation, it becomes mandatory to encrypt the credit card number in the database. Likewise, related personal information, such as name and address, should be stored separately in a database separate from credit card information. To further increase the security of the data, consider using separate user IDs and passwords for the database that stores personal information and the database that stores credit card information. Ideally, neither database should use default database passwords.

We conclude this chapter by noting that a successful architecture is created solely to support business processes and not the reverse. Many organizations fail in this undertaking by defining business objects and respective data elements that are never utilized. Even worse, they miss essential pieces of data used in business processes or they collect data that provide zero value to the organization. Remember: The purpose of an architecture is to support business processes, nothing else. This is what will allow an organization to stay agile.

In this chapter we have covered the following:

- Baseline data architecture
- Frameworks
- Metadata
- Data modeling
- Data warehousing
- Data security
- Agile databases
- Best practices

We have outlined an ideal vision of how enterprise architecture should function in an agile enterprise. If you follow the guidelines presented, you are guaranteed that the enterprise has achieved the required preparation to create an invaluable and consistent data architecture.

Conclusion

chapter 12

Thought Leadership

Never tattle; always make fun of people who appear differently from you. Never say anything unless you're sure that everyone feels exactly the way you do.

Homer Simpson, *Rules of the Playground*

The members of this author team play an active role in shaping the future of enterprise architecture. We have participated in various standards committees and collectively authored about a dozen books in subject areas including Web services, XML, project management, and software development. The refinement of provocative ideas coupled with practical examples throughout our collective body of knowledge will help extend this notion even further. You will find us participating at many industry conferences and serving as keynote speakers.

The savage pursuit of excellence in our professional lives has caused us to explore passionately how architecture is best created and realized. Many times, the best approach is not the prescription found elsewhere. Sometimes, we have good information we would like to share, but it does not fit into a particular chapter or is hard to classify, though it has merit for inclusion in a discussion.

Sometimes, thought leadership involves the ability to throw out ideas in a rough form and allow others to react and provide further refinement. This chapter departs from the typical literary formulas and opens doors you may choose to close or open further. With this in mind, we offer you short narratives, varied thoughts and diagrams we feel will bring value to your enterprise architecture. We consider this our manifesto.

Many organizations have struggled with the creation of a team responsible for the formation of an enterprise architecture. We firmly believe that the champion of enterprise architecture should be a high ranking individual (e.g., vice president). Figure 12–1 presents a representative organizational chart that can serve as a guide. We hope it provides appropriate information for responding to those who can't get behind the enterprise architecture concept.

Organizational Matrix

257

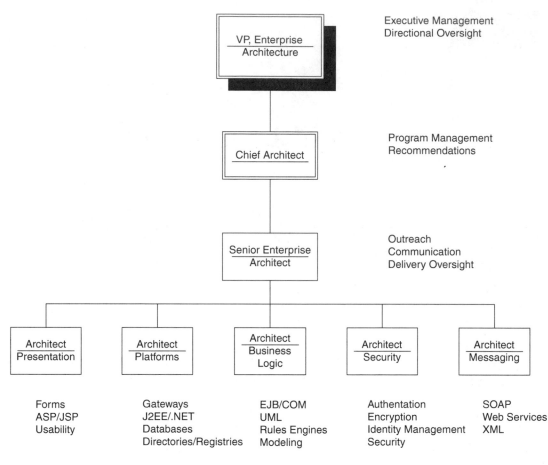

Figure 12–1
Organizational matrix.

It is a sad state of affairs in the world of enterprise architecture when executives want to outsource critical information technology functions. The root cause of this train wreck is the continued failure of enterprise architects to empower businesses to accelerate. This has caused a chain reaction that leads to outsourcing (nuclear implosion) until it results in a total meltdown (destruction of the business). Let's come to the heart of the problem. The proper reaction of an architect to outsourcing should be as follows.

Outsourcing results in taking the core competencies of an organization and moving them elsewhere. This is, of course, inappropriate once you understand the true goal of enterprise architecture. Many people are led down a rat hole with the notion that information technology is just a computerized administration function, which is the most mindless of all strategies. Imagine if Canaxia outsourced production of its cars. What would be left?

If you follow this line of thought further, you will realize that many of the large Fortune 500 organizations' primary business is information technology. For example, insurance companies don't sell manufactured products that are physical; they sell policies, which are contracts. The contracts themselves are promises of a particular behavior for the future that is essentially information. Insurance companies are really in the information management business. They take information and manipulate it to create policies (contracts). What is left of an insurance company if it outsources its core competency?

In many cases, outsourcing is not black and white. Sometimes outsourcing is a viable business decision to reduce costs; however, this can be achieved using alternative methods. For example, Canaxia can move its call center from New York City to Boise, Idaho, where labor costs are much lower. Furthermore, if going outside of the United States proves cost-effective, outsourcing in the same time zone is an option. Countries such as Barbados, Trinidad, Antigua, and so on have English as their native language and are knowledgeable about U.S. culture and lifestyles. We suggest you maintain the ability to check up at a moment's notice on whatever entity provides your outsourcing services. This can only be accomplished by outsourcing to countries with direct flights from major cities such as New York and Miami.

Usually the decision to outsource is done without any input from architects. The only thing I would recommend being passionate about is that a corporation maintain architecture and business control within its corporate headquarters.

Today's global economy demands strong technical leadership, the kind that can only be provided by enterprise architects. Many organizations have been led astray by the focus on putting project managers into leadership positions. It would be great if an organization could be successful simply by having a plan of action that is drilled into project managers through high-cost courseware and certifications. Sadly, this is not the reality. Project management is important, but strong technical leadership from enterprise architects is even more important.

Strong Technical Leadership

Enterprise architecture overlaps many project management disciplines, but with a fundamental difference. Enterprise architects focus on teams and improve the way they interact, solve problems, and work effectively instead of worrying about project plans (e.g., comprehensive documentation). Leadership in the technology sector is a rare commodity.

Fundamentally, it is easier to lead others if they believe you have walked in their shoes before. The vast majority of enterprise architects retain working knowledge of the systems over which they have stewardship. The same cannot be said of the masses of project managers. Organizations would be well served by adjusting their HR processes to incorporate the hiring and promotion of strong technical leaders.

Architects have the sole responsibility for dealing with constructive disruptive technologies such as the Internet, wireless, and so on. In essence, they become the solutions architect for many business problems. Typically, management does not impose a solution because it fears losing developers or, even worse, does not care enough about the practice to enforce a solution. Only an enterprise architect can assume this role.

Technical leadership influences the responses of others in the enterprise to the demands of adaptive change. Leaders should be empowered and bear sole responsibility for people who are managing processes with well-defined techniques. An enterprise architect should be in charge of influencing people performing technical functions, whether for a single project or an ongoing operation.

Architects Stand the Test of Time

While some people enter the technology field early in life, architects in many of the Fortune 500 enterprises tend to be older, a phenomenon we will refer to as the "wise dinosaur." The fact that many organizations are pushing the notion of architects in their twenties is laughable. Those who are successful have figured out not only the technology aspects of enterprise architecture and how to sell them to management but also how to sell themselves.

Several career pointers arise when one thinks about the characteristics of those who are successful versus those who aren't. The first problem is the competition between old and young. Younger people grow up with new technologies, are generally cheaper to hire, say "no" less often than their wiser peers, and don't have many other commitments. These traits are attractive to many employers.

Other architects develop a sense of arrogance (prima donnas in their ivory towers) over time, and they believe that others cannot be more intelligent or superior. Sadly, this leads not only to the downfall of the individual but also hurts the profession as a whole. Other architects do not expand their horizons and lash out at foreigners who are in many ways smarter and more expert.

I remember a presentation given by Ken Schwaber on protecting oneself in a down job market. and I have merged his thoughts with my own. Architects can fight back in many ways. For the weak minded, ask your representatives in Washington to support caps on the H1B visa program, to support tariffs on imported software, and to create bills such as New Jersey Senate Bill 1349. Consider spending time mastering new technologies such as Bayesian belief networks, grid computing, the semantic Web, and so on. Speak to the head of your network and infrastructure organization, and encourage them to think about IP telephony, instant messaging, tablet PCs, wireless, and server blades. Observe industry trends, and follow fundamental paradigm shifts before they occur. Paradigms this team currently follows include these:

- Future state implementations of Service-Oriented Architectures that incorporate the notion of ontologies and are model-driven
- The pervasive growth of business-rules engines within the enterprise and how they eventually will cause the enterprise to repeat the same mistakes made 20 years ago
- To increase business agility, incorporation of Bayesian belief networks as an alternative to declarative rules approaches
- The failure of organizations who migrate to new technologies, such as Web services, but still build business logic behind their screens and how UI standards such as XUL and XForms may help

A simple investment of 5 percent of one's time will put you ahead of your peers by 50 percent or more. Consider learning a foreign language or two. Members of this author team speak French, Hindi, Korean, Arabic, and Hebrew. The biggest investment one can make is in oneself. Invest regularly. Make sure you set aside at least 3 hours per week in the name of career development. Remember: *Past performance is no guarantee of future results.*

Many architects are pummeled by management (not leaders) with the idea that an organization should create initiatives that focus on the capture of best practices so others can benefit from them later. The mind-set that supports archiving these practices facilitates efficient problem solving, which leads over time to the way business should be conducted.

Of course, this goes against many agile approaches and is, in many ways, diametrically opposed to the agile manifesto of preferring interactions to comprehensive documentation. Solutions to business challenges are typically containerized by memorization of various "measures of goodness" (Booch) that also have embedded assumptions, nonpublic views of organizational strategy, and unwritten reward systems (e.g., what do I need to do to make my boss believe I am competent). The sad fact of many enterprises is that this mind-set breeds doing more of the same better, which only provides marginal returns that diminish over time.

For example, a frog is unable to detect gradual changes in temperature. A frog that is put into boiling water quickly has instincts that will tell it to jump out, but when it is put into room temperature water that is slowly brought to a boil (the vast majority of significant projects fall into this category), the frog will ultimately boil to death. The mantra of doing more of the same will result in locking in both desired and undesired behaviors that result in a death march. In other words, more of the same doesn't help. The status quo mind-set must be abolished.

This mind-set is further compromised by the notion that knowledge can be stored by using information technology. We are aware that databases and

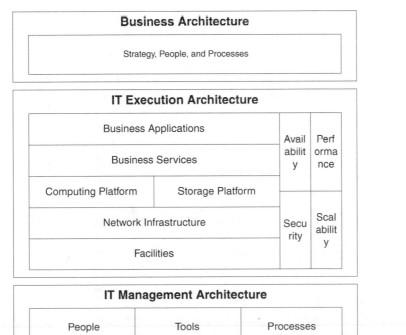

Figure 12–2
Core competencies reference architecture.

groupware applications can store information that is structured and unstructured, but in the end that amounts simply to storing bits of data. Neither solution today can store the rich schemas that people possess for making sense of those bits. One fundamental truth exists that is often ignored: the simple fact that information is context-sensitive. The same data will elicit different responses from different people. When someone invents the technology that can scan a person's mind and store it directly in a database, people will be able to experience the reality of another person. Since that isn't possible, it is important to focus on interaction.

This does not mean we are not for knowledge management or best practices. Rather, we think they are useful tools for creating a consensus-driven view of the business problem. However, it must be acknowledged up front that this information is static, rational, and without context, but our business problems are anything but static, border on the line of insane, and definitely have context. These tools do not truly help with what is important, which is the ability to renew existing knowledge and assist in the creation of new knowledge.

The best practice that is never spoken about is the one that allows a culture to be unlearned. What is "best" today may be "garbage" tomorrow.

The Agile CIO

Many of the great CIOs realized early in their careers that to rise on the organizational ladder, one must find alternative approaches for software development that focuses on customer satisfaction through continuous delivery of useful software. Others still use the questionable wisdom of developing software in the same manner it was done 30 years ago, which leads to the vast majority of projects falling to the demons of total failure, budget overruns, and release with less functionality than initially promised. Only the agile CIO has the answer to this conundrum. Let's look at the answers provided by Kello James, our agile CIO.

Kello James believes that requirements for software at the outset of a project should be kept to a minimum. He counsels not to enumerate every possible facet of what you want software to accomplish. Simply start with what functions the software must absolutely have. Kello also believes that one should not be savage at this stage about writing down all the needs of the software (comprehensive documentation) because requirements will change during the course of the project.

Our agile CIO has also instituted a process whereby the business leaders test the application on a monthly basis and provide additional guidance (customer interaction) and approval. This allows developers to get immediate feedback on areas that require additional concentration. Furthermore, it ensures that developers are focused solely on a hard-target deadline for which his staff will always rise to their finest hour. Any software that the business community tests at this stage is not released to production, but it must be functional (preferably working software).

Kello is also a fan of the movie *Sniper* and frequently uses the phrase "One shot, one kill" in his staff meetings. He advocates shooting a belief if it doesn't work. Bringing together businesspeople and IT frequently to evaluate software allows Kello the opportunity to determine immediately whether or not his team is satisfying the goals of its business partners. At a minimum, any software that doesn't meet the needs of the customer is killed.

The typical organization has incorporated the notion of *triage* into their methodology, but it usually comes too late in the game. Frequent evaluation of software with customer involvement provides the ideal opportunity to kill a software project. Kello once learned of a feature that was being developed by his application architect when he realized that no one had actually expressed a desire for the feature. Without hesitation, Kello killed it right then. Organizations no longer can afford to burn precious time and money only to realize what they are working on isn't useful.

Over the objections of his staff, Kello frequently slashes the budgets of many of the software projects, even those in progress. He has realized that small budgets force his development team to focus only on essential functionality. It also makes it more acceptable to kill failing projects. Kello's success rate has significantly increased using this approach.

Kello's nonagile CIO industry peers frequently commit to big-dollar projects that frequently crash. One of his peers is struggling to figure out how to rescue a project that has already burned through $40 million. At this stage, the only thing his peers can do is to attempt throwing more money at the problem in a rather futile attempt to rescue it rather than taking a huge loss. At the end of the day, Kello's nonagile peers further increase their losses using this approach.

Our agile CIO has mandated that the development team have direct access to the end business customer as they are in the best position to conduct tests and determine whether the customer's needs are being met. Using this approach has resulted in two separate successes for Canaxia. First, the business community can no longer claim ignorance about the software development process and cannot honestly say that they were in the dark. Second, through synergistic interaction with business communities, Canaxia has created the perfect developer: half businessperson, half programmer.

The Mysteries of Open Source

In many organizations, the architecture is determined by vendors selling miraculous wares to executives in exchange for golf outings. To prevent any dissent among the ranks, vendors distribute T-shirts, coffee mugs, and assorted trinkets as forms of bribery. The grand vision of becoming an organizational hero simply by championing the purchase of big-dollar expenditures on hardware and software is rapidly disappearing.

Open source and GNU (www.gnu.org) will sooner or later penetrate the enterprise architecture of many organizations—it is inevitable. The practical architect will embrace open source as a solution to business problems and may even become an advocate of it. Others will remain hesitant to consider it because of beliefs perpetuated by software vendors who hint that it is unsupported and written by shaggy college kids who may disappear for year-long sabbaticals in China or Germany. Nothing could be further from the truth.

A recent study by Boston Consulting Group found that professional network administrators and developers with an average of 11 years of information technology experience comprise the open source community. Furthermore, 30 percent of that community indicated that they will have to answer to their bosses if they *don't* write open source code.

Many well-respected Fortune 500 organizations are not only using open source but actively contributing to its development. Technologies such as Apache, Linux, JBoss, and JUnit are dominant within their respective categories. Many of the Web sites for open source initiatives contain links for making donations. Consider having your CIO click on such a link. Others have figured out that supporting open source is also good for other reasons.

One agile organization was spending over $1 million on a particular J2EE application server when it realized it could avoid further expenditures by embracing open source. It figured that the salaries for two highly compensated Java developers working on open source J2EE application servers would be much cheaper than paying the support charges of the respective J2EE vendor. Furthermore, having access to code and two individuals in-house with intimate knowledge helped the organization solve problems faster. It also noticed that morale increased because junior developers appreciated having at-will access to two developers. The two newly hired developers also conducted application design reviews, which further increased the quality of software within the organization.

Enterprises should consider contributing to the open source movement as an investment. Organizations that leverage open source for competitive advantage save money by utilizing the output from various projects. It is in their best interest to give something back, whether it is in the form of financial support or contributing a developer's time to extend the platforms the enterprise depends on.

Consultant 101

Every member of this author team has been a consultant, and what will be said here may be shocking but is based upon actual consulting experiences. Many organizations successfully hire consultants to provide guidance on IT strategy and enterprise architecture, while others fail to do likewise. Some people are not savvy to the tricks of the consulting trade and are clueless about what to look for. Since advice from others can result in the success or failure of enterprise architecture, we provide several tips to make sure you get the right consultant.

First, make sure that what you see is what you get. In larger consulting firms, typically a partner and one or more of the best employees will make sales calls to impress their potential client. Since many enterprises are slow to make decisions, this usually results in the original stars on the sales call being unavailable at engagement time. Consider putting the names of the people you met on the first sales call into your contract, which will guarantee that they show up for the engagement.

Next, consultants usually are not around long enough to see their advice come to fruition. It is important for consultants and their firms to have some skin in the game. Many enterprise initiatives may take a number of years before problems are discovered or the architecture is working correctly. Consider inserting a clause into the contract that requires the consultants to come back at a reduced rate if the product doesn't work as advertised.

Also, though reference checks are important, most organizations conduct them incorrectly. We recommend that you check the references of the project manager and architect assigned to your company, not only the references of the consulting firm. Consulting firms have an easy time securing references, especially if they have hundreds of clients. Of course, each reference you receive will be hand picked. The liability for delivery is in the hands of the people on your project, so their references are more important.

In addition, consulting arrangements should be structured around business improvement, not around installation of systems. Many consultancies that focus on installation of packages in the CRM, ERP, and systems management space are always successful in getting installations to work and past some form of technical sign-off but rarely demonstrate any cost savings or increased flexibility. Many technology magazines frequently publish articles about how initiatives such as these actually cost more after they have been implemented. Ensuring that these consultancies are doing the right thing for your enterprise requires incentives such as tying payment to improved productivity or reduced costs.

Consultancies are infamous for marketing their methodologies to those who are unfamiliar with what a methodology is supposed to contain. Some consultancies never actually make the effort to create or adopt a methodology, but promote a methodology merely for marketing reasons. Some consultancies have internal project documentation that they share and leverage across companies but not with their customers. Wise enterprises should consider mandating that the consulting firm provide access to the Web sites and tools the consultants use. Minimally, an organization should be able to see at will all documentation related to the project at hand.

Many consulting firms have a fast-track career path for their youngest and brightest. However, be careful in employing consulting firms without age diversity. Contract with firms offering an equal distribution of people in their thirties and forties. If a firm is overloaded with those in their twenties, especially in an outsourcing model, run in the other direction. Years of experience cannot be easily substituted.

Finally, in many organizations, enterprise architecture is determined on the golf course by the CIO. Unfortunately, the CIO does not typically purchase enterprise software; business executives do. Many consultancies understand this and do everything in their power to bypass enterprise architects, and this is best accomplished while playing golf. The best way to get hold of this type of problem is to build relationships with business executives so that they will, at the very least, check with you before any payment is issued.

Why I Should Be a CIO

The vast majority of architects worth their salt traditionally fail as managers. Having come from technical backgrounds, many architects prefer to lead by example. The preference for technical excellence and demonstrated ability gets in the way of processes and decision making by those who are uninformed. Many enterprises do not leverage expertise to their competitive advantage and fail to recognize the potential of those who push the envelope or think outside the box.

Many of today's respected executives were architects in their own domains. They found creative solutions to difficult problems, possessed a savage desire to succeed, and—most importantly—never stopped learning. Leaders such as Jack Welsh (former CEO of General Electric) and Rudolph

Giuliani (former mayor of New York City) had more desire to succeed than fear of failure. We hope executives will ensure future prosperity of their enterprise architectures by ensuring that stewards exist today but also are being grown for the future.

Sadly, for too long the development of new leaders within most enterprises has taken a back seat to other issues. Smart leaders understand that having talented leadership at all levels of an organization is necessary for a business to meet the challenges faced in today's business economy. Some executives believe that leaders can be built by sending them off to a leadership training class or by buying books about cheese and fish.

The problem is further compounded when this approach is taken with IT leadership. Today's IT departments face the challenge of understanding both the business of the company and the business of IT. Leaders within IT provide guidance to the business while simultaneously providing services for it. Their business partners may make flawed assumptions about the role of technology and how it can solve business problems and provide corrective action while also correcting flaws within their own organizations. Leaders within IT must constantly adapt their approach to fit their IT organizations' capabilities and still create attractive environments for talented technology staff.

To the CIOs who are reading this book: We ask you to seriously consider establishing a formal leadership development program for your organization and to staff it with people with diverse experiences and backgrounds. Include architects, developers, and even help desk personnel. Provide mentoring and continuous feedback, and you will be able to grow a constant supply of leaders. Don't settle for managers.

The Next Minute

We have noticed many boutique consulting firms that sell enterprise architecture frameworks and tools to large organizations with even larger purse strings by using the terminology of the next minute. Many of them use fluffy words to make themselves look smarter while they are merely focusing on drawing better PowerPoint diagrams. For us, *next minute* should be the term used for what you need to think about in the future: those problems that all enterprises will address. Let's dive into what we feel is the next minute.

The first next-minute challenge an enterprise architect will need to start thinking about is the nature of collaboration. With the advent of Web services, businesses can create relationships dynamically and on the fly. Today's model of security, integration, management, and such is heavily embedded with the notion of long-term relationships. In a dynamic model, organizations will need a substitute for trust. Many organizations will scratch their heads on this one.

Some enterprise architects believe they should position their organizations for future opportunities in the way of mergers and acquisitions. Of course, this falls in line with our best practices thinking. The new model for enterprise architecture has to be extremely agile. The architecture should support the ability for decisions to be made in real-time. If this can be solved for, the need to support mergers and acquisitions should dwindle. If organizations can interoperate in a fluid manner, they will not waste time or money or even incur risk to acquire each other.

Other enterprise architects maintain the notion of separate business and technology strategies. In the next minute, the business and technology strategy shall be unified. Technology will no longer be the hindrance that stands in the way of the organization's goals. Technology will no longer be the electronic filing cabinet but rather the engine that pushes forward.

Conclusion

This book explored a variety of concepts surrounding architecture, agile methods and processes, and summarized thoughts that will help you think practically about your approach to enterprise architecture. The authors have distilled important principles that warrant additional research. The remainder of this book contains appendices you may find useful. We encourage you to seek out the recommended books, magazine articles, and other source materials and to become savage in the pursuit of excellence.

Business Case

You do not build a business by reading Sun Tsu's Art of War.
Steve Mills, Senior VP and Group Executive, IBM

Examples within this book are based upon a fictitious auto manufacturer, Canaxia, based in the United States with locations throughout North America, the Caribbean, South America, Europe, and Africa. Canaxia is headquartered in Bloomfield, Connecticut, and was incorporated on August 24, 1967. It is a public company listed on the New York Stock Exchange and has 50,000 employees worldwide.

To maintain a competitive business advantage, this manufacturer needs to modernize its supply chain and other internal systems. The infrastructure (sometimes referred to as the *nervous system*) for the organization consists of a mix of applications written in different languages and run on various platforms. The vast majority of the applications are written in COBOL running on two IBM mainframes in two different data centers. The organization is working diligently to migrate legacy COBOL applications off the mainframe and has adopted Java and J2EE as its future application environment of choice.

> For more information on J2EE, see *java.sun.com/j2ee*.

The overall architecture of Canaxia has remained largely unchanged for 20 years. The lack of willingness to fund technology upgrades over time has caused Canaxia's systems to become difficult to maintain. Canaxia's CIO, Kello James, has mandated that all future applications be developed in a modular manner and that they use the architecture principles contained within this book. The first mandate was to select a Java-based application server and write all future business logic using Enterprise JavaBeans™ (EJBs).

Kello James would also like to integrate several disparate systems that exist throughout the organization, and he requires that all systems communicate in a loosely coupled manner.

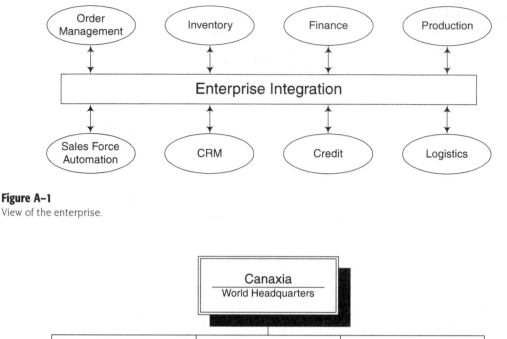

Figure A–1
View of the enterprise.

Figure A–2
Canaxia organizational structure.

Canaxia's CIO wants to make sure that all information is fully integrated and that any proposed solution provides seamless access. All systems should be fully accessible from not only the headquarters but also from the regional offices, provided that the user has the appropriate permissions.

Furthermore, Canaxia would like to extend access to its internal systems to customers, suppliers, and business partners to reduce support in its call centers, as well as to allow for automated invoicing, ordering, and purchasing.

Canaxia has unique problems in that it currently does not have the ability to create reports in a timely manner on key business processes. The ideal enterprise architecture would allow extraction of information from multiple systems and creation of a consolidated view at any time. Users have requested ad hoc reporting capabilities against several systems to help them accept last-minute changes to the cars they produce, even while they are on the assembly line.

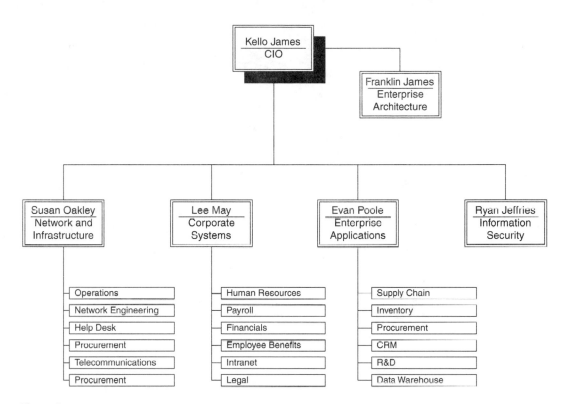

Figure A-3
Canaxia organizational chart.

The CIO of Canaxia, Mattie Lee Mitchell, has encouraged the CTO, Kello James, to adopt wherever appropriate the use of open standards and frameworks. Mattie Lee hopes that by using products and tools that adhere to open standards, Canaxia can lower its acquisition and licensing costs for software, as well as leverage knowledge among different project teams. Mattie Lee also requires a waiver be obtained when technology choices go against open standards.

Any examples, companies, organizations, products, domain names, email addresses, people, places, and events depicted herein are fictitious. No association with any real company, organization, product, domain name, email address, person, place, or event is intended or should be inferred.

Practical Considerations

I have three precious things which I hold fast and prize. The first is gentleness; the second is frugality; the third is humility, which keeps me from putting myself before others. Be gentle and you can be bold; be frugal and you can be liberal; avoid putting yourself before others and you can become a leader among men.

Lao-Tzu (604–531 B.C.), Chinese philosopher
and founder of Taoism

Many books that present architecture-related topics always have some mention of best practices. This book is no different. One thing missing from many of the other books is guidance on how best practices should be propagated throughout an organization.

We found an old copy of the "Systems Thinker," newsletter from 1997 that discussed putting best practices into practice. Back then, the notion of being agile was not even a thought in the minds of the founding fathers of the movement. Borrowing some of the concepts presented in this newsletter, we have adjusted for today's enterprise architecture. Following are several methods in which learning organizations can start the process of sharing best practices in an agile manner:

1. *Publish the business case.* Evangelists of best practices should be able to clearly articulate answers to questions such as "What problem or opportunity does this initiative address in terms of the organization's larger goals?

2. *Adapt the practice to fit local conditions.* What was successful in one situation may result in a total failure in another. It is vital to refine the essence of the best practice by defining a complete description that details the level of abstraction. This should point out whether it is the process or the product that is at the root of the practice. Of course, in the spirit of remaining agile, this should not turn into a large documentation exercise.

3. *Understand how your practice really works.* Many practices contain hidden individual and team knowledge associated with it. Sometimes, the creation and success of a practice are tied directly to specific team dynamics and those highly motivated individuals who promote the success of the practice. In many situations, the best practice may turn out to prefer individuals and interactions to processes and tools.

4. *Collaboration must be part of the organizational culture.* The vast majority of large enterprises prevent the development and adoption of best practices based on their reward systems. Individuals will not be successful in making global changes in an organization's structure, but individuals can gain support for acceptance of changes by attaching a new practice to an ongoing activity. Ideally, the IT senior leadership team will adopt an IT governance approach to solving this problem.

5. *Don't allow the jewels to get lost in the computer.* Many organizations think about best practices occurring in the form of repositories, which results in massive documentation. This approach reduces access to best practices. The focus should be on collaboration between matchmaker and information broker, which is the only action that will result in valuable best practice riches.

The Seven Habits of an Agile Enterprise Architecture

Some schools and teachers are better than others, but my level of effort, dedication, curiosity, and willingness to grow determine what I learn.

Larry Elder, KABC Radio, Los Angeles

While this book provides practical advice on enterprise architecture, the book would be incomplete without outlining seven action items that every architect should make a habit:

1. *Architecture Is Business-Driven.* This is the first and most important habit of an architect. All architectural undertakings should be done for the sole reason of solving business problems. Architecture planning is a continuous process that requires full alignment with business goals.

2. *Communication Is King.* Enterprise architecture must be communicated to all parties across all IT organizations and lines of business on an ongoing basis. This should include strategy, goals, and objectives. Its purpose is to increase awareness throughout an enterprise. It must also include a statement of shared values that are endorsed and supported by the executive team and incorporated into the IT governance model.

3. *Unification Is Queen.* For enterprise architecture to succeed, it must be unified across the enterprise. Success and failure of all forms of architecture depend upon the joint efforts of all business and IT areas, their support of the architecture, and consistent implementation.

4. *The Frog Is a Prince.* Support from the executive team is essential for the practice of architecture, but a successful architecture starts almost at a grass-roots level by seeking support from line managers and their direct reports where the sell is the hardest.

Getting buy-in from the troops (Seek first to understand, then be understood) will shield the architecture from passive resistance.

5. K.I.S.S.: *Keep Infrastructure Simple.* Information technology assets and the elimination of the endless combinations of platforms that use disparate technologies are the main inhibitors of change and result in an inflexible architecture. A goal of sound enterprise architecture is the destruction of incompatible technologies. If infrastructure is kept simple and consistent, enterprise architecture can leverage existing skill sets, training, support, and services in a cost-effective and agile manner.

6. *Agility Is Key.* Sometimes the best solution for a particular business problem requires adoption of a technology and/or approaches that are not mainstream. Agile enterprise architecture will allow the modification of standards to support business requirements, and it will seek out alternate ways to integrate the technology with the current architectural model.

7. *Crawl Before You Walk.* Expectations should be managed. The best architecture for an enterprise is one that evolves versus one that is created. Each iteration of the architecture should build upon previous versions and provide an incremental improvement to the organization. Enterprise architecture should also focus initial efforts on near-term opportunities—what is within reach—that can provide immediate business benefit. Small but quick wins will help win allies from both the business and technology areas and will best demonstrate the value of agile enterprise architecture.

Models

You never change things by fighting the existing reality. To change something, build a new model that makes the existing model obsolete.

Buckminster Fuller

Sound enterprise architecture can be described (modeled) using a layered approach. Each layer brings enlightenment to the mission of the organization, allowing all parties to become active participants in defining the near-term architecture.

The business model specifies the enterprise's business goals, the products and services it produces, what additional products and services it desires to produce in the future, and the constraints restricting how these goals can be accomplished. It also includes such factors as time, budget, legal and regulatory restrictions, and so on. The ultimate goal of the business model is to define in a single location the near-term and strategic intent of the organization.

Information models demonstrate how business functions within an enterprise coalesce as a cohesive business unit. Business analysts and executives review the output of the business model and decide what processes and integration are required to achieve the goals of the business. The key to success in this layer is having sufficient information to make a valid conclusion. This model contains information about processes, resources, how processes interact, and associations among data elements being used to drive the business. Lack of information within this model points to weak data architecture within an enterprise.

An operation model describes the structure of a business and provides for allocation of resources to optimally address elements of an enterprise's information model. This model specifies the organization chart and assigns resources (people and materials) to the specified hierarchy. Many organizations have struggled with creating the right organization chart. Paradigm shifts occur at this level due primarily to many organizations adopting traditional organizational structures rather than aligning to their stated informational models.

277

Figure D-1
Business technology
integration.

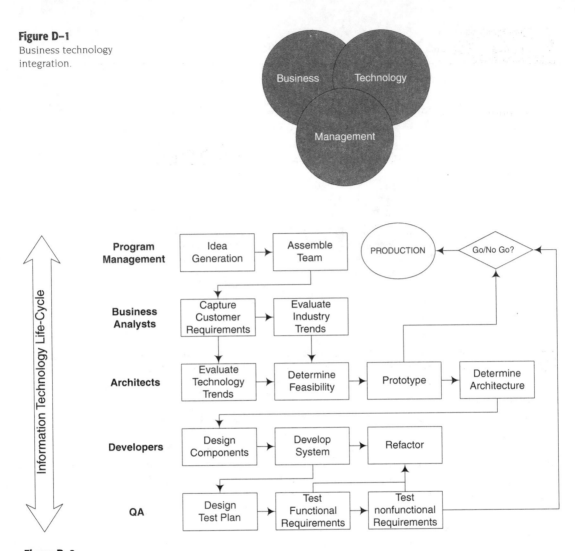

Figure D-2
Roles and responsibilities.

Organizational models scrutinize the processes described within the informational model and endeavor to provide optimal execution of those processes by creating diverse operational entities. This model contains an enterprise's various departments and traditionally includes functional areas such as engineering, sales and marketing, administration, and research and development.

Architecture models study the previous models and define the optimal technology topology for information systems. They will take into account systems or services being served today by humans who could allow for the business to increase agility if they were to automate using systems. This usually results in the creation of an architecture that includes distributed processing, middleware, and open systems.

Models of the current technology infrastructure capture the current state of technology decisions that have been made in the past and have been implemented. The model at this layer is constantly evolving and has the least amount of stability when compared to other models. Some components of an infrastructure have lives of only several weeks or months.

No enterprise architecture can be considered complete unless it addresses all the above layers. To be successful with enterprise architecture may require a divide-and-conquer approach since no one individual can do all the work. Figure out how to engage other resources within your organization to assist you with the task.

References

It is amazing what can be accomplished when nobody cares about who gets the credit.

Robert Yates

Abowd, G., Bass, L., Clements, P., Kazman, R., Northrop, L., & Zamerski, A. (1996). *Recommended Best Industrial Practices for Software Architecture Evaluation.* (CMU/ SEI-96-TR-025). Pittsburgh: Software Engineering Institute, Carnegie Mellon University.

Abrams, M., & Helms, J. (2002, February). *User Interface Markup Language (UIML) Specification, Version: 3.0.*

Agile Alliance (2001a). *Manifesto for Agile Software Development. www.agilealliance.org.*

Agile Alliance (2001b). *Principles: The Agile Alliance. www.agilealliance.org/principles.html.*

Agile Databases. *Groups.yahoo.com/group/agiledatabases.*

Ambler, S. W. (2001a). *The Object Primer 2nd Edition. The Application Developer's Guide to Object Orientation.* New York: Cambridge University Press. *www.ambysoft.com/theObjectPrimer.html.*

Ambler, S. W. (2001b). *Enterprise Unified Process Home Page. www.enterpriseunifiedprocess.info.*

Ambler, S. W. (2001c). *Agile Modeling Home Page. www.agilemodeling.com.*

Ambler, S. W. (2002a). *The Agile Data Home Page. www.agiledata.org.*

Ambler, S. W. (2002b). *Agile Modeling: Best Practices for the Unified Process and Extreme Programming.* New York: John Wiley & Sons. *www.ambysoft.com/agileModeling.html.*

Ambler, S. W. (2002c). *Different Projects Require Different Strategies. http://www.agiledata.org/essays/differentStrategies.html.*

Ambler, S. W. (2002d). Refactoring for Fitness. *Software Development. www.sdmagazine.com.*

Ambler, S. W. (2003a). *The Elements of UML Style.* New York: Cambridge University Press. *www.ambysoft.com/elementsUMLStyle.html.*

Ambler, S. W. (2003b). *Agile Database Techniques: Handbook for Agile DBAs.* New York: John Wiley & Sons. *www.ambysoft.com/agileDatabaseTechniques.html.*

ANSI INCITS 345-2001, CIF. *http://www.techstreet.com/cgi-bin/joint.cgi/incits/ cgi-bin/detail?pro%0D%20duct_id5%0D%0D%20%20%20673198*

Architectural reasoning; balancing genericity and specificity (n.d.) *www.extra.research.philips.com/ natlab/sysarch/ArchitecturalReasoningBook.pdf.*

Assessing Web Site Usability from Server Log Files. (1999). White Paper, Microsoft Tec-Ed.

Atkinson, C., Bayer, J., Bunse, C., Kamsties, E., Laitenberger, O., Laqua, R., Muthig, D., Paech, B., Wust, J., & Zettel, J. (2002). *Component-Based Product Line Engineering with UML*. London: Pearson Education.

Bass, L., Clements, P., & Kazman, R. (1997). *Software Architecture in Practice*. Reading, MA: Addison-Wesley Publications.

Bass, L., John, B. E., & Kates, J. (2001, March). "Achieving Usability Through Software Architecture.@CQU: *Technical Report Carnegie Mellon Software Engineering Institute* CMU/SEI-2001-TR-005 ESC-TR-2001-005.

Beck, K. (2000). *Extreme Programming Explained: Embrace Change*. Reading, MA: Addison-Wesley Longman.

Beck, K., & Fowler, M. (2000). *Planning Extreme Programming*. Reading, MA: Addison-Wesley Publications.

Beedle, M., & Schwaber, K. (2001). *Agile Software Development with SCRUM*. Upper Saddle River, NJ: Prentice Hall, Inc.

Bevan, 1995.

Beyen, N. (1997). *Quality and Usability: A New Framework*.

Bosch, J. (2000). *Design and Use of Software Architectures*. Reading, MA: Addison-Wesley.

Bredemeyer, D. (2003c). *Bredemeyer Web site. www.bredemeyer.com.*

Bredemeyer, D. (n.d.) Architecture Definition. *Bredmeyer Consulting. www.bredemeyer.com/pdf_files/ArchitectureDefinition. pdf.*

Bredemeyer, D. (n.d.) Role of the Architect. *Bredmeyer Consulting. www.bredemeyer.com/ pdf_files/role.pdf.*

Bredemeyer, D. (n.d.) Role of the Architect. *Bredmeyer Consulting. www.bredemeyer.com/ pdf_files/ArchitectRole.pdf.*

Brooks, F. P. (1975). *Mythical Man Month*. Reading, MA: Addison-Wesley.

Brooks, F. P. (1995). *The Mythical Man Month: Essays on Software Engineering, Anniversary Edition*. Reading, MA: Addison-Wesley.

Burrows, P. (2001). *Field and Data Validation with N-Tier Architecture*.

Buschmann, F., et al. (1996). *Pattern-Oriented Software Architecture*. New York: John Wiley & Sons.

Carnegie Mellon Software Engineering Institute. (2003). *Capability Maturity Models. www.sei.cmu.edu/managing/managing.html.*

Clements, P., Kazman, R., & Klein, M. (2002). *Evaluating Software Architectures*. Reading, MA: Addison-Wesley.

Clements, P., & Northrop, L. (2001). *Software Product Lines: Practices and Patterns*. Reading, MA: Addison-Wesley.

Cockburn, A. (1997, December). *Surviving Object-Oriented Projects* (The Agile Series for Software Developers). Reading, MA: Addison-Wesley.

Cockburn, A. (2001, December). *Agile Software Development*. Reading, MA: Addison-Wesley.

Cockburn, A. (2002). *Agile Software Development*. Reading, MA: Addison-Wesley Longman.

Connecticut Object Oriented Users Group. (n.d.) Presentation by Pramod Sadalage, Thoughtworks, Chief Data Architect. *www.cooug.org*.

Constantine, L. *Can UML and Unified Process Meet?*

Constantine, L. (2001). *Process Agility and Software Usability: Toward Lightweight Usage-Centered Design*.

Constantine, L. L., & Lockwood, L. A. D. (1999). *Software for Use: A Practical Guide to the Models and Methods of Usage-Centered Design*. New York: ACM Press.

Fowler, M. (2001a). *Is Design Dead? www.martinfowler.com/articles/designDead.html*

Gamma, E., Helm, R., Johnson, R., & Vlissides, J. (1995, January) *Design Patterns. Elements of Reusable Object-Oriented Software*. Reading, MA: Addison-Wesley.

Gane, C., & Sarson, T. (1979). *Structured Systems Analysis: Tools and Techniques*. Englewood Cliffs, NJ: Prentice Hall, Inc.

Garlan & Perry. (1992, April). Guest editorial to the IEEE Transactions on Software Engineering

Hay, D. C. (2003). *Requirements Analysis: From Business Views to Architecture*. Upper Saddle River, NJ: Prentice Hall, Inc.

Herzum, P., & Sims, O. (2000). *Business Component Factory: A Comprehensive Overview of Component-Based Development for the Enterprise*. New York: John Wiley & Sons.

Hofmeister, C., Nord, R., & Soni, D. (1999). *Applied Software Architecture*. Reading, MA: Addison-Wesley.

IBM Ease of Use: Out-of-box experience section. *http://www-3.ibm.com/ibm/easy/eou_ext.nsf/Publish/1534*

IESE PuLSE. (Product Line Software Engineering Method.) (n.d.) *www.iese.fhg.de/PuLSE*.

ISO/DIS 9241–11 Ergonomic requirements for office work with visual display terminals (VDTs) Part 11: Guidance on usability.

Jacobson, I., Griss, M., & Jonsson, P. (1997). *Software Reuse: Architecture, Process, and Organization for Business Success*. New York: ACM Press.

Jacobssen, I, Booch, G., & Rumbaugh, J. (1998). *The Unified Software Development Process*. Reading, MA: Addison-Wesley.

Jeffries, R., Anderson, A., & Hendrickson, C. (2001). *Extreme Programming Installed*. Reading, MA: Addison-Wesley.

Jones, O. D., Beyen, N., & Thomas, C. (n.d.) *Handbook of User-Centered Design, Telematics*. Applications Project IE 2016 INUSE European Usability Support Centers.

Kerievsky, J. (2001). *Patterns and XP: Extreme Programming Examined*. Succi, G., & Marchesi, M., eds. Reading, MA: Addison-Wesley, pp. 207–220.

Kruchten, P. (1999, February). *The Archictects: The Software Architecture Team*. Proceedings of the First Working IFIP Conference on Software Architecture.

Kruchten, P. (2000). *The Rational Unified Process: An Introduction*, 2nd Edition. Reading, MA: Addison-Wesley Longman.

Krutchen, P. (1995, November). The 4 + 1 View Model of Architecture. IEEE *Software*, pp. 42–50.

Krutchen P., Thompson C., Bell D., Devlin J., Booch G., Royce W., Marasco, Reitman M., Ohniec W., & Schonberg A. (n.d.) *4+1 View Model: Rational, Hughes Aircraft, and Alcatel*.

Lozoic, N. v. (2003). Newsletter.

Mackinnon, T., Freeman, S., & Craig, P. (n.d.) *Endo-Testing: Unit Testing with Mock Objects*. *www.connextra.com/about/xp_approach.htm*.

Macleod, M., Bowden, R., Beyan, N., & Curson, I. (1997). The MUSiC Performance Measurement Method. *Behaviour and Information Technology*, 16, pp. 279–293.

Malveau, R., & Mowbray, T. J. (2001). *Software Architect Bootcamp*. Upper Saddle River, NJ: Prentice Hall, Inc.

Marco, D. (2000). *Meta Data Repository: A Full Lifecycle Guide*. New York: John Wiley & Sons.

McBreen, P. (2001, August). *Software Craftmanship: The New Imperative*. Reading, MA: Addison-Wesley.

McGovern, J., Kagle, C., Bothner, P., Linn, J., & Nagarajan, V. (2003, September). *XQuery: Kick Start*. Indianapolis: Sam's Publishing.

McGovern, J., Tyagi, S., Stevens, M., & Mathew, S. (2003). *Java Web Services Architecture*. San Francisco: Morgan-Kaufmann.

Merriam-Webster's 10th Collegiate Dictionary. New York: Merriam-Webster.

Microsoft Windows 2000 Server. Redmond, WA: Microsoft Press.

Microsoft.NET Architecture.

Moriarty, T. (2001, April). To Unify Architecture with Methodology: The Rational Unified Process Meets the Zachman Information Systems Architecture. *Intelligent Enterprise*. *www.intelligententerprise.com/010416/metaprise1_2.html*.

Morris, C., & Ferguson, C. (1993, March). How Architecture Wins Technology Wars, *Harvard Business Review*.

Object Management Group. (2001a). *The Unified Modeling Language (UML) Specification*. *www.omg.org/technology/documents/formal/uml.htm*.

Object Management Group (2001b). *Model Driven Architecture (MDA)*. *ftp.omg.org/pub/docs/ormsc/01-07-01.pdf*.

Orr, K. (2001, July). *One Minute Methodology*. New York: Dorset House.

Ozsu, M. T., & Valduriez, C. (1999, January). *Principles of Distributed Database Systems*. Upper Saddle River, NJ: Prentice Hall, Inc.

Palmer, S. R., & Felsing, J. M. (2002). A *Practical Guide to Feature-Driven Development*. Upper Saddle River, NJ: Prentice Hall PTR.

Pérez-Quiñones, M. A. (2002). A *Software Architecture Approach to a User Interface Software Course*, Manuel A., D Sc.

Rational Corporation. (2003). *Rational Unified Process Home Page*. *www.rational.com/products/rup/index.jsp*.

Schwaber, K., Beedle, M., & Martin, R. (2001). *Agile Software Development with SCRUM*. Upper Saddle River, NJ: Prentice Hall, Inc.

The SEI Product Line Practice Initiative. (n.d.) *www.sei.cmu.edu/plp*.

Service Oriented Architecture Concepts. (2001). *Talking Blocks*. *www.talkingblocks.com/resources.htm*.

Stapleton, J. (2003). DSDM: Business Focused Development. Harlow, England: Addison-Wesley.

Stevens, M. (2002). Multi-Grained Services. *www.developer.com/article.php/114661*.

System Architecting. (n.d.) *www.extra.research.philips.com/natlab/sysarch/SystemArchitectureBook.pdf*.

Weiss, D., & Lai, C. (1999). *Software Product-Line Engineering: A Family-Based Software Development Process*. Reading, MA: Addison Wesley.

Wells, D. (n.d.) *XP and Databases*. *www.extremeprogramming.org/stories/testdb.html*.

Yourdon, E. (1989). *Modern Structured Analysis*. Upper Saddle River, NJ: Prentice-Hall, Inc.

ZIFA. (2003). The Zachman Institute for Framework Advancement. *www.zifa.com*.

Additional Reading

A positive attitude may not solve all your problems, but it will annoy enough people to make it worth the effort.

Herm Albright (1876–1944)

We have composed a list of our favorite books to further guide you on the path to becoming a superior architect. The books listed below span multiple subject areas but are mandatory for the architect to learn and master.

The Agile Manager's Guide to Getting Organized
Jeff Olson
Velocity Publications, January 2001

Agile Modeling: Effective Practices for Extreme Programming and the Unified Process
Scott Ambler, Ron Jeffries
John Wiley and Sons, March 2002

Agile Software Development Ecosystems
Jim Highsmith
Addison-Wesley, March 2002

Agile Software Development with SCRUM
Ken Schwaber, Mike Beedle, Robert C. Martin
Prentice Hall, October 2001

Agile

Building and Managing the Meta Data Repository: A Full Lifecycle Guide
David Marco
John Wiley and Sons, July 2000

Data Sharing Using a Common Data Architecture
Michael H. Brackett
John Wiley and Sons, July 1994

Database Design for Smarties: Using UML for Data Modeling
Robert J. Muller
Morgan Kaufmann, February 1999

Data Architecture and Databases

287

Joe Celko's Data & Databases: Concepts in Practice
Joe Celko
Morgan Kaufmann, August 1999

Metadata Solutions
Adrienne Tannenbaum
Addison-Wesley, August 2001

Development

Effective Java
Joshua Bloch
Addison-Wesley, June 2001

Mastering Enterprise JavaBeans
Ed Roman, Scott Ambler, Tyler Jewell
John Wiley and Sons, December 2001

Enterprise Architecture

e-Enterprise: Business Models, Architecture, and Components
Faisal Hoque
Cambridge University Press, April 2000

Enterprise Architecture and New Generation Information Systems
Dimitris N. Chorafas
Saint Lucie Press, December 2001

Enterprise Architecture Planning: Developing a Blueprint for Data, Applications, and Technology
Steven Spewak, Steven Hill
John Wiley and Sons, September 1993

Guide to Enterprise IT Architecture
Tony Beveridge, Col Perks
Springer Verlag, October 2002

Patterns

Core J2EE Patterns: Best Practices and Design Strategies
Deepak Alur, John Crupi, Dan Malks
Prentice Hall, June 2001

Design Patterns
Erich Gamma, Richard Helm, Ralph Johnson, John Vlissides
Addison-Wesley, January 1995

Design Patterns Java Workbook
Steven John Metsker
Addison-Wesley, March 2002

Patterns of Enterprise Application Architecture
Martin Fowler
Addison-Wesley, November 2002

Process Patterns: Building Large-Scale Systems Using Object Technology
Scott Ambler
Cambridge University Press, January 1999

Designing Web Usability: The Practice of Simplicity
Jakob Nielsen
New Riders, December 1999

Don't Make Me Think: A Common Sense Approach to Web Usability
Steven Krug, Roger Black
Que Publishing, December 2000

Homepage Usability: 50 Websites Deconstructed
Jakob Nielsen, Marie Tahir
New Riders, November 2001

Web Style Guide: Basic Design Principles for Creating Web Sites
Patrick Lynch, Sarah Horton
Yale University Press, March 2002

Presentation and Usability

The Pragmatic Programmer: From Journeyman to Master
Andrew Hunt, David Thomas, Ward Cunningham
Addison-Wesley, October 1999

Software Architect Bootcamp
Thomas Mowbray, Raphael Malveau
Prentice Hall, October 2000

The Software Architect's Profession: An Introduction
Marc Sewell, Laura Sewell
Prentice Hall, September 2001

The Profession

Building Web Services with Java
Steve Graham, Simeon Siemonov, Toufic Boubez, Glen Daniels, Doug Davis,
    Yuichi Nakamura, Ryo Neyama
Sams Publishing, December 2001

Java Web Services Architecture
James McGovern, Sameer Tyagi, Michael E. Stevens, Sunil Mathew
Morgan Kaufmann, April 2003

Service-Oriented Architecture

Design and Use of Software Architectures
Jan Bosch
Addison-Wesley, May 2000

Evaluating Software Architectures: Methods and Case Studies
Paul Clements, Rick Kazman, Mark Klein
Addison-Wesley, January 2002

Software Architecture in Practice
Less Bass, Paul Clements, Rick Kazman, Ken Bass
Prentice Hall, May 2000

Software Architecture: Organizational Principles and Patterns
David M. Dikel, David Kane, James R. Wilson
Prentice Hall, December 2000

Software Architecture

Software Architecture: Perspectives on an Emerging Discipline
Mary Shaw, David Garlan
Prentice Hall, April 1996

Software Product Lines: Practices and Patterns
Paul Clements, Linda M. Northrop
Addison-Wesley, August 2001

UML

Applying UML and Patterns
Craig Larman
Prentice Hall, July 2001

Developing Applications with Java and UML
Paul R. Reed Jr.
Addison-Wesley, January 2002

Elements of UML Style
Scott Ambler
Cambridge University Press, December 2002

Executable UML: A Foundation for Model Driven Architecture
Stephen Mellor, Marc Balcer
Addison-Wesley, May 2002

Teach Yourself UML in 24 Hours
Joseph Schmuller
Sam's Publishing, August 2001

UML Distilled: A Brief Guide to the Standard Object Modeling Language
Martin Fowler, Kendall Scott
Addison-Wesley, August 1999

Various Topics

Dogbert's Top Secret Management Handbook
Scott Adams
Harper Collins, October 1997

First, Break All the Rules: What the World's Greatest Managers Do Differently
Marcus Buckingham, Curt Coffman
Simon & Schuster, May 1999

Good to Great: Why Some Companies Make the Leap . . . and Others Don't
Jim Collins
Harper Collins, October 2001

How to Open Locks with Improvised Tools
Hans Conkel
Harper Collins, October 1997

The Mythical Man-Month: Essays on Software Engineering
Frederick P. Brooks
Addison-Wesley, August 1995

The Open-Book Experience: Lessons from Over 100 Companies Who Successfully Transformed Themselves
John Case
Perseus Publishing, January 1999

Please Understand Me II: Temperament, Character, Intelligence
David Keirsey
Prometheus Nemesis Books, May 1998

Rapid Development: Taming Wild Software Schedules
Steve McConnell
Microsoft Press, July 1996

Zen and the Art of Motorcycle Maintenance
Robert Pirsig
Bantam Books, April 1984

Future Books

Teamwork represents a set of values that encourage behaviors such as listening and constructively responding to points of view expressed by others, giving others the benefit of the doubt, providing support to those who need it, and recognizing the interests and achievements of others

Jon R.Katzenbach and Douglas K. Smith

Enterprise architecture spans many topics. To cover all topics in a single book is not realistic. This is the first book of many to come from this author team. Listed below are books planned for the future.

Agile Enterprise Architecture

Publication Date: Summer 2004

This book will bring you methodologies and best practices for implementing enterprise architecture within your organization and will provide guidance on increasing the productivity of other disciplines. Following are some of the topics that will be covered:

- Business architecture
- Portfolio management
- IT governance
- Software risk management
- Enterprise project management
- Quality assurance
- Configuration and release management
- The role of the architect
- Architectural assessments
- Thought leadership

Enterprise SOA
Publication Date: Fall 2004

A Service-Oriented Architecture (SOA) is made up of components and interconnections that stress interoperability, location transparency, and platform independence. SOA is not just about the technology used in Web services, but designing and building systems using diverse software components. Following are some of the topics that will be covered:

- Concepts of distributed computing
- Component-based services
- Model-driven architecture
- Orchestration
- Security
- QoS and dynamic routing
- Transactions
- Grid computing
- Namespaces, semantic and ontology's

Enterprise Service Patterns
Publication Date: Summer 2005

Service-Oriented Architectures are becoming the golden hammer for solving integration issues in corporate America. This book will cover architectural patterns that readers can use to quickly jump-start their own development efforts. Some of the patterns covered include the following:

- Self-service
- Information aggregation
- Extended enterprise
- Event monitor
- Business process locator
- Distributed value chain
- Asyncronous transactions
- Managed public process

About the Authors

James McGovern is an industry thought leader and the author of best-selling books: *Java Web Services Architecture*, *Enterprise SOA*, and *Agile Enterprise Architecture*. He has served as technical editor for five different books on various computer topics and has 16 years of experience in information technology. He is employed as an enterprise architect for The Hartford Financial Services Group, Inc. He holds industry certifications from Microsoft, Cisco, and Sun and is a member of the Java Community Process, IEEE, and the Worldwide Institute of Software Architects.

Scott W. Ambler is a senior object-oriented (OO) development consultant with Ronin International, Inc. (www.ronin-intl.com) and works in software analysis and design, Agile Modeling, agile database techniques, training, mentoring, and architectural audits of mission-critical systems. He is the coauthor of the best-selling books: *The Elements of UML Style*, *Agile Modeling*, *Mastering Enterprise JavaBeans 2/e*, *The Elements of Java Style*, *The Object Primer*, and the forthcoming *Agile Database Techniques*. He has a master's degree in information science from the University of Toronto. He is a senior contributing editor with *Software Development* magazine, a columnist with *Computing Canada*, and a member of Flashline Inc.'s Software Development Productivity Council.

Michael E. Stevens is employed as a software architect for The Hartford Financial Services Group, Inc. He specializes in service-oriented architectures and is a coauthor of a recent book, *Java Web Services Architecture*. He is a columnist on various software development topics for Developer.com. He received his B.S. degree in computer science from Central Connecticut State University and is a candidate for a master's degree in computer science from Rensselaer Polytechnic Institute. He has more than 14 years of experience in information technology and founded a software company that developed solutions for the mailing industry. He is a certified Java programmer, a member of the IEEE, the IEEE Computer Society, the ACM, and the ACM SIGSOFT.

James Linn is the coauthor of a recent book, *XQuery—Kick Start*. He has 8 years of experience in software development and has worked with Java, C++, and MFC. He has master's degrees in biochemistry and software engineering. He is a member of the consulting arm of The Hartford Financial Services Group, Inc.

Vikas Sharan is Lozoic's cofounder and currently a managing partner. He has spent 10 years defining, developing, and selling software and Internet services in various technical management and entrepreneurial positions. Before starting Lozoic, Vikas was a director with a services firm in the Silicon

Valley. Prior to this, he founded and set up a successful usability practice for PRT Group, a large system integrator on the East Coast with a development center in Barbados.

Sharan is currently a part of the architecture team at Baypackets, a telecom application platform engineering company. Vikas has a strong telecom, supply-chain, and financial services background, and he has worked with computer-based training systems and mobile communication products. He has a background in design and human factors. His master's degree from the Indian Institute of Technology, Bombay, is in industrial design.

Elias Jo is the systems architect for *New York Times Digital* and is responsible for the technical direction of the company's enterprise Web site. He has a background in deploying enterprise scale Web applications and middleware products for the media and the financial services industry. Jo was previously the architect/lead developer for multimillion-dollar project deployments at Deutsche Bank, Citibank, Standard & Poors, Guardian, AMKOR, and ADP. He has been published in *ColdFusion Developer's Journal* and has participated as a technical editor for O'Reilly's technical publications. Jo is a graduate of Columbia University and holds a degree in industrial engineering with a minor in computer science.

Index

D

Damage or compromise of business data, 30
Data access logic components, accessing, 201–202
Data architecture
  access rules to protect data, use of, 249
  advanced metadata architecture, 239–241
  agile approach, 225, 233
  agile database techniques, 242–255
  allowances for rapid changes in business
    requirements and database technologies, 248
  architectural process, 232–233
  baseline data architecture, 227–229
  business architecture (conceptual
    architecture), 231
  business data, 231–232
  business object modeling, 231
  business problem, 226–227
  centralization of shared and current data,
    248–249
  credit card information, protection of, 254
  data integrity, ensuring, 252
  data security, 241–242
  data validation, 250
  database iterations, 245
  development timeline, 244
  encryption methods, 254–255
  federated metadata approach, 235–236
  frameworks, 230–234
  layered data architecture, 230
  master lineage, 246
  metadata, 234–239
  monolithic database designs, 249
  normalization, 247–248
  OAGIS virtual business object model, 238
  online transaction processing (OLTP)
    databases, 247
  open standards to proprietary extensions,
    preference for, 253–254
  organizational context, 226–227
  replication of data, 250–251
  scripts, working with, 246–247
  star schemas, 246–248
  total performance *versus* local performance, 253
  transparency of location of data, 251–252
  validation/final review, 233–234
Data integrity, ensuring, 252
Data mining, 8
Data security, 241–242
Data tier, 181, 187
Data validation, 250
Database iterations, 245

Database management, 181
Decomposition, 99
Defined level, 123–124
Denial-of-service (DOS) attacks, 30–31
Development department, 104
Development environment, setting up a, 44
Development timeline, 244
DHTML (Dynamic Hyper Text Markup Language),
  192, 193
Diary methods, 218
Direct attached storage (DRS), 24, 27
Disaster recovery plan (DRP), 3, 31–34
Discovery, concept of, 75
Document-based user interfaces, 196–197
DOM (Domain Object Model), 192
Domain engineering unit, 106
DOS. *See* Denial-of-service (DOS) attacks
DRP. *See* Disaster recovery plan (DRP)
DRS. *See* Direct attached storage (DRS)

E

EbXML, 77
Empathic modeling, 220
Encryption methods, 254–255
Enhancing system value, role in, 15–17
Enterprise application integration (EAI), 7
Enterprise architectural model, 1
Enterprise management discipline, 146–147
Enterprise Unified Process (EUP)
  additions to the RUP life cycle, 142–143
  adoption of, 147
  advantages of, 142
  enterprise management discipline, 146–147
  life cycle of, 143
  operations and support discipline, 145
  production phase, 144
  retirement phase, 144–145
Error handling, 69
Ethernet, 18, 20
Ethnographic approach, 218
EUP. *See* Enterprise Unified Process (EUP)
Expected inputs and outputs, 69
EXtended IDE (XIDE), 103–104
EXtreme programming (XP)
  acceptance tests, creation and execution of, 119
  advantages of, 120
  approach, 114–115
  Class, Responsibility and Collaboration (CRC)
    card, 118
  coding the unit, 118–119
  communication, 115

Index

300

W

Walk-through, 221
WAN technologies, 18
Web Service Description Language (WSDL), 76, 77, 78
Web-Based User Interface (WUI), 208–209
Well-defined interfaces and polices, 67–71
Widgets, 185
Wizard of Oz prototyping, 219

X

XIDE. *See* eXtended IDE (XIDE)
XML Metadata Interchange (XMI), 130
XML/XSLT (Extensible Markup Language/Extensible Stylesheet Language Transformation), 192
XP. *See* EXtreme programming (XP)
XUnit. *See* Unit testing framework (XUnit)

Z

Zachman Framework (ZF)
  advantages of, 129–130
  agile architecture, in, 163
  development of, 126
  disadvantages, 129–130
  framework, 127–128
  principles of, 126

informIT

TOMORROW'S SOLUTIONS FOR TODAY'S PROFESSIONALS

Prentice Hall Professional Technical Reference

| Browse | Book Series | What's New | User Groups | Alliances | Special Sales | Contact Us |

Search | Help | Home

Quick Search

PTR Favorites

Find a Bookstore

Book Series

Special Interests

Newsletters

Press Room

International

Best Sellers

Solutions Beyond the Book

Shopping Bag

Keep Up to Date with
PH PTR Online

We strive to stay on the cutting edge of what's happening in professional computer science and engineering. Here's a bit of what you'll find when you stop by **www.phptr.com**:

What's new at PHPTR? We don't just publish books for the professional community, we're a part of it. Check out our convention schedule, keep up with your favorite authors, and get the latest reviews and press releases on topics of interest to you.

Special interest areas offering our latest books, book series, features of the month, related links, and other useful information to help you get the job done.

User Groups Prentice Hall Professional Technical Reference's User Group Program helps volunteer, not-for-profit user groups provide their members with training and information about cutting-edge technology.

Companion Websites Our Companion Websites provide valuable solutions beyond the book. Here you can download the source code, get updates and corrections, chat with other users and the author about the book, or discover links to other websites on this topic.

Need to find a bookstore? Chances are, there's a bookseller near you that carries a broad selection of PTR titles. Locate a Magnet bookstore near you at www.phptr.com.

Subscribe today! Join PHPTR's monthly email newsletter! Want to be kept up-to-date on your area of interest? Choose a targeted category on our website, and we'll keep you informed of the latest PHPTR products, author events, reviews and conferences in your interest area.

Visit our mailroom to subscribe today! **http://www.phptr.com/mail_lists**